EGYPTIAN MYSTERIES
VOLUME 2

The Gods and Goddesses of Shetaut Neter- Ancient Egyptian Religion

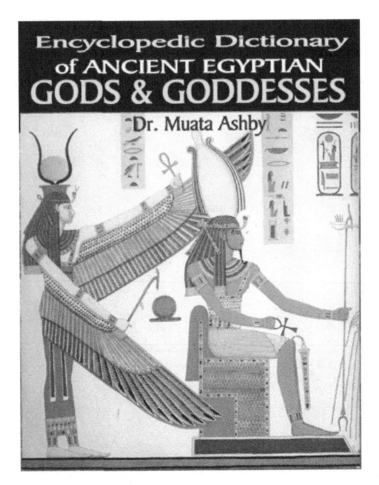

ON THE COVER: The God Asar sits on the divine throne (Which is Aset), as the goddess Aset embraces him with her wings.

Cruzian Mystic Books
P.O. Box 570459
Miami, Florida, 33257
(305) 378-5432 Fax: (305) 378-6253

First U.S. edition 2003

The author is available for group lectures and individual counseling. For further information contact the publisher.

Ashby, Reginald Muata Abhaya
Egyptian Mysteries Volume 2: Dictionary of Ancient Egyptian Gods and Goddesses ISBN: 1-884564-23-2

Library of Congress Cataloging in Publication Data

1- Ancient Egyptian Religion, 2- Ancient Egyptian Gods and Goddesses, 3- African Religion, 4- African Philosophy.

Sema Institute of Yoga
Cruzian Mystic Books and Music

Sema Institute of Yoga

Sema ($\downarrow$) is an Ancient Egyptian word and symbol meaning union. The Sema Institute is dedicated to the propagation of the universal teachings of spiritual evolution which relate to the union of humanity and the union of all things within the universe. It is a non-denominational organization which recognizes the unifying principles in all spiritual and religious systems of evolution throughout the world. Our primary goals are to provide the wisdom of ancient spiritual teachings in books, courses and other forms of communication. Secondly, to provide expert instruction and training in the various yogic disciplines including Ancient Egyptian Philosophy, Christian Gnosticism, Indian Philosophy and modern science. Thirdly, to promote world peace and Universal Love.

A primary focus of our tradition is to identify and acknowledge the yogic principles within all religions and to relate them to each other in order to promote their deeper understanding as well as to show the essential unity of purpose and the unity of all living beings and nature within the whole of existence.

The Institute is open to all who believe in the principles of peace, non-violence and spiritual emancipation regardless of sex, race, or creed.

About the Author

Who is Sebai Muata Abhaya Ashby D.D. Ph. D.?

Priest, Author, lecturer, poet, philosopher, musician, publisher, counselor and spiritual preceptor and founder of the Sema Institute-Temple of Aset, Muata Ashby was born in Brooklyn, New York City, and grew up in the Caribbean. His family is from Puerto Rico and Barbados. Displaying an interest in ancient civilizations and the Humanities, Sebai Maa began studies in the area of religion and philosophy and achieved doctorates in these areas while at the same time he began to collect his research into what would later become several books on the subject of the origins of Yoga Philosophy and practice in ancient Africa (Ancient Egypt) and also the origins of Christian Mysticism in Ancient Egypt.

Sebai Maa (Muata Abhaya Ashby) holds a Doctor of Philosophy Degree in Religion, and a Doctor of Divinity Degree in Holistic Health. He is also a Pastoral Counselor and Teacher of Yoga Philosophy and Discipline. Dr. Ashby received his Doctor of Divinity Degree from and is an adjunct faculty member of the American Institute of Holistic Theology. Dr. Ashby is a certified as a PREP Relationship Counselor. Dr. Ashby has been an independent researcher and practitioner of Egyptian Yoga, Indian Yoga, Chinese Yoga, Buddhism and mystical psychology as well as Christian Mysticism. Dr. Ashby has engaged in Post Graduate research in advanced Jnana, Bhakti and Kundalini Yogas at the Yoga Research Foundation. He has extensively studied mystical religious traditions from around the world and is an accomplished lecturer, musician, artist, poet, screenwriter, playwright and author of over 25 books on Kamitan yoga and spiritual philosophy. He is an Ordained Minister and Spiritual Counselor and also the founder the Sema Institute, a non-profit organization dedicated to spreading the wisdom of Yoga and the Ancient Egyptian mystical traditions. Further, he is the spiritual leader and head priest of the Per Aset or Temple of Aset, based in Miami, Florida. Thus, as a scholar, Dr. Muata Ashby is a teacher, lecturer and researcher. However, as a spiritual leader, his title is Sebai, which means Spiritual Preceptor.

Sebai Dr. Ashby began his research into the spiritual philosophy of Ancient Africa (Egypt) and India and noticed correlations in the culture and arts of the two countries. This was the catalyst for a successful book series on the subject called "Egyptian Yoga". Now he has created a series of musical compositions which explore this unique area of music from ancient Egypt and its connection to world music.

Who is Hemt Neter Dr. Karen Vijaya Clarke-Ashby?

Karen Clarke-Ashby (Seba Dja) is a Kamitan (Kamitan) priestess, and an independent researcher, practitioner and teacher of Sema (Smai) Tawi (Kamitan) and Indian Integral Yoga Systems, a Doctor of Veterinary Medicine, a Pastoral Spiritual Counselor, a Pastoral Health and Nutrition Counselor, and a Sema (Smai) Tawi Life-style Consultant." Dr. Ashby has engaged in post-graduate research in advanced Jnana, Bhakti, Karma, Raja and Kundalini Yogas at the Sema Institute of Yoga and Yoga Research Foundation, and has also worked extensively with her husband and spiritual partner, Dr. Muata Ashby, author of the Egyptian Yoga Book Series, editing many of these books, as well as studying, writing and lecturing in the area of Kamitan Yoga and Spirituality. She is a certified Tjef Neteru Sema Paut (Kamitan Yoga Exercise system) and Indian Hatha Yoga Exercise instructor, the Coordinator and Instructor for the Level 1 Teacher Certification Tjef Neteru Sema Training programs, and a teacher of health and stress management applications of the Yoga / Sema Tawi systems for modern society, based on the Kamitan and/or Indian yogic principles. Also, she is the co-author of "The Egyptian Yoga Exercise Workout Book," a contributing author for "The Kamitan Diet, Food for Body, Mind and Soul," author of the soon to be released, "Yoga Mystic Metaphors for Enlightenment."

Hotep -Peace be with you!
Seba Muata Ashby & Karen Ashby

TABLE OF CONTENTS

FOREWORD: THE IMPORTANCE OF GODS AND GODDESSES

The Importance of Neteru

This book is about the mystery of *neteru*, the gods and goddesses of Ancient Egypt (Kamit, Kemet). Neteru means "Gods and Goddesses." But the Neterian teaching of Neteru represents more than the usual limited modern day concept of "divinities" or "spirits." The Neteru of Kamit are also metaphors, cosmic principles and vehicles for the enlightening teachings of Shetaut Neter (Ancient Egyptian-African Religion). Actually they are the elements for one of the most advanced systems of spirituality ever conceived in human history. Understanding the concept of neteru provides a firm basis for spiritual evolution and the pathway for viable culture, peace on earth and a healthy human society.

Why is it important to have gods and goddesses in our lives? In order for spiritual evolution to be possible, once a human being has accepted that there is existence after death and there is a transcendental being who exists beyond time and space knowledge, human beings need a connection to that which transcends the ordinary experience of human life in time and space and a means to understand the transcendental reality beyond the mundane reality. Therefore, the sages of ancient times devised a system of symbols and metaphors that allow the mind to receive the wisdom of the higher consciousness.

It is important to realize that two processes must occur in order for a human being to experience higher consciousness. The first is feeling and the second is wisdom. Intellectual studies and the practice of the spiritual disciplines lead to a certain level of wisdom but this is not enough to reach the summits of spiritual awakening and enlightenment. For that it is also important that the teaching should reach to the depths of the personality. Otherwise the intellectual knowledge will remain superficial and ultimately ineffectual. The personality needs to feel the teaching as well as know it intellectually. The feeling aspect of spiritual evolution is promoted when a human being opens up the capacity to awaken divine love. That is, love for the Divine, i.e. God(dess).

Divine love allows the pretentiousness, pride, hubris, and narcissism of the personality to be broken down into humility and purity of heart, leading to bright intellect, and a virtuous personality that will develop clear vision of the higher self.

The gods and goddesses are the bridge between the world of human experience and the transcendental absolute. The religion encompasses higher and lower levels of divinities. As the lower echelon of divinities to the higher ranks are studied, they lead to other relative divinities who represent higher and higher principles of philosophy and consciousness through their iconography, interrelationships and mythic teachings embedded in the myths, which are the vehicles for getting to recognize and become familiar with the neteru.

As the familiarity increases and as there is frequency of interaction between an aspirant and the divinities, an aspirant gains a unique insight into their nature and in so doing the aspirant gains insight into the nature of him/her self since the neteru are merely reflections of higher human potential.

"The neteru are immortal human beings,
and human beings are mortal Neteru (Gods and Goddesses)."
-Ancient Egyptian-African Proverb of Shetaut Neter

The Neteru allow us to propitiate for Divine Grace and Divine Grace opens the door to spiritual realization. It is the passageway to the *Sekhtet Hetep* or "field of peace" in which the answers to all questions of life are discovered.

What is Divine Grace? God does not grant Nehast (Spiritual awakening-enlightenment). That is not within God's power to give. As a spark of the Divine every human being is essentially one with God and as such partakes in Divine Power. Every human being has the power to lead him or her self to exaltation or degradation. The soul, as that spark, has led itself to ignorance, forgetfulness of its immortality and freedom, and so by itself must lead itself to awakening. Spiritual preceptors and the gods and goddesses lead willing souls to understand and practice the disciplines that lead to spiritual enlightenment but they cannot do the disciplines for spiritual aspirants. Spiritual aspirants must diligently follow the teaching. Practicing devotion to God has the effect of turning the mind towards the Divine and this leads to purity of feeling and thinking. Essentially, spiritual practice is a worship of the Divinity within oneself. When the divinity within is worshipped as opposed to the world, it allows that divinity to emerge as the preeminent aspect of life and the mind AWAKENS to its presence and the true nature of the personality which is not the egoistic notion but the heretofore unknown Divine Spirit-God within. Devotional exercises and rituals bestow propitious conditions to practice and advance in spiritual attainment. The Gods and Goddesses do not grant enlightenment but only open the door as an aspirant worships the Divine in order to promote Divine Grace. To be successful, the spiritual practice needs propitious conditions for spiritual evolution including promoting balance and peace of mind, encounters with spiritual preceptors, and reduction of pressure of egoistic tendencies that act as obstacles to spiritual attainments. When Divine Grace dawns the aspirant gains spiritual strength and increasing desire to study and practice the teaching as well as increasing pleasure and fulfillment through the practice and increasing dispassion about the worldly objects and worldly desires. Divine Grace is propitiated through Devotion to the Divine and Right Action-righteousness.

"Seekest thou God, thou seekest for the Beautiful. One is the Path that leadeth
unto It - Devotion joined with Knowledge."
-Ancient Egyptian-African Proverb of Shetaut Neter

The gods and goddesses are to be worshipped and studied in order to lead oneself to discover the Supreme Being. Devotion to Gods and Goddesses allows the depth of the teaching to be revealed. Approaching the teaching intellectually will only promote a superficial understanding and therefore a limited attainment. Intellectual study allows the teaching to be thought about but this thinking process can become circular if the depth of the teaching is not approached. Devotion-Divine Love towards God allows the depth of the teaching to be approached. In essence the teaching must be felt as well as known. In order to be effective, intellectual knowledge must be augmented by spiritually feeling the teaching. The feeling aspect of the soul, when tapped into, does not allow the intellectual aspect to become deluded. In fact, it will plague the intellect with insecurities, torment the intellect with doubts until the right path is pursued and this is the deeper conscience of a person-whose source is their own soul. This cannot occur if the divine feeling is dulled due to delusion and worldly desire. Devotional exercises and rituals allow the intellectual teaching to be experience as well as thought. So this book is dedicated to gaining insight into the nature of the philosophy of Neteru that leads to higher self-knowledge and the science of spiritual evolution through Shetaut Neter-Ancient Egyptian religion.

"O behold with thine eye God's plans. Devote thyself to adore God's name. It is
God who giveth Souls to millions of forms, and God magnifyeth whosoever
magnifyeth God."

-Ancient Egyptian-African Proverb of Shetaut Neter

The Deeper Symbolism of the Neteru

Much of the current general world knowledge about the Ancient Egyptian gods and goddesses was formulated based on the concepts established by early and present day followers of and scholars of the Judeo-Christian-Islamic faiths. The Jewish theolosians who wrote the Old Testament tried to supplant the Ancient Egyptian gods and goddesses through the story of the Exodus where Moses defeats the gods of the Egyptians with the healof the "Hebrew God." The Muslims consider the Ancient Egyptians as polytheists and consequently have an even lower opinion of them than they do of Jews or Christians.

As for the Islamic views on the followers of the Ancient Egyptian religion, they are indirectly mentioned as polytheists and are grouped together with the Jews and Christians as well as other non-Islamic groups, i.e. any groups that do not believe "the truth" as espoused by Islam. The Polytheists as well as the Jews and Christians will be "judged by Allah" (22:17) and since they have an "evil opinion of Allah" (48:6), and they "reject truth (true faith) (98:5-6) they will go to hell (48:6).

> 22:17 (Koran) Those who believe (in the Koran), those who follow the <u>Jewish (scriptures)</u>, and the Sabians, <u>Christians</u>, Megians, and <u>Polytheists</u>, -- Allah will judge between them on the Day of Judgment: For Allah is witness of all things.

> 48:6 (Koran) And that He may punish the Hypocrites, men and women, and the <u>Polytheists</u>, men and women, <u>who imagine an evil opinion of Allah</u>. On them is a round of Evil: The Wrath of Allah is on them: <u>He has cursed them and got Hell ready for them: and evil is it for a destination.</u>

> 98:5 (Koran) And they have been commanded no more than this: To worship Allah, offering Him sincere devotion, <u>being True (in faith);</u> to establish regular Prayer; and to practice regular Charity; and that is the Religion Right and Straight.

> 98:6 (Koran) <u>Those who reject (Truth),</u> among the People of the Book and among the <u>Polytheists</u>, will be in Hellfire, to dwell therein (for aye). They are the worst of creatures.

The purported founder of Christian-Egyptian monasticism, Saint Anthony, led his followers in active attacks against the Ancient Egyptian Temples, their priests and priestesses which practiced the ancient Egyptian religion. The ignorance, intolerance and denigration of the Kamitan Temples and their images are readily evident in the following quote by Saint Anthony.

> "Which is better, to confess the cross or to attribute adulteries and pederastys to these so called gods, beasts, reptiles and the images of men? The Christians, by their faith in God prove that the demons whom the Egyptians consider gods are no gods! The Christians trample them underfoot and drive them out for what they are, deceivers and corruptors of men. Through Jesus-Christ our lord, Amen"

In its beginning Christianity was seen as a pagan and alien religion. Its followers were the persecuted, but ironically, in the late Roman times when the Roman emperors adopted Christianity as the state religion, the Christians murdered priests and priestesses of other faiths whom they called pagan and led a persecution against all non-Christians, forcing new symbols and teachings on the populace. Intolerance and fundamentalism were integral aspects of early Christianity. "Fundamentalism" is a modern interpretation of orthodox Christianity, but its roots are deeply embedded into the fabric of the Roman Catholic Church and the later protestant sects that emerged. This was expressed later in history as the Crusades, the destruction of Native American culture, the African slave trade, African missionary movements and efforts to convert peoples around the world to Christianity and at the same time eradicate all other religions, something which has angered many nations around the world including China and the

Muslim countries. Due to the persecution and wonton destruction of the Ancient Egyptian scriptures along with the murder of those who were knowledgeable about the symbolism, the initiatic (mystical) teachings were lost to the orthodox Western Culture from this time on but they remained dormant and embedded in the traditions of the church itself as well as in "pagan" religions and mystical sects that carried on the ancient traditions as best they could. Ironically, the main teachings of Judaism and Christianity have been found to be based on the teachings and philosophy of Ancient Egypt.[1] The wisdom related to the Ancient Egyptian symbolism such as that displayed by Dionysus the Areopagite was misunderstood and misrepresented by the orthodox Church leaders in favor of the simple but limited symbolism of orthodox Christianity. The Gnostic Christianity followed more closely the Ancient Egyptian teachings.[2]

> "If anyone suggests that it is disgraceful to fashion base images of the Divine and most Holy orders, it is sufficient to answer that the most holy Mysteries are set forth in two modes: one by means of similar and sacred representations akin to their nature, and the other to unlike forms designed with every possible discordance ... Discordant symbols are more appropriate representations of the Divine because the human mind tends to cling to the physical form of representation believing for example that the Divine are "golden beings or shining men flashing like lightning." But lest this error befall us, the wisdom of the venerable sages leads us through disharmonious dissimilitudes, not allowing our irrational nature to become attached to those unseemly images ... Divine things may not be easily accessible to the unworthy, nor may those who earnestly contemplate the Divine symbols dwell upon the forms themselves as final truth."
>
> – Dionysus the Areopagite

Mysticism is the essence of Ancient Egyptian religion and that had a profound effect on some of the creators of the Christian faith and those who helped its early and later development.[3] However, even mysticism did not escape the process of co-optation. Many of the teachings that already existed in Ancient Egypt were adopted but the source was not cited or acknowledged but rather disavowed and sometimes maligned. The same Dionysus the Areopagite who wrote the statement above, which is in direct contradiction with that of Saint Anthony (above), was accepted into the Christian Church albeit in an altered form. Also, traditional Christian literature and scholarship have recognized St. Paul as an important Christian theologian even though some of his writings have a mystic quality. There is a Christian mystical tradition. The New Testament writings best known for their mystical emphasis are Paul's letters and the Gospel of John (John 10:30-34). Christian mysticism, as a philosophical system, is derived from Gnosticism, and Neo-Platonism through the writings of Dionysus the Areopagite, or Pseudo-Dionysus. The original Dionysus the Areopagite, who wrote the statement above, lived in the 1st century A.C.E. He became first bishop of Athens and was martyred about 95 A.C.E. He is often confused with the Pseudo-Dionysus (c. 500 A.C.E) who created mystical writings using the name of Dionysus the Areopagite. He (the first Dionysus) was later canonized as a Catholic Saint. Dionysus was converted to Christianity when he heard Paul preach the sermon concerning the nature of "the unknown God" on the Hill of Mars or Areopagus in Athens, as described in Acts 17:15-34. However, while some aspects of mysticism can still be found reflected in the Christian church teachings, they are heavily veiled and misunderstood. They are also de-emphasized by the church leadership as anomalies and thus, negated and consequently nullified in the course of Church activities.[4]

Even though Judaism, Christianity and Islam drew from Ancient Egyptian religion in order to develop their spiritual philosophies it is not correct to say that they are based in Ancient Egyptian or African theology. In order to truly understand the African theology and the gods and goddesses and the religious

---

[1] See the book *The Mystical Journey From Jesus to Christ* by Muata Ashby, See the book *African Origins of Civilization* by Muata Ashby

[2] See the book *The Mystical Journey From Jesus to Christ* by Muata Ashby

[3] ibid

[4] ibid

philosophy of Ancient Egypt itself, it is necessary to remove the context of Western preeminence and to see Kamitan (Ancient Egyptian) culture in its own right and as part of the greater context of African religious thought in which the divinities have deeper teachings. Thus the views of Dionysus the Areopagite and Plutarch is more appropriate to our study.

> *"When therefore, though hearest the myths of the Egyptians concerning the Gods - wanderings and dismemberings and many such passions, think none of these things spoken as they really are in state and action. For they do not call Hermes "Dog" as a proper name, but they associate the watching and waking from sleep of the animal who by Knowing and not Knowing determines friend from foe with the most Logos[5] like of the Gods."*

–Plutarch (c. 46-120 ACE)

There is something important and even imperative in the study of the neteru that orthodox religions have lost in their effort to distance themselves from what they call pagan or polytheistic. That deep essential philosophy is still available to those who open themselves up to the science of neteru, the gods and goddesses.

---

[5] Divine creative intelligence expressed through the divine speech and manifest in all objects in creation.

Preface: A Long History

For a period spanning over 10,000 years the Neterian religion served the society of ancient Kamit. It is hard to comprehend the vastness of time that is encompassed by Ancient Egyptian culture, religion and philosophy. Yet the evidence is there to be seen by all. It has been collected and presented in the book *African Origins of Civilization, Religion and Yoga Philosophy.* This volume serves as the historical record for the Neterian religion and as record of its legacy to all humanity. It serves as the basis or foundation for the work contained in all the other books in this series that have been created to elucidate on the teachings and traditions as well as disciplines of the varied Neterian religious traditions.

The book *African Origins of Civilization, Religion and Yoga Spirituality and Ethics Philosophy,* and the other volumes on the specific traditions detail the philosophies and disciplines that should be practiced by those who want to follow the path of Hm or Hmt, to be practitioners of the Shetaut Neter religion and builders of the Neterian faith worldwide.

Plate 1: The Great Sphinx of Ancient Egypt-showing the classical Pharaonic headdress popularized in Dynastic times. Also, the water damage can be seen in the form of vertical indentations in the sides of the monument.

INTRODUCTION: The Origins of African Kamitan Culture and Neterian Spirituality

When Was Neterian Religion Practiced in Ancient Times?

Chronology of Ancient Egyptian Religion Based on Confirmed Archeological Dating of artifacts and Monuments[6]

Major Cultural-Theological Developments

c. 10,000 B.C.E. Neolithic – period

c. 10,500 B.C.E.-7,000 B.C.E. Creation of the Great Sphinx Modern archeological accepted dates – Sphinx means Hor-m-akhet or Heru (Horus) in the horizon. This means that the King is one with the Spirit, Ra as an enlightened person possessing an animal aspect (lion) and illuminated intellect. Anunian Theology – Ra

c. 10,000 B.C.E.-5,500 B.C.E. The Sky GOD- Realm of Light-Day – NETER Androgynous – All-encompassing –Absolute, Nameless Being, later identified with Ra-Herakhti (Sphinx)

>7,000 B.C.E. Kamitan Myth and Theology present in architecture

5500+ B.C.E. to 600 A.C.E. Amun -Ra - Ptah (Horus) – Amenit - Rai – Sekhmet (male and female Trinity-Complementary Opposites)

5500+ B.C.E. Memphite Theology – Ptah

5500+ B.C.E. Hermopolitan Theology- Djehuti

5500+ B.C.E. The Asarian Resurrection Theology - Asar[RA3]

5500+B.C.E. The Goddess Principle- Theology, Isis-Hathor-Net-Mut-Sekhmet-Buto

5500 B.C.E. (Dynasty 1) Beginning of the Dynastic Period (Unification of Upper and Lower Egypt)

5000 B.C.E. (5th Dynasty) Pyramid Texts - Egyptian Book of Coming Forth By Day - 42 Precepts of MAAT and codification of the Pre-Dynastic theologies (Pre-Dynastic period: 10,000 B.C.E.-5,500 B.C.E.)

4950 B.C.E. Neolithic – Fayum

4241 B.C.E. The Pharaonic (royal) calendar based on the Sothic system (star Sirius) was in use.

3000 B.C.E. Wisdom Texts-Precepts of Ptahotep, Instructions of Any, Instructions of Amenemope, Etc.

2040 B.C.E.-1786 B.C.E. Coffin Texts

1800 B.C.E.-Theban Theology - Amun

1570 B.C.E.-Books of Coming Forth By Day (Book of the Dead)

1353 B.C.E. Non-dualist Philosophy from the Pre-Dynastic period was redefined by Akhenaton.

712-657 B.C.E. The Nubian Dynasty

Early Beginnings: The First Religion in Human History

Shetaut Neter[7] is Ancient Egyptian Religion and Philosophy. Ancient Egypt was the first and most ancient civilization to create a religious system that was complete with all three stages of religion, as well as an advanced spiritual philosophy of righteousness for social and spiritual order, called Maat Philosophy, that also had secular dimensions. Several temple systems were developed in Kamit and they were all related. The pre-Judaic/Islamic religions that the later Jewish, Christian and Muslim religions drew from in order to create their religions developed out of these, ironically enough, only to later repudiate the source from whence they originated. In any case, the Great Sphinx remains the oldest known religious monument in history that denotes high culture and civilization as well. Ancient Egypt and Nubia produced the oldest extensive philosophically and literally based religious systems and their contact with the rest of the world led to the proliferation of advanced religion and spiritual philosophy. People who were practicing simple animism, shamanism, nature based religions and witchcraft were elevated to the level of not only understanding the nature of the Supreme Being, but also attaining salvation from the miseries of life through the effective discovery of that Transcendental Being, not as an untouchable aloof Spirit, but as the very essence of all that exists.

---

[6] For more details see the Book *African Origins of Civilization, Religion and Yoga Spirituality and Ethics Philosophy* by Muata Ashby

[7] For more details see the Book *Egyptian Mysteries Volume 1.* by Muata Ashby

The Far Reaching Implications of the New Evidence Concerning the Sphinx and Other New Archeological Evidence in Egypt and the Rest of Africa

In the last 20 years traditional Egyptologists, archeologists and others have been taking note of recent studies performed on the Ancient Egyptian Sphinx and Pyramids which sit at Giza in Egypt. Beginning with such students of Ancient Egyptian culture and architecture as R. A. Schwaller de Lubicz in the 1950's, and most recently, John Anthony West, with his book *Serpent In the Sky*, many researchers have used modern technology to study the ancient monument and their discoveries have startled the world. They now understand that the erosion damage on the Sphinx could not have occurred after the period 10,000 B.C.E. - 7,000 B.C.E. because this was the last period in which there would have been enough rainfall in the area to cause such damage. This means that most of the damage which the Sphinx displays, which would have taken thousands of years to occur, would have happened prior to that time (10,000 B.C.E.).

The following evidences must also be taken into account when examining the geology of the Sphinx and the Giza plateau.

> ➢ The surrounding Sphinx Temple architecture is similarly affected.

> ➢ Astronomical evidence agrees with the geological findings.

> ➢ Ancient Egyptian historical documents concur with the evidence.

> ➢ The Sphinx Temple Architecture matches the architecture of other buildings in other parts of the country

It is important to understand that what we have in the Sphinx is not just a monument now dated as the earliest monument in history (based on irrefutable geological evidence). Its existence signifies the earliest practice not only of high-art and architecture, but it is also the first monumental statue in history dedicated to religion and mystical philosophy. This massive project including the Sphinx and its attendant Temple required intensive planning and engineering skill. Despite its deteriorated state, the Sphinx stands not only as the most ancient mystical symbol in this historical period, but also as the most ancient architectural monument, and a testament to the presence of Ancient African (Egyptian) culture in the earliest period of antiquity. Further, this means that while the two other emerging civilizations of antiquity (Sumer and Indus) were in their Neolithic period (characterized by the development of agriculture, pottery and the making of polished stone implements), Ancient Egypt had already achieved mastery over monumental art, architecture and religion as an adjunct to social order philosophy, as the Sphinx is a symbol of the Pharaoh (leader and upholder of Maat-order, justice and truth) as the god Heru. The iconography of the Sphinx is typical of that which is seen throughout Ancient Egyptian history and signals the achievement of a culture of high morals which governs the entire civilization to the Persian and Greek conquest.

> The water erosion of the Sphinx is to history what the convertibility of matter into energy is to physics.
> -John Anthony West, *Serpent In the Sky*

The findings related to the Sphinx have been confirmed by seismographic tests[8] as well as examination of the water damage on the structures related to the Sphinx and the Sphinx Temple, as compared to the rest of the structures surrounding it which display the typical decay due to wind and sand. It has been conclusively found that the Sphinx and its adjacent structures (Sphinx Temple) were built in a different era and that the surrounding structures do not display the water damage. Therefore, the wind and sand

---

[8] *Traveler's Key to Ancient Egypt*, John Anthony West

damaged structures belong to the Dynastic Era and the Sphinx belongs to the Pre-Dynastic Era. Therefore, the evidence supporting the older dating of the Sphinx is well founded and confirmed.

Plate 2: Sphinx rump and Sphinx enclosure show detail of the water damage (vertical damage).

This is a momentous discovery. It demands an opening up of the closely held chronologies and timelines of ancient cultures for revision, thereby allowing the deeper study of the human experience on this earth and making the discovery of our collective past glory possible. Thus, it is clear to see that the problem in assigning dates to events in Ancient Egypt arises when there is an unwillingness to let go of closely held notions based on biblical based assumption biased information that is accepted as truth and passed on from one generation of orthodox Egyptologists to the next generation, rather than on authentic scholarship (constant search for truth). This deficiency led to the exclusion of the ancient historical writings of Ancient Egypt (*Palermo Stone, Royal Tablets at Abdu, Royal Papyrus of Turin,* the *Dynastic List* of Merndjehuti- Manetho ᗰᗰᗰ). However, now, with the irrefutable evidence of the antiquity of the Sphinx, the carbon dating of the Great Pyramid and the excavations at Abdu (Greek-Abydos) and Nekhen (Greek-Hierakonpolis), the mounting archeological evidence and the loosening grip of Western scholars on the field of Egyptology, it is no longer possible to ignore the far reaching implications of the Ancient Egyptian historical documents.

New Evidence from the Great Pyramid

Newly refined radio carbon tests on organic material found in recent years in the Great Pyramid have shown that it "was built at least 374 years earlier" than previously thought.[9] The oldest radiocarbon dating of the organic material in the Great Pyramid yielded a date of 3,809 B.C.E. Further, there is evidence that the lower section of the Great Pyramid is older than the upper parts.

---

[9] *Egypt: Child of Africa,* Ivan Van Sertima 1994

Above: The Giza Pyramid Complex-with Great Pyramid.

While the date when the stone to create the Great Pyramid was originally cut apparently cannot as yet be dated with available instruments, tests performed on 16 samples of organic materials discovered in the Great Pyramid in Giza, Egypt, by a prominent orthodox Egyptologist (Mark Lehner) such as charcoal, showed that the pyramid was in use as early as 3,809 B.C.E. So on this evidence alone the chronologies given for the age of the Great Pyramid by traditional Egyptology as belonging to the reign of Pharaoh Khephren (Cheops) of 2551 B.C.E.- 2528 B.C.E. are simply untenable and must be revised forthwith. Therefore, while momentous, the evidence of the Sphinx fits into the larger scheme of scientific evidences, which are unraveling the mysteries of history, and leads us to the understanding of life in ancient Northeast Africa as a high point in human cultural achievement which was attained in Ancient Egypt and later spread out to the rest of the world.

Below: The Great Pyramid-new radio-carbon dating: older than 3,809 B.C.E.
A-older section, B-newer section

Where is Egypt?

Figure 1: Egypt is located in the north-eastern corner of the African Continent.

Below left: A map of North East Africa showing the location of the land of Ta-Meri **or** Kamit, **also known as Ancient Egypt and South of it is located the land which in modern times is called Sudan.**

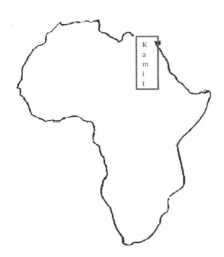

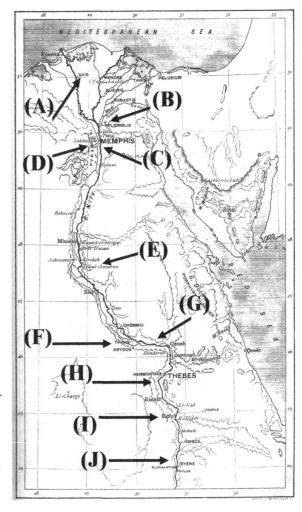

Figure: right- The Land of Ancient Egypt-Nile Valley

The cities wherein the theology of the Trinity of Amun-Ra-Ptah was developed were: A- Sais (temple of Net), B- Anu (Heliopolis- temple of Ra), C-Men-nefer or Hetkaptah (Memphis, temple of Ptah), and D- Sakkara (Pyramid Texts), E- Akhet-Aton (City of Akhnaton, temple of Aton), F- Abdu (temple of Asar), G- Iunet (Denderah) (temple of Hetheru), H- Waset (Thebes, temple of Amun), I- Djebu (Edfu) (temple of Heru), J- Pilak (Philae) (temple of Aset). The cities wherein the theology of the Trinity of Asar-Aset-Heru was developed were Anu, Abydos, Pilak (Philae), Iunet (Denderah) and Djebu (Edfu).

The Nubian Origins of Kamit -Ancient Egypt

In order to understand the Ancient Egyptians, we must also understand their origins in Nubia and their relationship to the Nubians (ancient Ethiopians). In this manner we will have a full grasp of the African origins of Kamitan culture as well as fathom the full impact that it had on the rest of Africa through the Nubian kingdoms, which in turn influenced other countries in the interior of Africa. So next we will explore the Nubian origins and history of Ancient Egypt.

> "Our people originated at the base of the mountain of the Moon,
> at the origin of the Nile river where the god Hapi dwells."
>
> -The Ancient Egyptian tradition.

> "They also say that the Egyptians are colonists sent out by the Ethiopians, Asar having been
> the leader of the colony.
>
> -Diodorus

The Ancient Egyptians themselves said that their ancestors originated in the very interior of Africa, the place known as the source of the Nile. The land they were referring to is up-river, in the area of modern day Africa that is today occupied by the countries Uganda and southern Sudan. The Nile River, which flows down to the Mediterranean Sea originates in a mountainous region from which several tributary rivers flow to make one main watercourse known as the Nile River. The mountains in this region have such an elevation that even though they are located close to the equator, one may experience not only extremely low temperatures, but extreme weather conditions as well. This topography is ideal for promoting rains at particular times of the year. The interaction between the mountains and the winds and the attendant atmospheric conditions which develop annually are the key to what causes the production of snow. Then the snow melts forming streams, which then coalesce into rivers, which in turn nourish the entire region. Thus it is not surprising that this region, which includes Tanzania, would have been the place where the remains of the oldest known human being were discovered.

Below: Map of Africa

The Ancient Egyptians referred to Nubia as Kash (precursor to Kush), and Ta *Seti* ("Land of the Bow") presumably because of the skill of the Nubian archers who served in the Egyptian armies. The Ancient Egyptians also referred to Nubia as Wawat and Yam, which were capitals or centers of power in Nubia. Thus, these names were used at different periods. The term Yam is not used after the Old Kingdom Period. The term Kush (Cush) appears at about 2000 B.C.E., and at this time Kerma was the capital of the Nubian nation.

THE TERM KAMIT AND THE ORIGINS OF THE ANCIENT EGYPTIANS

Ancient Origins

As we have seen, the terms "Ethiopia," "Nubia," "Kush" and "Sudan" all refer to "black land" and/or the "land of the blacks." In the same manner we find that the name of Egypt which was used by the Ancient Egyptians also means "black land" and/or the "land of the blacks." The hieroglyphs below reveal the Ancient Egyptian meaning of the words related to the name of their land. It is clear that the meaning of the word Qamit is equivalent to the word Kush as far as they relate to "black land" and that they also refer to a differentiation in geographical location, i.e. Kush is the "black land of the south" and Qamit is the "black land of the north." Both terms denote the primary quality that defines Africa, "black" or "Blackness" (referring to the land and its people). The quality of blackness and the consonantal sound of K or Q as well as the reference to the land are all aspects of commonality between the Ancient Kushitic and Kamitan terms.

Qamit - Ancient Egypt

Qamit - blackness – black

Qamit - literature of Ancient Egypt – scriptures

Qamiu or variant — Ancient Egyptians-people of the black land.

Who Were the Ancient Egyptians?

Diodorus Siculus (Greek Historian) writes in the time of Augustus (first century B.C.):

"Now the Ethiopians, as historians relate, were the first of all men and the proofs of this statement, they say, are manifest. For that they did not come into their land as immigrants from abroad but were the natives of it and so justly bear the name of autochthones **(sprung from the soil itself),** is, they maintain, conceded by practically all men..."

"They also say that the Egyptians are colonists sent out by the Ethiopians, Asar having been the leader of the colony. For, speaking generally, what is now Egypt, they maintain, was not land, but sea, when in the beginning the universe was being formed; afterwards, however, as the Nile during the times of its inundation carried down the mud from Ethiopia, land was gradually built up from the deposit...And the larger parts of the customs of the Egyptians are, they hold, Ethiopian, the colonists still preserving their ancient manners. For instance, the belief that their kings are Gods, the very special attention which they pay to their burials, and many other matters of a similar nature, are Ethiopian practices, while the shapes of their statues and the forms of their letters are Ethiopian; for of the two kinds of writing which the Egyptians have, that which is known as popular **(demotic)** is learned by everyone, while that which is called sacred **(hieratic)**, is understood only by the priests of the Egyptians, who learnt it from their Fathers as one of the things which are not divulged, but among the Ethiopians, everyone uses these forms of letters. Furthermore, the orders of the priests, they maintain, have much the same position among both peoples; for all are clean who are engaged in the service of the gods, keeping themselves shaven, like the Ethiopian priests, and having the same dress and form of staff, which is shaped like a plough and is carried by their kings who wear high felt hats which end in a knob in the top and are circled by the serpents which they call asps; and this symbol appears to carry the thought that it will be the lot who shall dare to attack the king to encounter death-carrying stings. Many other things are told by them concerning their own antiquity and the colony which they sent out that became the Egyptians, but about this there is no special need of our writing anything."

The Ancient Egyptian texts state:

"Our people originated at the base of the mountain of the Moon, at the origin of the Nile river."

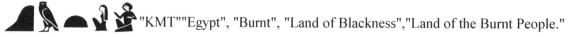"KMT""Egypt", "Burnt", "Land of Blackness","Land of the Burnt People."

KMT (Ancient Egypt) is situated close to Lake Victoria in present day Africa. This is the same location where the earliest human remains have been found, in the land currently known as Ethiopia-Tanzania. Recent genetic technology as reported in the new encyclopedias and leading news publications has revealed that all peoples of the world originated in Africa and migrated to other parts of the world prior to the last Ice Age 40,000 years ago. Therefore, as of this time, genetic testing has revealed that all humans are alike.

Therefore, there is only one human race who, due to different climactic and regional exposure, changed to a point where there seemed to be different "types" of people. Even in ancient times, differences were noted with respect to skin color, hair texture, customs, languages, and with respect to the essential nature (psychological and emotional makeup) due to the experiences each group had to face and overcome in order to survive. However, racial distinctions were not made. There is no such thing as races. There is only one human race.

From a philosophical standpoint, the question as to the origin of humanity is redundant when it is understood that <u>ALL</u> come from one origin which some choose to call the "Big Bang" and others "The Supreme Being."

> "Thou makest the color of the skin of one race to be different from that of another, but however many may be the varieties of mankind, it is thou that makes them all to live."
>
> —Ancient Egyptian Proverb from The Hymns of Amun

> "Souls, Heru, son, are of the self-same nature, since they came from the same place where the Creator modeled them; nor male nor female are they. Sex is a thing of bodies not of Souls."
>
> —Ancient Egyptian Proverb from The teachings of Aset to Heru

Historical evidence proves that Ethiopia-Nubia already had Kingdoms at least 300 years before the first Kingdom-Pharaoh of Egypt.

> "Ancient Egypt was a colony of Nubia - Ethiopia. ...Asar having been the leader of the colony..."

> "And upon his return to Greece, they gathered around and asked, "tell us about this great land of the Blacks called Ethiopia." And Herodotus said, "There are two great Ethiopian nations, one in Sind (India) and the other in Egypt."
>
> **-Recorded by** Diodorus **(Greek historian 100 B.C.)**

The pyramids themselves however, cannot be fully dated, but indications are that they existed far back in antiquity. The Pyramid Texts (hieroglyphs inscribed on pyramid walls) and Coffin Texts (hieroglyphs inscribed on coffins) speak authoritatively on the constitution of the human spirit, the vital Life Force along the human spinal cord (known in India as "Kundalini"), the immortality of the soul, reincarnation and the law of Cause and Effect (known in India as the Law of Karma).[10]

---

[10] For more detail see the book *African Origins of Civilization* by Muata Ashby

ANCIENT KAMITAN TERMS AND ANCIENT GREEK TERMS

Kamitan (Ancient Egyptian) Names	Greek Names
Amun	Zeus
Ra	Helios
Ptah	Hephastos
Nut	Rhea
Geb	Kronos
Net	Athena
Khonsu, Heryshaf	Heracles
Set	Ares or Typhon
Bast	Artemis
Uadjit	Leto
Asar (Ausar), Asar-Hapi	Osiris or Hades
Asar	Dionysus
Aset (Auset)	Isis or Demeter
Nebthet	Nephthys
Anpu or Apuat	Anubis
Hetheru	Hathor (Aphrodite)
Heru	Horus or Apollo
Djehuti	Thoth or Hermes
Maat	Astraea or Themis
Nekhebit	Eileithyia
Banebdjedut	Priapus and Pan
Sefer	Griffin
Hapi (bull of Menefer)	Apis
Nem-ur (bull of Anu)	Mnevis
Asar-Hapi (bull of Ptah-Sokar-Asar)	Serapis
Imhotep	Asclepius

Ancient Egyptian and Greek or Arabic

Djebu (Greek or Arabic= Edfu)
Pilak (Greek or Arabic= Philae)
Iunet (Greek or Arabic= Denderah),
Abdu (Greek or Arabic= Abydos)
Anu (Greek or Arabic= Heliopolis)
Waset (Greek or Arabic= Diospolis (i.e., Thebes))
Menefer (Greek or Arabic= Memphis)
Zau (Greek or Arabic= Sais).

In keeping with the spirit of the culture of Kamitan Spirituality, in this volume we will use the Kamitan names for the divinities through which we will bring forth the Philosophy of the Neteru. Therefore, the Greek name Osiris will be converted back to the Kamitan (Ancient Egyptian) Asar (Ausar), the Greek Isis to Aset (Auset), the Greek Nephthys to Nebthet, Anubis to Anpu or Apuat, Hathor to Hetheru, Thoth or Hermes to Djehuti, etc. (see the table below) Further, the term Ancient Egypt will be used interchangeably with "Kamit", or "Ta-Meri," as these are the terms used by the Ancient Egyptians to refer to their land and culture.

Chapter 1: What is Religion and What is the Nature of the Divine?

Introduction to Religion and Religious Studies

The Ancient Egyptian religion (⬚⬚⬚⬚⬚⬚⬚ Shetaut Neter), and its language and symbols provide the first "historical" record of mystical religion and Yoga Philosophy and Religious literature. Egyptian Yoga (*smai-tawy* ⬚⬚⬚⬚⬚) is what has been commonly referred to by Egyptologists as Egyptian "Religion" or "Mythology", but to think of it as just another set of stories or allegories about a long lost civilization is to completely miss the greatest secret of human existence. This unique perspective from the highest philosophical system which developed in Africa over thousands of years ago provides a new way to look at life, religion, the discipline of psychology and the way to spiritual development leading to spiritual Enlightenment. Egyptian mythology, when understood, gives every individual insight into their own divine nature and also a deeper insight into all religions and Yoga systems.

Those who wish to become Shemsu Neter (followers of the Kamitan (Ancient Egyptian) spiritual teaching, are initiated into Shetaut Neter and Smai Tawi. Shetaut Neter is the religion and its mythic teachings based on the varied traditions centered around one or more of the different gods and goddesses. Smai Tawi are the yogic disciplines, techniques or metaphysical technologies used to transform a human being. These disciplines promote a transformation through a movement that purifies the personality and renders it subtle enough to perceive the transcendental spiritual reality beyond time and space-called Nehast, Enlightenment, resurrection. This is a movement from ignorance to enlightenment, from mortality and weakness to immortality and supreme power, to discover the Absolute from whence the gods and goddesses and all Creation arose. This is a movement towards becoming one with the universe and the consciousness behind it, which is eternal and infinite. This is the lofty goal of initiation. So those who tread this path must be mature and virtuous as well as strong, physically, mentally (intellectually and emotionally). The purpose of the religion and disciplines is to promote purity of heart and virtue and these lead to higher realization and spiritual enlightenment. The next section will present an overview of Shetaut Neter and later the main traditions within Shetaut Neter spirituality will be presented.

THE TRUE PURPOSE OF RELIGION AS A SPIRITUAL PATH TO ENLIGHTENMENT AND IMMORTALITY

The term religion comes from the Latin "Relegare" which uses the word roots "RE", which means "BACK", and "LIGON", which means "to hold, to link, to bind." Therefore, the essence of true religion is that of linking back, specifically, linking its followers back to their original source and innermost essence. In this sense the terms "religion" and "yoga" are synonymous. That source which is the underlying reality behind every object in Creation is described as unborn, undying, eternal and immortal, and is known by an endless number of names, some of which are: Consciousness, Self, Higher Self, God, Goddess, Supreme Being, Divine Self, Eternal Self, Soul, Neberdjer, Pure Consciousness, Brahman, All, Allah, Neter Neteru, Creator, Absolute, Divine Mother, Great Spirit. These various names, while arising from various traditions and separate cultures, in reality represent the same divine and transcendental principle.

Although religion in its purest form is supposed to be a mystical system, the original intent and meaning of the scriptures are often misunderstood, if not distorted. This occurs because the various religions have developed in different geographic areas, and therefore, the lower levels (historical accounts, stories and traditions) have developed independently, and sometimes without proper guidance. Political conflicts often spill over into religious practice, distorting it. Under these conditions, the inner meanings of the myths and symbols become lost and the exoteric, folkloric meanings are emphasized. This leads to deism and a phenomenal (an occurrence or fact which is perceptible by the senses) approach to religion rather than a mystical, symbolic and transcendental understanding.

Most religions tend to be dogmatic and deistic at the elementary levels. Deism, as a religious belief or form of theism (belief in the existence of a God or gods), holds that God's action was restricted to an initial act of creation, after which He retired (separated) to contemplate the majesty of His work. Deists hold that the natural creation is regulated by laws put in place by God at the time of creation which are inscribed with perfect moral principles. Therefore, deism is closely related to the exoteric or personal understanding of the Divinity.

Myth → Ritual → Mysticism

In its complete form, religion is composed of three aspects, myth, ritual and metaphysics or the mystical experience (mysticism - mystical philosophy). While many religions contain rituals, traditions, metaphors and myths, there are few professionals trained in understanding their deeper aspects and psychological implications (metaphysics and mystical). Thus, there is often disappointment, frustration and disillusionment among many followers as well as leaders within many religions, particularly in the Western culture, because it is difficult to evolve spiritually without the proper spiritual guidance and faith alone is not sufficient to promote the highest spiritual evolution. Through introspection and spiritual research, it is possible to discover mythological vistas within religion which can rekindle the light of spirituality and at the same time increase the possibility of gaining a fuller experience of life. The exoteric (outer, ritualistic) forms of religion with which most people are familiar is only the tip of an iceberg so to speak; it is only a beginning, an invitation or prompting to seek a deeper (esoteric) discovery of the transcendental truths of existence.

There are several "High God" systems in Ancient Egyptian Mythology. High God means that the highest God or Goddess within that a system of theology is considered to be the original deity from which all others emanated as cosmic forces. Thus, in Asarian myth, Asar is known as Pa Neter or The God (High God) and Creation is composed of the cosmic forces which originated from the High Divinity. The cosmic forces are known as neters or gods and goddesses. It is important to understand that the High Gods and Goddesses as well as the Egyptian Trinities* originated from the same transcendental Supreme Being which was without name or form, but was referred to as Neter Neteru (Neter of Neters - Supreme Being above all gods and goddesses) and Neb-er-djer.

In this manner, the initiate is to understand that all of the gods and goddesses are in reality symbols, with names and forms, which represent the Divine in the varied manifest forms of nature. This produces a two aspected format of religion in which there is a personal aspect and a transpersonal aspect of God. The personal aspect is fixed in time and space with a name and form. This form is readily understood by the masses of human beings with ordinary spiritual awareness and is used in myths and stories. The second aspect, the transpersonal side, points our interest towards that which lies beyond the symbolic form. This is the unmanifest form of the Divine as it is expressed in the mystical teachings of religious mythology. Thus, the High God is a personal symbol or representation, with a name and form, of the nameless, formless, unmanifest and transcendental Supreme Being.

There are several forms of the Trinity in Ancient Egyptian religion depending on the geographic locality where the teaching was espoused. These included: Amun-Mut-Khons, Ptah-Sekhmet-Nefertum, Heru-Hetheru-Harsomtus (Heru the Younger), Khnum-Anukis-Satis, Ptah-Sokar-Asar. However, the most popular Trinity throughout all of Ancient Egypt was that of Asar-Aset-Heru.

Single Supreme, Transcendental Being - Pa Neter - Neter Neteru - Neberdjer
(unmanifest realm beyond time and space - names and forms)

High Gods and Goddesses manifesting as a Trinity: Amun-Ra-Ptah; Asar-Aset-Heru

The activity or awareness within the manifest or symbolic area of religious practice is within the purview of the mythological and ritual stages of religious practice while the activity within the unmanifest area is covered by the third and final level of religious practice, the mystical or metaphysical level.

The first sophisticated system of religion and yoga mystical philosophy in historical times occurred in Ancient Egypt. This system included all of the gods and goddesses which in later times became individually popular in various cities throughout Ancient Egypt. At the heart of this system of gods and goddesses was *Shetai*, the hidden and unmanifest essence of the universe, also known as Neberdjer and Amun. The system of religion of Ancient Egypt was called Shetaut Neter or the *Hidden Way of The Unmanifest Supreme Being.*

Hidden Way of The Unmanifest Supreme Being.

The term *shetaut* "unmanifest" relates to the fact that the Ancient Egyptians realized the illusory nature of physical reality. The phenomenal world, as it is perceived by the ordinary senses in a human being, is not the absolute reality of existence. In modern times, quantum physics experiments have uncovered the fact that "physical matter" is not "physical" at all, that it is "energy" in various states of manifestation or vibration. That energy is held together and sustained as well as given order by God through certain cosmic forces. Those forces are what Shetaut Neter calls *neteru* (gods and goddesses). However, physical experiments can only lead to indications about the neteru. In order to have a deeper understanding there must be also subtle spiritual experiments and communions with them. Thus, the Ancient Egyptians discovered that the phenomenal universe is only a "manifest" form which arises from a deeper, unmanifest source. This notion was extensively explained in Memphite Theology.[11] The theory of relativity relating to time and space was also expressed in the Ancient Egyptian creation stories long before Albert Einstein proposed his theory of relativity.

The entire system of mystical philosophy of the hidden Supreme Being, as well as the method through which that Being manifests in the form of the phenomenal physical universe and individual human consciousness, was explained in progressive stages in the theology of the Trinity known as Amun-Ra-Ptah, which was said to have arisen out of the Supreme Being: Neberdjer. As Ancient Egyptian history moved on through thousands of years, each segment of this Trinity was adopted by a particular priesthood and locality which then set about to explain and expound the philosophy of that particular segment of the Trinity. The priests and priestesses of the Ancient Egyptian city of Anu adopted Ra, the priests and priestesses of the Ancient Egyptian city of Hetkaptah adopted Ptah, and the priests and priestesses of the Ancient Egyptian city of Waset or Newt (Thebes) adopted Amun.

In a similar manner, the theology of the city of Abdu centered around the myth of Asar while the theology of Pilak (Philae) and other localities centered around the teachings of Aset. One of the reasons why the Asarian Trinity of Asar, Aset and Heru was so powerful is that it incorporated the teachings given in the entire primordial Trinity system of Neberdjer: Amun Ra Ptah, and brought them to the level of the common folk. It personalized the Divinity in such a way that every man and woman could partake of the myth and practice the rituals in everyday life, thereby attaining greater and greater closeness to the Divine. In this sense, every Ancient Egyptian citizen and the followers of the Asarian religion outside Egypt understood that the myth was in reality about every individual.

The mystical philosophy concerning the Trinity myth is so powerful, especially the Trinity of Asar-Aset-Heru, that when correctly understood, it holds the key to understanding the nature of Creation and of the nature of human consciousness. This is why the system of a Trinity was used in the religious system of India and later in Christianity, the former being modeled after the Ancient Egyptian system indirectly and the latter being directly modeled after the Ancient Egyptian system of the Asarian Resurrection.

The portrayal of God as a Father who begets a son who becomes his paraclete and revealer occurs first, and with most primacy, in Ancient Egypt, in the mythology of Neberdjer and Asar. Heru, in Egypt, was the reincarnation of Asar, his father, who was himself an incarnation of the High God Ra, the Absolute abode of all things. At the same time, Heru is the symbol of the human soul, the essential nature and the

---

[11] See the book *Memphite Theology* by Muata Ashby

innate hero/heroine within every human being. In much the same way, Jesus is the revealer and paraclete of God, The Father. In Eastern mystical philosophy, Buddha and Krishna are considered to be Avatars or incarnations of God. The original idea of Avatarism was that from time to time when unrighteousness reaches a certain level and threatens to overwhelm righteousness, God would manifest on earth in human form to restore virtue in the world. The purpose of Avatarism from the divine point of view is to sustain creation by maintaining the balance between the pairs of opposites in Creation. The disparity in the pairs of opposites is most evident in the rise of unrighteousness in society. In Ancient Egyptian mythology, the concept of Avatarism goes back in the predynastic era to the incarnations of Hetheru, as the destructive Eye of Ra, and Asar and Aset.

In Ancient Egyptian Mythology, the children of God (the Company of Gods and Goddesses) are not only Avatars, but they are also symbols or aspects of the human soul, and of creation itself. They, through their symbolic forms, are to be treated as models for the kind of behavior which leads to happiness and spiritual freedom. In this respect, the incarnation of God as an Avatar is really a metaphor which relates to the potential within every human being to discover and manifest their divine nature, and in so doing, become an Avatar. Thus, the passions, actions, relationships, teachings and fates of the gods and goddesses reveal the story of the human soul and the path it must follow in order to attain knowledge of its true divine nature and achieve liberation from ignorance, pain and suffering due to bondage to the world of time and space.

In Ancient Egypt, the concept of God, the ultimate and absolute reality behind all physical manifestations, was called Amn or Amun[12] or Neberdjer or Pa Neter (The God, The Supreme Being). In Hindu mythology, it is Brahman; to the Taoists, it is The Tao.

> "God is a metaphor for a mystery that transcends all human categories of thought...It depends on how much you want to think about it, whether or not it's doing you any good, whether it's putting you in touch with the mystery which is the ground of your own being."

> —**Joseph Campbell**

In this manner, the ancient Sages who originally established the teachings of mystical philosophy used metaphors and symbols to describe the ultimate and transcendental reality which is beyond the grasp of the ordinary human senses and mind. To describe this transcendental reality, the terms "God", "Supreme Being", "The Absolute", Pa Neter", "Neberdjer", etc., were created in an attempt to provide a concept which the human mind could understand.

MYTH, RELIGION, PSYCHO-MYTHOLOGY AND THE GODS AND GODDESSES

The Language of Myth

Myth is a fluid language. It is the language of concepts, which are represented through the symbols, themes, legends, traditions, heritage and philosophy contained in the myth. Myths are representations of the higher transcendental spiritual experience. Myth is the language of transcendental consciousness and a means for the ordinary unenlightened mind to relate to transcendental spiritual concepts. Myths use celestial beings, spirits, gods and goddesses and other special beings such as fantastic animals, journeys, struggles, etc to metaphorically relate the wisdom and pathway for those who wish to tread a path of life that leads to the discovery of the true meaning of life.

The gods and goddesses of Neterian religion may be thought of as the elements of myth and the mythology (study) of the Neterian Myths is a specialized discipline engaged by the elevated philosophers,

---

[12] Other spellings include Amun, Amen, Amon, Amonu, Amunu.)

priests and priestesses and mystics. In this capacity myth is to be understood as a psycho-spiritual language and code for penetrating the mysteries of life as related through the stories, legends and exploits of the gods and goddesses and their interaction with human beings, especially as they relate to the deification of human existence or rather the elevation and transformation of human existence into god and goddess existence. This I call psycho-mythology.

PSYCHOMYTHOLOGY

Mystical teaching holds that the essence of Creation and therefore, of each individual human being, is transcendental; it transcends the ordinary bounds of mental perception and understanding. However, all human experiences occur in and through the mind. Therefore, the heart of all human experiences, be they painful or pleasurable, is rooted in the mind. The purpose of myth is to bridge the gap between the limited human mind and its conscious, worldly level and that which transcends all physicality as well as the mind and senses. Thus, religious myths, which will be our primary focus in this volume, must be understood in the light of their psychological and mystical (transcending body, mind and senses) implications. We will refer to this concept by a new term: *"Psycho-Mythology."*

So the term *"psycho,"* as it is used here, must be understood as far more than simply that which refers to the mind in the worldly sense. The term "psycho" must be understood to mean everything that constitutes human consciousness in all of its stages and states, but most importantly, the subconscious and unconscious levels of mind. *"Mythology"* here refers to the study of the codes, messages, ideas, directives, stories, culture, beliefs, etc., that affect the personality through the conscious, subconscious and unconscious aspects of the mind of an individual, specifically those effects which result in psycho-spiritual transformation, that is, a transpersonal or transcendental change in the personality of an individual which leads to the discovery of the transcendental reality behind all existence.

A myth should never be understood literally even though some of its origins may involve actual events or actions, otherwise one will miss the transcendental message being related through the metaphor. This would be like going to a theater to see a fictional movie or reading a fantasy novel, and believing it to be real. However, as a movie or novel may be based on unreal events and yet carry an important message which is imparted through the medium of actors, a plot and so on, mystical myths are not to be understood as being completely baseless nor as having been put together purely for entertainment or as "primitive mumbo-jumbo." Myths constitute a symbolic language that speaks to people in psycho-symbolic ways, satisfying their conscious need for entertainment, but also affecting the subconscious and unconscious mind and its need for spiritual evolution. This psychological language of myths can lead people to understand and experience the transcendental truths of existence, which cannot be easily expressed in words.

Myth is the first stage of religion and the reenactment of the myth constitutes the second level religion: Ritual.[13] Myths constitute the heart and soul of rituals. Myth is a mystical language for transmitting and teaching the principles of life and creation. Rituals are the medium through which the myths are practiced, lived and realized.

The study of religious mythical stories is important to gain insight into the *"Psycho-Mythology"* or psychological implications of myth for the spiritual transformation of the individual which leads to the attainment of Enlightenment. Enlightenment implies the attainment of an expanded state of consciousness, termed as *"awet ab,"* dilation (expansion) of the heart in Ancient Egyptian Mystical Philosophy, in which there is a full and perfect awareness of one's existence beyond the mind and body. Thus, when you delve into a myth, you must expect more than just entertainment. You should be equipped with the knowledge which will allow you to decipher the hidden meanings in the story so that you may also begin to experience and benefit from them on a personal level, i.e. live the myth and on a spiritual level, i.e. attain enlightenment. Only then will a person be able to engender a real transformation in their life which will lead you to true fulfillment and happiness as well as contentment. This is the third level of religious practice, the mystical or metaphysical level.

---

[13] *Resurrecting Osiris*, Muata Ashby, 1997

Myth in Orthodox Religion

As stated earlier, religion is composed of three aspects, *mythological, ritual* and *metaphysical* or the *mystical experience* (mysticism - mystical philosophy). Mystical philosophy is the basis of myth. It is expressed in ritual and experienced in the metaphysics (spiritual disciplines, yoga) of the given religion.

An important theme, which will be developed throughout this volume, is the understanding of complete religion, that is, in its three aspects, *mythological, ritual* and *metaphysical* or the *mystical experience*. At the first level, a human being learns the stories and traditions of the religion. At the second level, rituals are learned and practiced. At the third level the practitioner, now called a spiritual aspirant, is led to actually go beyond myths and rituals and to attain the ultimate goal of religion. This is an important principle, because many religions present different aspects of philosophy at different levels, and an uninformed onlooker may label it as primitive or idolatrous, etc., without understanding what is going on. For example, Hinduism[14] and Ancient Egyptian religion present polytheism and duality at the first two levels of religious practice. However, at the third level, mysticism, the practitioner is made to understand that all of the gods and goddesses being worshipped do not exist in fact, but are in reality aspects of the single, transcendental Supreme Self. This means that at the mystical level of religious practice the concept of religion and its attendant symbols must also be left behind, that is to say, transcended. The mystical disciplines constitute the technology or means by which the myth and ritual of religion, and the spiritual philosophy can be developed to its highest level.

In contrast, orthodox religions present images as if they are in fact mundane realities as well as transcendental reality. By definition, idolatry is the presentation of an image of the divine as if it is a reality. Therefore, orthodox traditions are the true idolaters and mystical religions, since they do not ascribe absolute or abiding qualities to their images, are not idolatrous.

In order to fully understand the message of myth it is important to keep in mind some important keys.

The Keys to Reading and Understanding a Myth

Key #1: Myths (Religious/Mystical) are relevant to our lives in the present.
Key #2: Myth is a journey of spiritual transformation.
Key #3: Myths are to be lived in order to understand their true meaning.
Key #4: Myth points the way to victory in life.

---

[14] The word "Hinduism" is a Western term. The religion called Hinduism is actually referred to by the Hindus themselves as "Sanatana-Dharma," which means "the eternal law" or "the path or righteous actions or way of life." The major religion of the Indian subcontinent is Hinduism. The word derives from an ancient Sanskrit term meaning "dwellers by the Indus River," a reference to the location of India's earliest known civilization in what is now Pakistan. (*Feuerstein, Georg, The Shambhala Encyclopedia of Yoga* 1997 and *Compton's Interactive Encyclopedia.* Copyright (c) 1994, 1995 Compton's NewMedia, Inc. All Rights Reserved) .

Summary of African Shetaut Neter Religion and Philosophy

The Spiritual Culture and the Purpose of Life: Shetaut Neter

"Men and women are to become God-like through a life of virtue and the cultivation of the spirit through scientific knowledge, practice and bodily discipline."

-Ancient Egyptian Proverb

The highest forms of Joy, Peace and Contentment are obtained when the meaning of life is discovered. When the human being is in harmony then it is possible to reflect and meditate upon the human condition and realize the limitations of worldly pursuits. When there is peace and harmony a human being can practice any of the varied disciplines, designated as Shetaut Neter, to promote the evolution of the human being towards the ultimate goal of life which is Spiritual Enlightenment. Spiritual Enlightenment is the awakening of the human being to the awareness of the transcendental essence which binds the universe and which is eternal and immutable. In this discovery is also the sobering and ecstatic realization that the human being is one with that transcendental essence. With this realization come great joy, peace and power to experience the fullness of life and to realize the purpose of life during the time on earth. The lotus is a symbol of Shetaut Neter, meaning the turning towards the light of truth, peace and transcendental harmony.

Shetitu

The Shetaut (mysteries- rituals, wisdom, philosophy) about the Neter (Supreme Being) are related in the *Shetitu* or writings related to the hidden teachings (the mysteries). Those writings are referred to as *Medu Neter* or "Divine Speech," are the writings of the god Djehuti (Ancient Egyptian god of the divine word) – and also refers to any hieroglyphic texts or inscriptions generally. The term Medu Neter makes use of a special hieroglyph, which means "*medu*" or "staff - walking stick, speech." This means that speech is the support for the Divine, . Thus, just as the staff supports an elderly person, the hieroglyphic writing (the word) is a prop (staff) which sustains the Divine in the realm of time and space. That is, the Divine writings contain the wisdom which enlightens us about the Divine, *Shetaut Neter.*

If Medu Neter is mastered then the spiritual aspirant becomes *Maakheru* or true of thought, word and deed, that is, purified in body, mind and soul. The symbol *medu* is static while the symbol of *kheru* is dynamic.

This term (Maakheru) uses the glyph *kheru* which is a rudder – oar (rowing), symbol of voice, meaning that purification occurs when the righteous movement of the word, when it is used (rowing-movement) to promote virtue, order, peace, harmony and truth. So Medu Neter is the potential word and Maa kheru is the perfected word in action.

The hieroglyphic texts (Medu Neter) become (Maakheru) effective in the process of religion when they are used as *hekau* - the Ancient Egyptian "transformative words of power" when the word is *Shedy,* studied, *Hesi,* chanted and *Shmai*- sung and thereby one performs **or** *Dua* or worship of the Divine. The divine word allows the speaker to control the gods and goddesses, i.e. the cosmic forces, and thereby reshape the reality of life. This concept is really based on the idea that human beings are higher order beings if they learn about the nature of the universe and elevate themselves through virtue and wisdom.

Fundamental Principles of Shetaut Neter African Religion

What is Shetaut Neter? The Ancient Egyptians were African peoples who lived in the north-eastern quadrant of the continent of Africa. They were descendants of the Nubians (Kushites-present day Sudan), who had themselves originated from farther south into the heart of Africa at the great lakes region, the sources of the Nile River. They realized that the universe has certain absolute truths and regularities such as the order of the heavens and the annual Nile flood and the daily rise and setting of the sun. These reflections led to the realization that there is a transcendental being who ordered Creation and who sustains it and that acting in harmony with that truth allows a human being to discover peace and universal self-knowledge but most people are unaware of that truth; it is a mystery to them. They created a vast civilization and culture earlier than any other society in known history and organized a nation which was based on the concepts of balance and order as well as spiritual enlightenment. These ancient African people called their land Kamit and soon after developing a well-ordered society they began to realize that the world is full of wonders but life is fleeting and that there must be something more to human existence. They developed spiritual systems that were designed to allow human beings to understand the nature of this secret being who is the essence of all Creation. They called this spiritual system *"Shtaut Ntr."*

Definitions:

Shetaut means hidden, secrets, mysterious things.

Neter means Divinity.

The Religion of Ancient Kamit (Egypt) is *Neterianism.* The terms "Shetaut Neter" and "Neterianism" will be used interchangeably throughout this work.

The Origin of the Term Shetaut

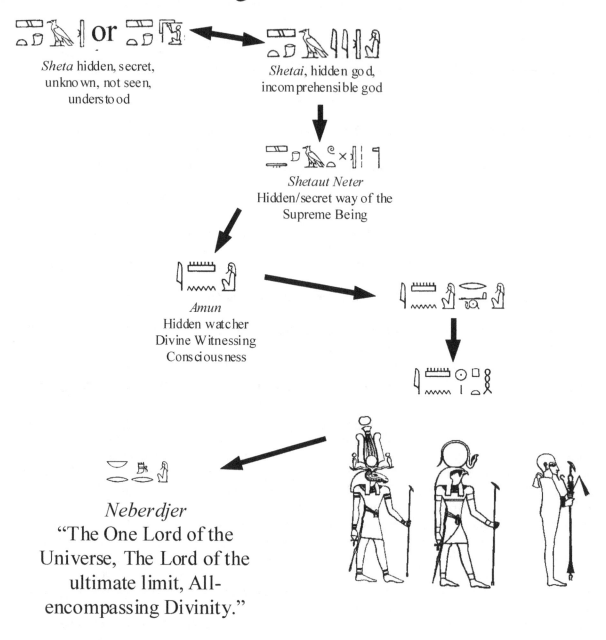

Sheta hidden, secret, unknown, not seen, understood

Shetai, hidden god, incomprehensible god

Shetaut Neter
Hidden/secret way of the Supreme Being

Amun
Hidden watcher
Divine Witnessing
Consciousness

Neberdjer
"The One Lord of the Universe, The Lord of the ultimate limit, All-encompassing Divinity."

Neberdjer Speaks:
"I was One
And then I
became three"

The term *"Shetaut"* has its root in the term *Sheta* which means "hidden" or "Secret," i.e. a mystery. The Divine (Neter) is a mystery because it is hidden from the physical senses and the simple-minded personalities. So religion is the study of the hidden Divinity (Shetaut Neter, lit. hidden Divine Self). The term Amun also means Hidden. Amun is the first aspect in a Triune manifestation of spirit (Amun-Ra-Ptah) which emanates from the "All-Encompassing" Divinity called "Neberdjer."

Who is Neter?

"Ntr"

The symbol of Neter was described by an Ancient Kamitan sage as:

"That which is placed in the coffin"

The term Ntr , or Ntjr, comes from the Ancient Egyptian hieroglyphic language which did not record most of its vowels. However, the term survives in the Coptic language as *"Nutar."* The same Coptic meaning (divine force or sustaining power) applies in the present as it did in ancient times, It is a symbol composed of a wooden staff that was wrapped with strips of fabric, like a mummy. The strips alternate in color with yellow, green and blue. The mummy in Kamitan spirituality is understood to be the dead but resurrected Divinity. So the Nutar is actually every human being who does not really die, but goes to live on in a different form. Further, the resurrected spirit of every human being is that same Divinity. Phonetically, the term Nutar is related to other terms having the same meaning, the Latin "natura," Spanish "naturaleza," English "nature" and "nutriment", etc. In a real sense, as we will see, *Ntr* means power manifesting as Neteru and the Neteru are the objects of creation, i.e. "nature."

THE FOLLOWER OF NETERIANISM

"Shemsu Neter"

"Follower (of) Neter"

The term "Neterianism" is derived from the name "Shetaut Neter." Those who follow the spiritual path of Shetaut Neter are therefore referred to as "Neterians."

Neterianism is the science of Neter, that is, the study of the secret or mystery of Neter, the enigma of that which transcends ordinary consciousness but from which all creation arises. The world did not come from nothing, nor is it sustained by nothing. Rather it is a manifestation of that which is beyond time and space but which at the same time permeates and maintains the fundamental elements in time and space. In other words, it is the substratum of Creation and the essential nature of all that exists.

The Neterian Philosophy of God

"God is the father of beings. God is the eternal One... and infinite and endures forever. God is hidden and no man knows God's form. No man has been able to seek out God's likeness. God is hidden to Gods and men... God's name remains hidden... It is a mystery to his children, men, women and Gods. God's names are innumerable, manifold and no one knows their number... though God can be seen in form and observation of God can be made at God's appearance, God cannot be understood... God cannot be seen with mortal eyes... God is invisible and inscrutable to Gods as well as men."

-Portions from the Egyptian Book of Coming forth by Day and the papyrus of Nesi-Khonsu

The Neterian statements above give the idea that God is the unfathomable mystery behind all phenomena, which cannot be discerned "even by the gods." However, God is the unfathomable mystery as well as the innermost essence of his children. This means that God is transcendental, the unmanifest, but also what is manifest as well. In order to perceive this reality it is necessary to transcend ordinary human vision. When this transcendental Self is spoken about through different names and metaphors, the idea often emerges that there are many faces to the ultimate deity or Supreme Being. Nevertheless, as has been previously discussed, it must be clear that all the Neterian spiritual traditions and divinities are in reality referring to the same Supreme Being, the transcendental reality. The following Neterian texts encapsulate the Neterian concept of God as nondual, all-encompassing divinity.

UA ⟨hieroglyphs⟩ or "One,"

UA UA ⟨hieroglyphs⟩ "One One"

UA NETER ⟨hieroglyphs⟩ or "One God,"

UA NETER UA UR ⟨hieroglyphs⟩, "Only Great One"

UA UA UR AN TIF ⟨hieroglyphs⟩ "Only One Without a second"

The following passages come from the Egyptian Book of Coming Forth By Day (Chapter. clxxiii):

"I praise thee, Lord of the Gods, God One, living in truth."

The following passage is taken from a hymn where princess Nesi-Khonsu glorifies Amen-Ra:

"August Soul which came into being in primeval time, the great god living in truth, the first Nine Gods who gave birth to the other two Nine Gods,[15] the being in whom every God existeth One One, ⟨hieroglyphs⟩ the creator of the kings who appeared when the earth took form in the beginning, whose birth is hidden, whose forms are manifold, whose germination cannot be known."

Philosophy of The Great Awakening

"Nehast"

---

[15] Ancient Egyptian mythology conceives of creation as an expression of God in which there are nine primordial cosmic principles or forces in the universe. These first nine may be seen as the cause from which all other qualities of nature *(the other two Nine Gods)* or creative forces in nature arise.

Nehast means to "wake up," to Awaken to the higher existence. In the Prt m Hru Text it is said:

Nuk pa Neter aah Neter Ejah asha ren[16]

"I am that same God, the Supreme One, who has myriad of mysterious names."

The end of all the Neterian disciplines is to discover the meaning of "Who am I", to unravel the mysteries of life and to fathom the depths of eternity and infinity. This is the task of all human beings and it is to be accomplished in this very lifetime.

This can be done by learning the ways of the Neteru, emulating them and finally becoming like them, Akhus, (enlightened beings), walking the earth as giants and accomplishing great deeds such as the creation of the universe!

The General Principles of Shetaut Neter African Religion

1. The Purpose of Life is to Attain the Great Awakening-Enlightenment-Know thyself.

2. SHETAUT NETER enjoins the Shedy (spiritual investigation) as the highest endeavor of life.

3. SHETAUT NETER enjoins the responsibility of every human being is to promote order and truth.

4. SHETAUT NETER enjoins the performance of Selfless Service to family, community and humanity.

5. SHETAUT NETER enjoins the Protection of nature.

6. SHETAUT NETER enjoins the Protection of the weak and oppressed.

7. SHETAUT NETER enjoins the Caring for hungry.

8. SHETAUT NETER enjoins the Caring for homeless.

9. SHETAUT NETER enjoins the equality for all people.

10. SHETAUT NETER enjoins the equality between men and women.

11. SHETAUT NETER enjoins the justice for all.

12. SHETAUT NETER enjoins the sharing of resources.

13. SHETAUT NETER enjoins the protection and proper raising of children.

14. SHETAUT NETER enjoins the movement towards balance and peace.

---

[16] (Prt M Hru 9:4)

The Creation of The Universe and the Origin of the Gods and Goddesses

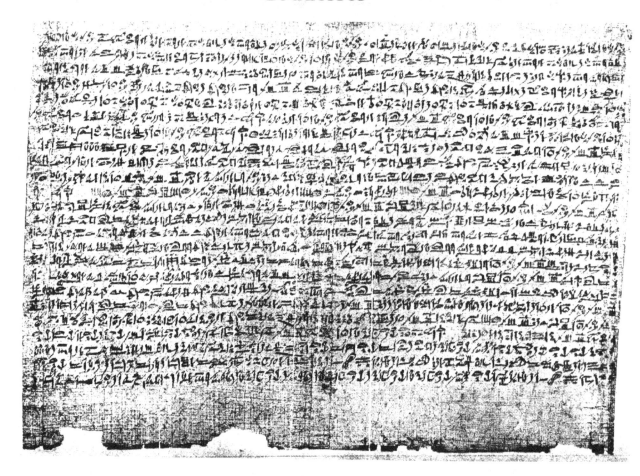

Above: The papyrus containing the ancient Egyptian myth of the History of Creation.

The process of creation of the universe is explained in the form of a cosmological system for better understanding. Cosmology is a branch of philosophy dealing with the origin, processes, and structure of the universe. Cosmogony is the astrophysical study of the creation and evolution of the universe. Both of these disciplines are inherent facets of Ancient Egyptian philosophy through the main religious systems or Companies of the gods and goddesses. A *pauti* or Company of Gods and Goddesses is a group of deities, which symbolize a particular cosmic force, or principles that emanates from the all-encompassing Supreme Being from which they have all emerged. The Self or Supreme Being manifests creation through the properties and principles represented by the *Pauti* Company of Gods and Goddesses - cosmic laws of nature. The system or Company of Gods and Goddesses of Anu is regarded as the oldest, and also forms the basis of the Asarian Trinity. It is expressed in the diagram of the *Pautti* **Of Anunian Cosmology** or Company of Gods and Goddesses who formed the creation of the universe based on the creation story of the theological teaching that was developed by the priests and priestesses of the Ancient Egyptian city of Anu (also known to the Greeks as "Heliopolis").

THE COMPANIES OF GODS AND GODDESSES

Study of the term "Pa"

Before going on it is important to understand the Neterian concept of Pauti. Pauti means Company of Gods and Goddesses. By studying the phonetic and pictorial (Kamitan language is not only phonetic, but also illustrative) etymology (the origin and development of a linguistic form) and etiology (the study of causes or origins) of names and applying the initiatic science, it is possible to decipher the mysteries of Creation by discovering the teachings embedded in the language by the Sages of Ancient Egypt.

For example, the Kamitan word "Pa" is central to understanding the deeper essence of nature, divinity and the gods and goddesses of the Neterian religion. In the study of the word "Pa," philosophy as well as pictorial and phonetic associations must be considered. Along with this, the variations in spellings act to expand the possible associations and thereby also the appropriate meaning in the given usage. Sometimes the very same words may be used, but the usage in different texts denotes a slight difference in the nuance of the meaning in accordance with the usage. This aspect of assigning the proper meaning of a word which is used sometimes even with the same spelling but in different contexts in different or even the same Kamitan scriptures, is an artistic development which comes to a translator with time. Thus, there is greater and greater approximation to the higher intended truth behind the teaching as advancement in the teaching moves forward. Also, it should be remembered that research here implies not only studying books, but also meditation and introspection, as well as living in accordance with the philosophy.

The Ancient Egyptian words and symbols related to the Company of Gods and Goddesses (*Pauti*) indicate several important mystical teachings. The root of the Ancient Egyptian word Pauti is *Pa* (Figure A- Above). *Pa* means "to exist." Thus, Creation is endowed with the quality of existence as opposed to non-existence. *Pau* (Figure B) is the next progression in the word. It means the Primeval Divinity, the source of Creation. *Paut* (Figure C and D) is the next evolution of the word, *Pau*, meaning primeval time and the very substance out of which everything is created is the one and the same. *Pauti* is the next expression of *Pa* and it has two major meanings. It refers to the Primeval Divinity or Divine Self (God) (Figure E). *Pautiu* refers to *Pauti* but in plural, as well as being a gender specific term implying, the Divinity as the source of the multiplicity in creation. In the Ancient Egyptian language, like Spanish for example, all objects are assigned gender. Also, *Pauti* refers to the deities who comprise the Company of Gods and Goddesses (Figure G and H). *Paut* (men) or *Pautet* (women) also refers to living beings, especially human beings (Figure I).

Pa ➔ Pau ➔ Paut ➔ Pauti ➔ Pautiu ➔ Paut and Pautet

The most important teaching relating to the nature of Creation is being given here. The neteru (gods and goddesses) are in a sense, iconographical and philosophical representations of cosmic principles that exist and manifest in Creation. If those philosophical principles were correctly understood, that is, realized spiritually, that would lead to knowing the secrets of the universe. In a higher sense, the neteru of the creation are not separate principles or entities. They are in reality one and the same as the Primeval Divinity. They are expressions of that Divine Self. However, they are not transformations of or evolutions from the Divine Self, but the very same Divine Self expressing as Creation temporarily. So even though God is referred to as a primordial deity who did something a long time ago or set into motion various things, in reality God and Creation are one and the same. With this understanding, it is clear to see that God is not distant and aloof, observing Creation from afar. The Divine Self is the very basis of Creation and is in every part of it at all times. This is why the terms *Pa-Neter* and *Neteru* both used to describe the Divine. Pa-Neter means "The Supreme Being" and Neteru means "the gods and goddesses." Also, the word "Neteru" refers to creation itself. So Neter-u emanates from Neter. Creation is nothing but God who has assumed various forms or Neteru: trees, cake, bread, human beings, metal, air, fire, water, animals, planets, space, electricity, etc. This is a profound teaching which should be reflected upon constantly so that the mind may become enlightened to its deeper meaning and thereby discover the Divinity in nature as well as the inner Higher Self.

The Etymological, Etiological, Phonetic and Pictorial Study of the Kamitan word "Pa"	Meaning
A-	A- **Pa**- demonstrative, this, the, to exist
B-	B- **Pau** - Primeval Divinity- The Existing One
C-	C- **Paut**- Primeval time - remote ages-beginning time
D-	D- **Paut**- stuff, matter, substance, components which make something up.
E-	E- **Pauti**- The Primeval God; Primeval Divinity who is self-Created; Dual form relates to rulership of Upper and Lower Egypt
F-	F- **Pauti-u**- Primeval Divinity with male or female determinative - source of all multiplicity in Creation.
G-	G- **Pat** (paut) **n Neteru**- Company of Gods and Goddesses
H-	H- **Pauti**- Company of nine gods and goddesses
I-	I- **Pau** or **Paut** -human beings, me, women

GOD IS CREATION

The *Pau* - self existent spirit, God, created all things out of *Paut*, the stuff or matter or substance or material out of which all is made (food-objects-people-gods-planets-stars-etc.). Thus, came into being the *Pauti* Company of Gods and Goddesses, and God is also known as Pauti because Creation is made of God stuff.

The Divine Self is not only in Creation but is the very essence of every human being as well. Therefore, the substratum of every human being, regardless of their ethnicity or religion is in reality God as well. The task of spiritual practice is to discover this essential nature within one's own heart. This can occur if one reflects upon this teaching and realizes its meaning by discovering its reality in the deepest recesses of one's own experience. When this occurs, the person who has attained this level of self-discovery is referred to as having become enlightened, awakened. They have discovered their true, divine nature. They have discovered their oneness with the Divine Self.

In conclusion, it must be understood that the Kamitan language is synonymous with Kamitan philosophy. As such, when speaking, one must adhere to truth. The ultimate truth is, that when we speak of objects, we are in reality speaking about principles, the deeper basis of which is the Divine Self. When words are spoken, they immediately take on the first level of reality as they engender an image in the mind of the listener. When a listener acts upon what has been heard, the speech takes on a reality in the physical plane. Therefore, the speech is a reflection of an idea, a concept, and the physical reality is a reflection of speech. The cause underlying the concept is the real name of a thing, its higher reality, and this essence has no name or form in its potentiality, but only in its relative manifestation. This relative manifestation is the world of time and space and all living and non-living objects in it. Therefore, we have three levels of reality, the thought, the word and the actual object existing in the physical world. However, these are only relative realities since they are all ephemeral in nature and not abiding. They require a mind (which is a relative object itself) to give them meaning. The creative essence (God-transcendental consciousness) which gave power to the thought, the concept, is the source and substratum which lends temporary reality to the projection (thought, the word and the actual object).

The Divinity Beyond Names

In Neterian philosophy the name is an extremely important aspect of being. Naming something, anything, imbues it with a certain reality, an existence that it does not have without the name. Transcending the name means transcending time and space for only things of time and space i.e. that come into the realm of relative existence, are namable. That transcendental essence, from which the named objects of Creation come, is the absolute, the Supreme essence, and that is the All-source. We all have an aspect which is that essence and that teaching is reflected in the following passages from the Ancient Egyptian Pert m Heru text wherein the initiate says the following:

> I am that same God, the Supreme One, who has myriad of mysterious names. I was born of Temu, the first divinity that came into existence. I know this! I am one possessing the knowledge of the innermost truth.

From Prt M Hru Chapter 9

> I am the substratum of all the gods and goddesses.

From Prt M Hru Chapter 26

> I am Ra! I am one whose name is unknown[17], Lord of Eternity...

From Prt M Hru Chapter 27

---

[17] one of the most ancient and mystical names to describe the transcendental Divinity, "Nameless One". This term also refers to the Primeval being who arose from the Primeval Ocean, bringing Creation into existence, i.e. Atum.

Neter and the Neteru

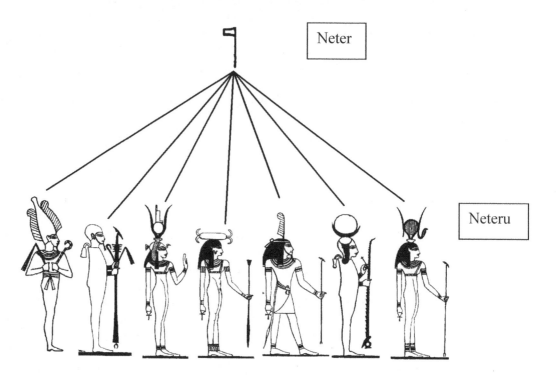

The concept of Neter and Neteru binds and ties all of the varied forms of Kamitan spirituality into one vision of the gods and goddesses all emerging from the same Supreme Being. Therefore, ultimately. Kamitan spirituality is not polytheistic, nor is it monotheistic in the sense espoused by the western religions, for it holds that the Supreme Being is more than a God but an all-encompassing Absolute Divinity.

"Neteru"

The term "Neteru" means "gods and goddesses." This means that from the ultimate and transcendental Supreme Being, "Neter," come the Neteru. There are countless Neteru. So from the one come the many. These Neteru are cosmic forces that pervade the universe. They are the means by which Neter sustains Creation and manifests through it. So Neterianism may be thought of as a kind of "monotheistic polytheism." The one Supreme Being expresses as many gods and goddesses and at the end of time, after their work of sustaining Creation is finished, these gods and goddesses are again absorbed back into the Supreme Being.

All of the spiritual systems of Ancient Egypt (Kamit) have one essential aspect that is common to all; they all hold that there is a Supreme Being (Neter) who manifests in a multiplicity of ways through nature, the Neteru.

Like sunrays, the Neteru emanate from the Divine and they are its manifestations. So by studying the Neteru we learn about and are led to discover their source, the Neter. And with this discovery we are enlightened.

The Neteru may be depicted anthropomorphically or zoomorphically or in a combination (composite) form in accordance with the teaching about Neter that is being conveyed through them.

Chapter 2: The Main Spiritual Traditions –Schools of Religious Philosophies of Neterianism Related to the Principal Gods an Goddesses

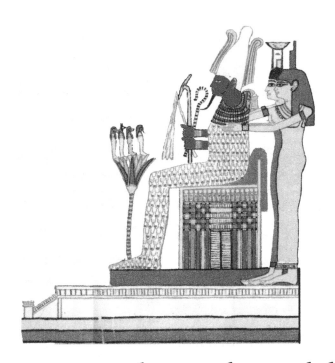

How many Gods and Goddesses?

Stipulation

It is important to understand that it is not possible to list all the gods and goddesses of Neterian Spirituality (Ancient Egyptian Religion). This is because they are too numerous. The reason for the large number is that in African religion all nature is seen as embodying some essential principle derived from the transcendental Divinity. Therefore, all is a manifestation of divinity in some form or another. However, what can be done is to list and describe the main divinities neteru (gods and goddesses) and supportive neteru and show how the divinities encompass the entire breadth of divinities in aggregate. Having a basic understanding about what each of the principal divinities represents provides insight into the nature of self and the divine essence behind all. This of course is the first step to understanding the code which is embedded in the myths. That code is the key to unlocking the Shetaut (Mysteries) of the mysticism of life and the means to attain spiritual awakening, which is the highest goal of all spiritual endeavors in any religion.

The Classes of Gods and Goddesses

Firstly, it must be understood that there are two categories of sentient being. Firstly, there are deities and human beings. Secondly, according to Maat philosophy all sentient beings fall into two categories, those who follow Maat and those who follow anMaat (unrighteousness). The deities may be divided into two classes, the Neteru or Gods and Goddesses and the Sebau or Demons. Both the Neteru and the Sebau emanate from Pa-Neter (The Supreme Being). They constitute the duality of Creation. Just as there are human beings who follow Maat and others who follow anMaat so too there are some divinities that follow Maat and others who follow anMaat. The Neteru lead to freedom, and spiritual expansion, what is good and true. The Sebau lead to worldliness, what is base, dull and painful and frustrating (bondage to the world of time and space).

Gods and Goddesses	**Demons**
Neteru- Gods and Goddesses	*Seba*- Demon enemy of Ra *Sebau*- Devils- associates of Seba *Sebaut*- evil things- demoniac things
Teaching	Notice that the terms for demons are phonetically synonymous with the terms for teachers. This is a Kamitan pun relating to the opposites. One enlightens and the other darkens.
Sba (or Seba) means teach, enlighten. *Sbaa* (or Sebaa) - teachers teach, bring up, educate, train, instruct. *Sbau* (or Sebau) are the teachers, instructors. *Sbai* is the Spiritual Preceptor.	The Neteru are teachers and leaders to the righteous. The priests and priestesses are their intermediaries in the world.

The neteru, gods and goddesses of Neterian religion may be grouped as follows. There are two main categories. First there is the transcendental, the Supreme Being; then there is the temporal, the gods and goddesses who emanate from the Supreme Being and do the work of creation and sustain life.

In the realm of time and space (Djeta) there are three divisions. There are gods and goddesses of the earth realm (Ta), gods and goddesses of the Duat (upper-Netherworld) realm and gods and goddesses of the Pet or heavenly (lower astral plane) realm.

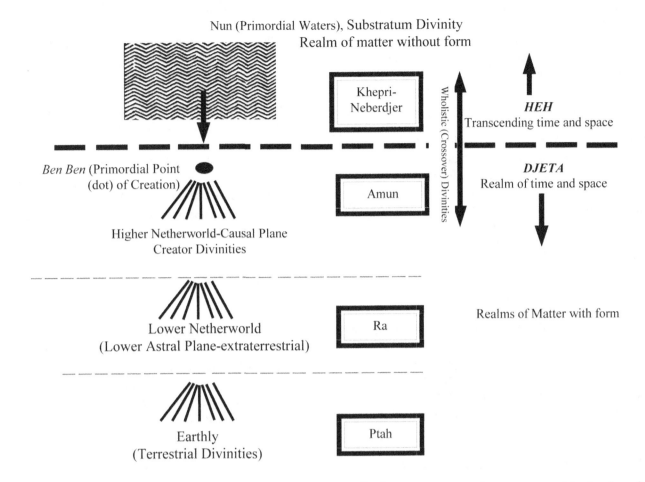

Nun (Primordial Waters), Substratum Divinity
Realm of matter without form

Khepri-Neberdjer

HEH
Transcending time and space

Wholistic (Crossover) Divinities

Ben Ben (Primordial Point (dot) of Creation)

Amun

DJETA
Realm of time and space

Higher Netherworld-Causal Plane Creator Divinities

Lower Netherworld
(Lower Astral Plane-extraterrestrial)

Ra

Realms of Matter with form

Earthly
(Terrestrial Divinities)

Ptah

TRANSCENDENTAL DIVINITIES

First of all it is important to understand that there is a concept in Neterian Religion of a nameless and formless Divinity that transcends concepts, and thought and cannot be circumscribed within the confines of philosophy. This is the ultimate and transcendental absolute, infinite and unfathomable essence. That Supreme Divinity has no name, no image, no origin; it is indefinable, unfathomable and unknowable through the ordinary mind in time and space but is referred to philosophically as *Khemn ren f- he whose name is not known - i.e. God.* That transcendental absolute is discovered only when the person transcends the mind and senses and time and space.

For purposes of divine worship and ordinary spiritual practice in religion the abstractness of an absolute divinity is impractical. The mind needs a firm image, *tut* (form-image), and concept to grasp hold of especially in the beginning practice of religion but even into the more advanced stages.

Having a concrete form to worship is therefore essential for the effective practice of religion. Through these forms the wisdom related to the nature of the Divine is related to the human mind in a manner that is accessible. When the mind is confronted with an abstract image it cannot easily relate to it. There must be much work done in order for that to happen. However, when the mind is confronted with images that are making use of concepts and images that the mind is already familiar with it is able to more easily comprehend the meaning of the teaching. A relationship needs to be established and for this purpose the sages have used basic human communication and relational modalities in order to convey the teachings of spirituality. This is the purpose of the neteru. In this sense all divinities besides the transcendental absolute are only manifestations in time, space imagery for the benefit of spiritual practice only. Therefore they are relative realities. The task of every aspirant is to discover the transcendental absolute reality of the God(dess). This is what bestows the sought after illumination, that *Nehast* (Great Awakening) that confers immortality and freedom from the bonds of ignorance and human delusion, pain, and sorrow. When the mind matures it is able to grasp the higher conceptualizations contained in the iconographies and myths. In this manner the mind is able to gradually become more purified in it's understanding of the Divine and thereby approach the Divine in a realistic manner. The neteru may therefore be considered as belonging to two classes: unmanifest and manifest. The manifest exists in a hierarchy stretching forth from the subtlest to the gross. Some have transitional qualities (they function between different levels or planes of existence. Through their interactions and capacities we learn the teaching of spirituality that is contained in the myths.

SUBSTRATUM DIVINITY

The manifested divinities constitute the physical creation itself. The first level of manifested divinity is the substratum from which all creation arises. Creation does not come from nothing but rather from the ever infinite and eternal essential essence of existence, called Nun or Nunu. Nun is commonly referred to as the "Primordial Waters."

CREATOR DIVINITIES

Out of the Nun an all-encompassing Creator divinity arises who causes the parts of the Nun to take on shapes and forms we call Creation. These divinities contain within themselves the entire matrix that becomes Creation. Therefore they are androgynous. It must be understood that there is only one Creator, but it can be named differently in different myths. However, we know that there is only one because the scriptures themselves tell us so. Therefore, the Creator divinities of the different Neterian traditions are actually manifestations of the same creative principle but described in different ways in order to highlight particular teachings. The main Creator Divinities are *Mehurt, Net, Neberdjer, Ra-Herakhti-Herumakhet, Amun-Ra, Asar, Ptah and Khepri*. Each divinity is endowed with a particular form, name and myth in order to convey the teaching of divine and human origins in a particular way. So, again, it is important to understand however that all of these divinities are related to each other and they all emanate from the same substratum, the primeval ocean, and thus their teaching is not contradictory but rather complementary.

The creator divinities emanate the rest of the gods and goddesses and human beings from themselves and thereby Creation comes into existence along with all of the life forms therein. This means that everything has a divine spark that sustains it and everything in manifested Creation is actually composed of that same primordial "stuff" which was given form by the Creator divinities. The Creative work occurs in the deeper recesses of the Netherworld Plane, the Causal Plane.

NETHERWORLD — (ASTRAL PLANE-EXTRATERRESTRIAL) AND EARTHLY (TERRESTRIAL DIVINITIES)

Another level of the Neteru are those that function within the earth and the nether planes. The Netherworld or astral plane is the plane of existence that is subtler than the Earth (Physical) Plane. The Netherworld is where most of the gods and goddesses reside and there is a lower and higher Netherworld and they have interactions on the physical plane with each other and with people. People can communicate with them through meditation or through the state in between waking and sleep.

Some divinities in this category have avian qualities and this signifies that they have a subtler nature while other divinities are quadruped, and this signifies that they have a grosser nature, they are earthbound. These divinities have local interest and so they are recognized as tutelary (caretaker) divinities of that particular locality on earth.

WHOLISTIC (CROSSOVER) DIVINITIES

The wholistic neteru are those who have qualities that allow them to appeal to the masses of people on earth in the form of local divinities and also they operate in the other planes of existence. Thus they fulfill the roles needed by people at every stage of spiritual evolution. They have human existence and incarnation but their higher aspects are of Creator Divinities. In order to promote spiritual evolution a human being needs to learn about and experience increasing and expanding consciousness on the higher planes of existence. Through the worship and increasing knowledge of these divinities a human being can discover deeper and deeper levels of existence by discovering the deeper levels of symbolism and mythic teaching contained in the iconography and mythic wisdom of their respective sagas and mystery systems (Shetaut Neter). The divinities in this category include Asar, Aset, Djehuti, Heru, and Hetheru. These divinities are related to the other Creator divinities an they also have a relationship to the Nun.

NATURAL DIVINITIES

The natural divinities are the neteru who compose the elements of nature. Divinities: Geb, Nut, Shu, Tefnut, etc.— divinities symbolizing the cosmic forces of nature.

LOCAL (WORLDLY) DIVINITIES

Divinities: worshipped at the particular nome (city-town) but not nationally throughout Egypt. Example of a local divinity is: Djedi-worshipped as a form of Asar in Djedu.

ANTHROPOMORPHIC ICONOGRAPHY

The term "Anthropomorphic" means with human form. This kind of imagery is the easiest for the human mind to identify with and recognize. It is the basic kind of iconography that people can adopt and follow since it allows them to quickly relate with the divinity. This kind of iconography is often used by those divinities who have human incarnation. The character, behavior, myth and costume of these divinities denote the energies and teaching of these divinities. By using particular kinds of headdresses and acting in the temple pageant as the divinity the cosmic force can be further experienced through empathy (identification) with the divinity. If the energy (cosmic force) of the particular divinity is understood the Divine quality being expressed is better understood and thus spiritual knowledge is increased. If all of the forms of manifestation were understood the Creative divinity who gave rise to them would also be understood and this would lead to spiritual awakening of the highest order.

ZOOMORPHIC ICONOGRAPHY

Zoomorphic means with animal qualities. Many divinities are depicted with animal qualities. This is to signify that they represent some quality or force of nature as expressed more purely through a particular animal. Animals have a particular way of being and acting and feeling as well as certain purity with which they manifest certain energies that is rarely manifested by human beings. Animals do not have conscience or inhibitions such as those of human beings. They operate more directly through instinct and thus their actions demonstrate particular forms or characteristics of a particular manifestation of energy in a more natural and powerful way. This way of imagery allows the avid student to study that particular force and understand it more clearly.

COMPOSITE ICONOGRAPHY

Various divinities use the composite form of iconography. This increases their flexibility and also allows the divinity to take on diverse characteristics to suit particular situations or manifestations in different planes of existence. For example, the God Asar manifests as an anthropomorphic male divinity in the physical plane as king of Egypt. After his death he becomes a hawk-headed man and operates as king of the netherworld. The avian quality relates him to Ra and Heru as well as the capacity to fly to the heavens. This kind of iconography is to be considered as a *Correlative Theological Statement,* a statement that links theological traditions that outwardly appear to be different and separate. There are many such statements in Neterian philosophy. They serve to show the underlying correlations between the divinities as well as the unifying principles of the philosophy.

The concept of iconography and the system of divinities also allows human beings to study creation in a dissected fashion so as to better understand the parts. The end of this study is the realization that human beings have all of the qualities represented in the divinities. If the divinities are eaten, as the Pyramid Texts explain, the power of the divinities reverts back to the eater, just as the energy or power of food reverts back to the eater. Thus as this eating process goes on a human being gradually becomes more and more complete and "whole." Putting the pieces back together is the task of spiritual study, worship and the ultimate goal of life. It is the unraveling of the mysteries of life. This is also the oldest and deepest philosophy behind what later came to be called *Eucharist.* Thus, we have two kinds of Eucharist in Neterian theology. One is the eye of Heru, which reconstitutes the body of Asar. The other is the neteru, which constitute the pieces of the eye of Heru itself.

THE DUAT NETERU OF ANUNIAN THEOLOGY AND THE ELEMENTS OF CREATION

The Anunian Theology informs us as to the nature and origin of the elements that go to form Creation. After Khepri-Ra-Atum emerged from the ocean as a focus of consciousness, the Ben-Ben dot, •, he caused part of the ocean ≋≋≋ to turn into the four primeval gods of the universe. This is represented in the hieroglyph of the encircled dot, ⊙. The outer circle circumscribes the Creation. All is within it and all arises from the dot. The gods and goddesses of Creation take on the form and quality of the elements which compose Creation. As the Creator names them they come into existence through the power of Divine speech which carries with it the force of cosmic vibration (Sekhem, dekh) that is conditioned by thought: *Neter kat-ab*  - Divine thought of the heart.

Nun Becomes Creation

The symbols for the elements are as follows. Each element has a mundane (related to the physical world) aspect and a cosmic aspect, related to the presiding divinity who controls the element. Human beings are composed of the mundane and cosmic aspects of the elements at the same time. Attaining the knowledge of the elements implies attaining knowledge of the divinity (Neteru) that presides over it and thereby controlling that element. In essence this effectively means discovering the element (divinity) within oneself and thereby becoming one with the knowledge of the divinity, thus expanding the sphere of self-awareness as a superhuman being, i.e. attaining self-mastery or enlightenment.

Element (English)	Hieroglyph Physical	transliteration	Hieroglyph Cosmic	God or Goddess
Fire		Asher	⊙	Ra
Water		Moo		Nun
Air		Shu		Shu
Earth		Ta		Geb
Ether		sehedj		Nut

The Characters of the Anunian Myth as Cosmic Principles of Creation: The Natural Divinities

The main characters in the Anunian Creation Myth may be understood as cosmic principles of Creation. Each represents a particular manifestation of material reality as envisioned by the Creator, Khepri-Ra, who brought them forth out of himself. The Creation myth informs us that Ra emerged from the primeval waters, i.e. the substratum, formless and timeless essential matter from and with, which Creation was created. The first four divinities who emerged from Ra represent the primary and subtlest essence of physical matter as well as the physical and subtle elements that constitute the three planes of relative existence.

Below: The Ancient Egyptian Conception of the Elements of Creation

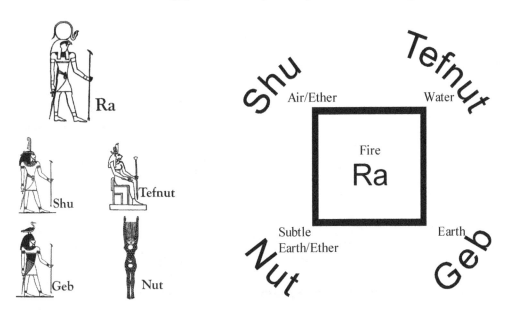

In Anunian Theology the first five divinities to emerge represent the principles of cosmic forces of the physical elements. Ra is fire; Shu is air and lower ether (space), the ether that is between earth and the heavens. Tefnut is water. Nut is upper ether (outer space) and the subtle physical part of Creation- the Universe. Geb is earth, the grosser part of the physical creation. Together and in combination, the elements form the basis upon which Creation is constituted and the substratum which sustains the physical forms of Creation. All matter (including subtle matter such as thoughts) is infused with these divinities. And all the divinities proceed from the transcendental and unseen Supreme Being who fashioned Creation out of an undifferentiated mass of matter, matter that did not have form or function, i.e. an elemental principle (fire, water, air, earth, ether.) operating through it- that was called *Nun* or *Paut*.

The Neteru Of the Three Main Neterian Theologies and Their Interrelationships

The image below provides an idea of the relationships between the divinities of the three main Neterian spiritual systems (traditions)-the Anunian tradition, the Wasetian tradition and the Memphite Tradition. The traditions are composed of companies or groups of gods and goddesses. Their actions, teachings, interactions, with each other and with human beings, provide insight into their nature as well as that of human existence and Creation itself. The lines indicate direct scriptural relationships and the labels also indicate that some divinities from one system are the same in others with only a name change. Again, this is attested to by the scriptures themselves in direct statements, like those found in the Prt m Hru text Chapter 4 (17).[18]

---

[18] For more details see the Book *The Egyptian Book of the Dead* by Muata Ashby

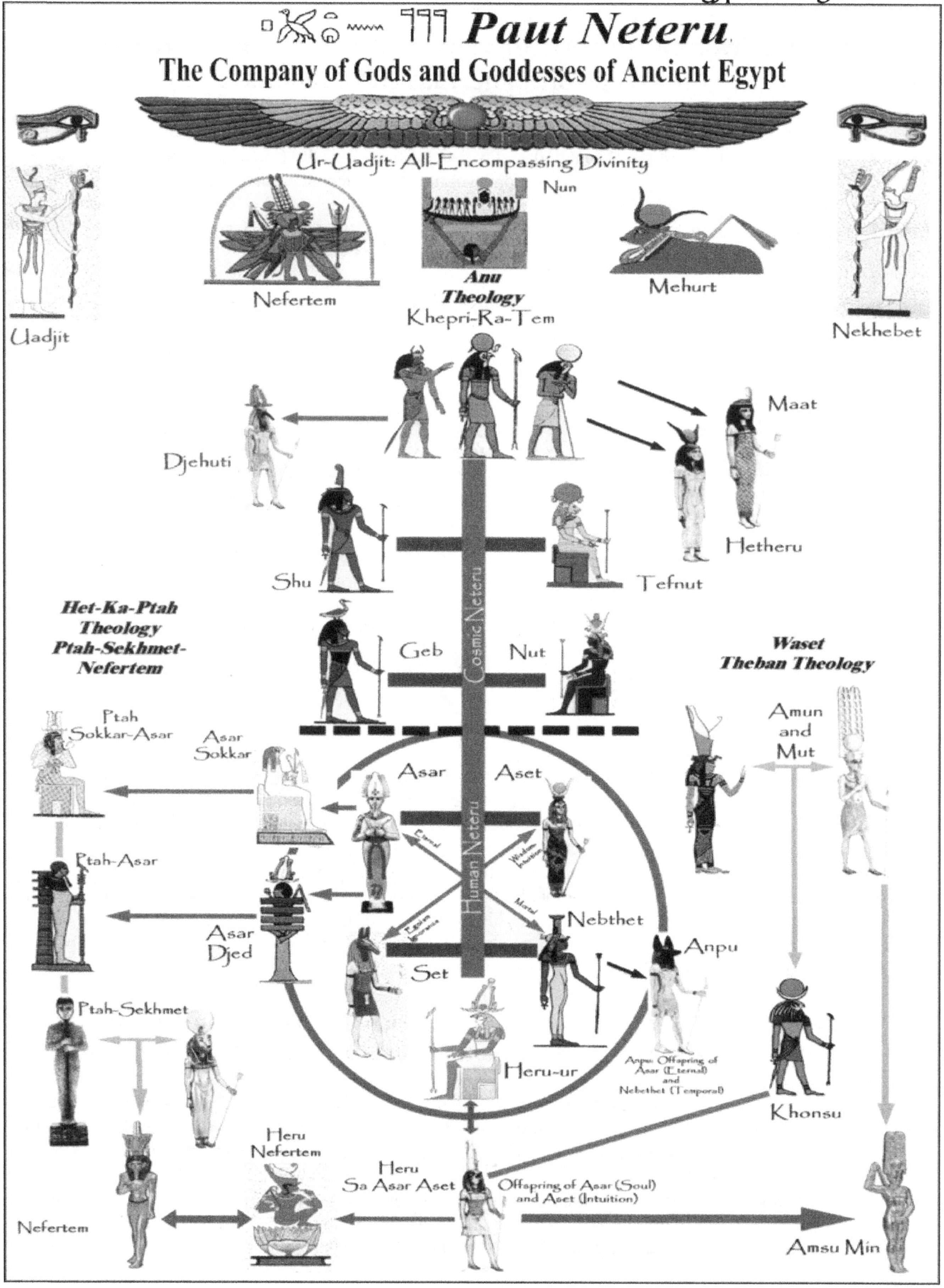

Paut Neteru

The Company of Gods and Goddesses of Ancient Egypt

Ur-Uadjit: All-Encompassing Divinity

Nun

Nefertem

Anu Theology
Khepri-Ra-Tem

Mehurt

Uadjit

Nekhebet

Djehuti

Maat

Shu

Hetheru

Tefnut

Het-Ka-Ptah Theology Ptah-Sekhmet-Nefertem

Geb

Nut

Cosmic Neteru

Waset Theban Theology

Ptah Sokkar-Asar

Asar Sokkar

Asar

Aset

Amun and Mut

Ptah-Asar

Human Neteru

Asar Djed

Nebthet

Anpu

Ptah-Sekhmet

Set

Heru-ur

Anpu Offspring of Asar (Eternal) and Nebethet (Temporal)

Khonsu

Nefertem

Heru Nefertem

Heru Sa Asar Aset

Offspring of Asar (Soul) and Aset (Intuition)

Amsu Min

The Main Trinity Gods and Goddesses of Ancient Egypt

THE GREAT TRINITY: AMUN-RA-PTAH

The Great Three Divinities: Amun-Ra-Ptah

Creation manifests as three aspects. This teaching is expressed in the Ancient Egyptian statement:

"I was One and then I became Three" and "Neberdjer: Everything is Amun-Ra-Ptah, three in one." Neberdjer manifests as Amun-Ra-Ptah. In this teaching, Amun represents the witnessing consciousness, Ra represents the mind and senses, and Ptah represents matter and all physical manifestation. Therefore, the Trinity owes its existence to the one. The realization of the underlying unity, the oneness behind the multiplicity of the Trinity, gives profound insight into the true nature of the Divine and the way to discover the Supreme Self. When a spiritual aspirant begins to understand that the underlying basis behind Creation, meaning the consciousness or identity, the senses and mind, the perceptions of the physical universe, is in reality the One Supreme Spirit, they begin to turn away from the world of ordinary human existence, to discover the Self within, and to *Know Thyself.*

Mehurt[19] – Neberdjer[20] – Net[21] - Heru[22]

⬇

Nun[23]

⬇

Khepri-Atum-Ra

⬇

	Khepri-Ra-Tem	
Amun	⬇	Ptah
⬇	⬇	⬇
Mut	**Asar**	Sekhmet
⬇	**Aset**	⬇
Khonsu	⬇	Nefertum
	Heru	

The table above is provided to show the relationship between the main Neterian divinities in the context of the overall scheme of Ancient Egyptian mythology. It should be noted that the hierarchy presented above should not be taken as an order of importance, but as an order of mythic emergence of the Divinity in the culture of Ancient Egyptian religious practice. There are four main Trinity systems which became prominent in Ancient Kamit. All the deities emerged at the same time, but their prominence as individually worshipped divinities occurred at

---

[19] ibid

[20] ibid

[21] ibid

[22] ibid

[23] One name used to describe the Supreme Being, the transcendental Spirit, beyond time and space.

different times in Ancient Egyptian history. Amun-Ra-Ptah is first. Arising out of each of these, a new Trinity of male (father), female (mother), and child emerges. Thus, we have: Amun-Mut-Khonsu (Wasetian tradition), Asar-Aset-Heru (Asarian tradition), and Ptah-Sekhmet-Nefertum (Memphite tradition). Khonsu and Nefertum are aspects of Heru. Therefore, the origin (Neberdjer) and product (Khonsu, Nefertum and Heru) of all the traditions are one and the same. This is another example of a *Correlative Theological Statement.* The main Trinity system related to the Prt m Hru is based on Ra, Asar-Aset and Heru. When dealing with Wasetian Theology, the Trinity system and mythology are related to Amun-Mut-Khonsu and the main scriptures of this tradition are the Hymns of Amun. When dealing with Hetkaptah or Menefer (Memphite) Theology, the main Trinity system and mythology are related to the divinities Ptah-Sekhmet-Nefertum and the main scripture of this tradition is the Shabaka Inscription. Thus, it is clear that while each divinity system has a clearly defined mythology and mystery teaching related to it, they all are in effect related to each other in the broad context of an all encompassing set of complementary principles which emerge from the same source and which together are more than the sum of their parts, i.e. when put together they transcend any polytheistic concept and produce a picture of universal wholeness. Indeed, they represent a harmonious family, whose members are all descended from the same ancestor. This *Correlative Theological Foundation* is the underlying philosophy of the science of the Neteru. It is manifested as *Correlative Theological Statements* throughout the myths, texts and iconographies of Neterian religion. This is why sometimes references are made in one tradition to other divinities in related Trinities identifying them as being manifestations of the same divinity and cosmic principle as the first tradition. Also, the divinities are presented in similar iconography, for example, Atum-Ra, Ra, Amun, and Asar have Divine Boats. They are used virtually interchangeably because their underlying origin and symbolism are so closely related. The differences presented in the myths and the icons are for the purpose of introducing and elucidating varying aspects of the Divine, just like in a modern big business, the marketing department may have several executives highlighting and promoting different aspects of the same company. The differences are not of substance but of manifested energy and these variations can be stark contrasts or subtle nuances. As they coordinate their work, they produce in the mind of the people, a view of the company, from different angles, creating a total view of the company. In a sense, the Sages of Ancient Egyptian mythology created a mythology with different names and forms to teach the masses about the glory and diversity of the Divine so as to show them the grandeur of the Spirit and engender in them the capacity to understand divinity and also the desire to move towards divinity. The purpose is not to lead people to divinity by fear or force but by understanding the kinship of spirit and its relation to humanity. So the idea of fearing God does not exist in Neterian spirituality as it does in the Jewish, Christian and Islamic faiths.

In this context, Atum-Ra is the primordial Divine principle which emanated from the Primeval Waters (Nun-Mehurt-Neberdjer) to engender Creation. Thus, Ra is the Supreme Being, and Asar is his incarnation, an avatar (divine incarnation on earth). Further, after Asar was killed by Set, he reincarnates as his son, Heru, and through him he ultimately attains victory over the forces of chaos, ignorance and egoism. So, although all of the gods and goddesses are related, the story of Asar was the most powerful in terms of popular appeal. It is upon the teachings related to Asar that the entire philosophy of the *Prt m Hru,* the most important text genre of Ancient Egypt, is primarily based.

The religion of Ancient Egypt revolved around four major Trinities of gods and goddesses who emanated from the one Supreme Being. These Trinities had major centers of worship in ancient times. They were Amun (city of worship-Thebes or *Waset*), Ra (city of worship-*Anu* or the city of the sun), Ptah (city of worship-*Hetkaptah*) and Asar (city of worship-*Abdu*). Along with these divinities, their female counterparts and their sons also had centers of worship. For example, Aset, the companion of Asar and mother of Heru, had a worship center at the island of Pilak (Philae). Heru had a worship center in the city of Neken. However, it must be clearly understood that all of these divinities were related. They emanated from Pa Neter or Neberdjer, the Supreme Being, and therefore, must all be considered as brothers and sisters and not as separate divinities.

The idea of classifying the Neteru or gods and goddesses comes about as the Sages of ancient times sought to explain the manifestations of the Divine in nature as well as in human psychology. However, they should not be understood just as divinities, but as cosmic forces and principals, their forms denoting the special qualities of those forces. The Ancient Egyptian word "Neteru," which is loosely translated as "gods and goddesses" or divinities therefore actually means "cosmic forces of creation." That term is the etymological origin of the Latin word "natura," and Anglo words "nature" and "natural." The Neteru (plural) emanate from Neter (singular)- meaning "Supreme Being-Supreme essential power. Thus, the Neteru have mythical references to nature and mystical references to human psychology which lead to greater understanding of the origins and destiny of human existence.

The Realm of Light

There is a very ancient philosophy from which the theology of the gods Heru and Ra and the goddess Net arises. In pre-dynastic times (before 5,500 B.C.E.), Egyptian doctrine held that there is a realm of light (beyond our physical universe) where food, clothing and our bodies are of light, and further, that we will exist for all eternity as beings of light along with other beings of light. This realm of light may be likened to the modern esoteric notion of an "Astral Plane" of existence. The physical realm (earth) is a reflection or shadow of this astral reality.

In dynastic times, the doctrine of the realm of light and of a single GOD of whom creation is composed survived in the earliest religious texts. In chapter 64 of the Egyptian Book of Coming Forth By Day (Prt m Hru), GOD is referred to as "The One Who Sees by His Own Light" and "Atum in the western horizon and Heru in the east". Hence, the "Lord of Two Faces", who is in reality only ONE, is similar to the Chinese *TAO* philosophy with the singularity which is composed of two opposite but complementary forces.

THE MAIN NETERU AND THEIR TEMPLES

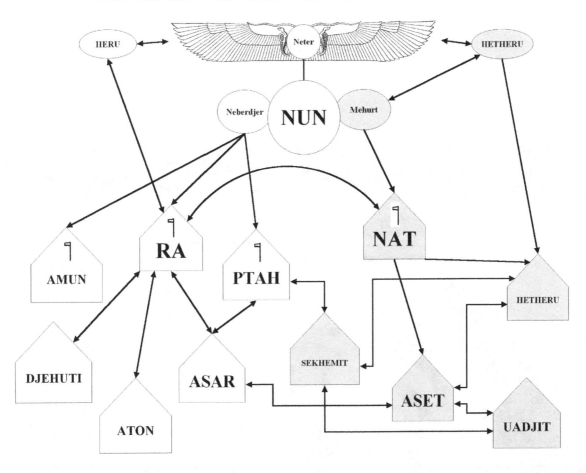

The sages of Kamit instituted a system by which the teachings of spirituality were espoused through a special kind of temple organization. The major divinities were assigned to a particular city and that divinity became the "patron" of that city. Also, the priests and priestesses of that temple were in charge of seeing to the welfare of the people in that district as well as to maintain the traditions and disciplines of the traditions based on the particular divinity being worshipped. So the original concept of "Neter" became elaborated through the "theologies" of the various traditions and variations on the teachings emerged that expressed nuances of variation in perspective on the teachings to suit the needs of varying kinds of personalities in the people of different locales.

In the diagram above the primary or main divinities are denoted by the Neter symbol ( ). The house structure represents the temple for that particular divinity. The interconnections with the other temples are based on original *Correlative Theological Statements*, which were espoused by the temples that linked them with the other divinities. So this means that the divinities should be viewed not as separate entities operating independently but rather as complementary and correlated entities, like family members who are in the same "business" together, i.e. the enlightenment of society, albeit through variations in form of worship, name and form, etc. Ultimately, all the divinities are referred to as Neteru and they are all said to be emanations from the ultimate and Supreme Being. Thus, the teaching from any of the temples leads to understanding the others and these lead back to the source, the highest Divinity, and with this attainment comes spiritual enlightenment, the Great Awakening.

The same Supreme Being, Neter, is the winged all-encompassing transcendental Divinity, the Spirit, which is in the early history called "Heru." The physical universe in which the Heru lives is called "Hetheru" or the house of Heru. This Divinity is also the Nun or primeval substratum from which all matter is composed and from this mass are composed the various Divinities and the material universe. Neter is actually androgynous and Heru, the Spirit, is also related as a male aspect of that androgyny. Heru gives rise to the solar principle and this is seen in both the male and female divinities.

Temple of Amun-Ra at Abu Simbel

Shetaut Anu

INTRODUCTION TO THE NETERU OF ANUNIAN THEOLOGY

Below: Fire ritual, offering to Ra, from the Amun temple at Abu Simbel

The Pautti Of Anunian Cosmology (The Ra Tradition)

Khepri-Ra-Tem   ⇨⇨⇨⇨↘

⇩   ⇩

         Hetheru

⇩   Djehuti (Thoth)

⇩   Maat

Shu ⇔ Tefnut
⇩

Geb⇔Nut
↖ ⇩ ↘

Set (Seth)   Asar ⇔ Aset   Asar⇔ Nebthet

⇩   ⇩

Heru   Anpu

The Mystery Teachings of the Anunian Tradition are related to the Divinity Ra and his company of Gods and Goddesses.[1] This Temple and its related Temples espouse the teachings of Creation, human origins and the path to spiritual enlightenment by means of the Supreme Being in the form of the god Ra. It tells of how Ra emerged from a primeval ocean and how human beings were created from his tears. The gods and goddesses, who are his children, go to form the elements of nature and the cosmic forces that maintain nature.

Shetaut Anu

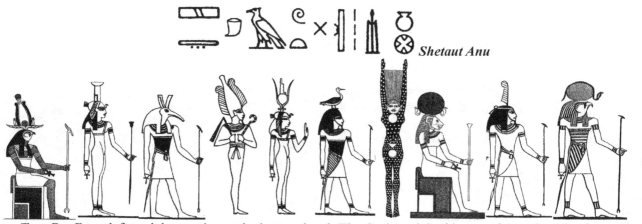

Top: Ra. From left to right, starting at the bottom level- The Gods and Goddesses of Anunian Theology: Shu, Tefnut, Nut, Geb, Aset, Asar, Set, Nebthet and Heru-Ur

The diagram below (Tree of Life of Anunian Theology) shows that the *Psedjet* (Ennead), or the creative principles which are embodied in the primordial gods and goddesses of creation, emanated from the Supreme Being. *Khepri-Ra* or *Ra-Tem* arose out of the *"Nu"*, the Primeval Waters, the hidden essence, and began sailing the *"Boat of Millions of Years"* which included the Company of Gods and Goddesses. On his boat emerged the "neters" or cosmic principles of creation. The neters of the Pautti (Ennead) are *Khepri-Ra-Atum, Shu, Tefnut, Geb, Nut, Asar, Aset, Set,* and *Nebethet.* Hetheru (Life Force), Djehuti (mind) and Maat (order-truth) represent attributes of the Supreme Being as the very *stuff* or *substratum* which makes up creation. Shu, Tefnut, Geb, Nut, Asar, Aset, Set, and Nebethet represent the principles upon which creation manifests. *Anpu* is a son of Asar and is not part of the Ennead. He represents the feature of intellectual discrimination in the Asarian myth. "Sailing" signifies the beginning of motion in creation. Motion implies that events occur in the realm of time and space, the realm of relativity and movement, thus, the phenomenal universe comes into existence as a mass of moving essence we call the elements. Prior to this motion, there was the primeval state of being without any form and without existence in time or space.

After emerging from the Nun and after Ra created Shu, Tefnut, Geb and Nut. Geb and Nut were locked in a loving sexual embrace and Ra decreed that they should be separated. After being separated, Geb and Nut formed our planet and the heavens. So, as the image below attests, Geb (the earth) rests under Nut (the sky), as Ra traverses the heavens in his Divine Boat and with him is Maat, who establishes order in the vibrations of time and space formed by the movement of the boat so that Creation may exist in an organized and logical manner.

Each Neteru listed above here has specific wisdom related to the nature of self, Creation and the Divine. Following this tradition means studying their mythic significance, their wisdom teaching and their mystical insight. Together, they constitute a wholistic teaching, integrating the philosophy of their own tradition and their relationship with the other traditions. These teachings, their understanding and application, are to be learned through the process of Shedy.

The divinities of the Myth of Creation (Company of Gods and Goddesses) and their various forms of interaction with each other are in reality an elaborate mystic code relating to understanding what Creation and God are, as well as the nature of human consciousness. The first thing that is noticed when the deities of the Ancient Egyptian Creation, based on the teachings of Anu, is that the neteru are placed in a hierarchical fashion based on their order of Creation by Ra, is that they arise in accordance with their level of density. Density here refers to their order of subtlety of the elements in Creation. Ra is the first principle which emerges out of the Primeval Waters. He is the subtle, singular principle of Creation, the focus of consciousness in time and space. The ocean itself transcends time and space and is beyond existence and non-existence. Ra is the first principle to emerge out of the Absolute and his emergence signifies the beginning of existence i.e. the conditioning or shaping of the ocean into the forms of Creation. Besides Ra, the Pauti refers to Creation itself. The deities of the Pauti are nine in number and include Shu, Tefnut, Geb, Nut, Asar, Aset, Set, Nebethet and Heru. Maati, Hetheru and Djehuti are not part of the Pauti itself. They are subtle principles which support its existence. The child form of Heru is a product of the union of Soul (Asar) and Intuitional Wisdom (Aset).

The second important idea derived from the Pauti (Company of Gods and Goddesses) is that they represent a whole number, 10 (Ra plus the nine gods and goddesses), and thus convey the idea of a special symmetry. The iconography has been likened to that of a tree and indeed, comparisons have been made to the Kabalistic Tree of Life as the study of the much earlier tree of Kamitan gods and goddesses that influenced Judaism and Hebrew culture reveals a subtlety of wisdom which leads to the discovery of the Divine Self, as symbolized by Ra. This Kamitan tree or ladder has its roots above, in the heavens with the Supreme Being, and its branches below, in the phenomenal universe with the gods and goddesses. The highest level, Ra, is juxtaposed against the lowest level of the Pauti with the image of Heru. So at one end we see the perfect singularity of the Supreme Self and at the other we see the perfect combination of Spirit and Matter in the form of Heru. Ra is perfection in the Transcendental Realm, Asar is perfection in the Astral Realm and Heru is perfection in the Physical Realm. While the diagram above may be understood as a reference to a "higher" and a "lower" idea, in reality the figure is not to be understood as a teaching of something that is above or better and something that is below or lesser. It is a teaching which expresses the essence of Creation, containing subtle as well as grosser objects which all emanate from the same source. The Ancient Egyptian teaching states: That which is above is the same as that which is below. If the "Above and Below" teaching is to be applied, it should be understood as referring to the idea that everything in Creation is a reflection of the spiritual essence which transcends physicality. The physical universe is an emanation from the spiritual essence and as such, is sustained by it. The very matter that constitutes Creation is in reality spirit in a condensed form, just as when a person falls asleep their dream world is condensed out of their own consciousness, conditioned by their thoughts, based on their desires and concept of self. Nun is the underlying primordial matrix of consciousness which gives rise to Creation. The following is a graphic representation of the neteru of Anunian Theology depicting their interrelationships and iconography.

The Tree of Life of Anunian Theology

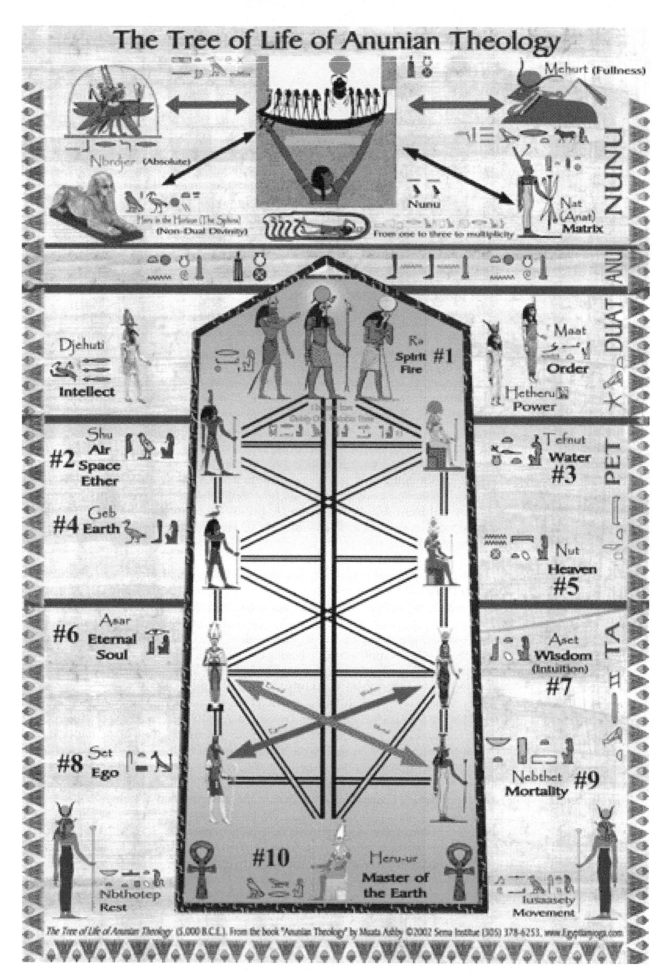

Nbrdjer (Absolute)

Mehurt (Fullness)

Heru in the Horizon (The Sphinx)
(Non-Dual Divinity)

Nunu

Nat (Anat)
Matrix

From one to three to multiplicity

NUNU

ANU

DUAT

Djehuti
Intellect

Ra
Spirit
Fire #1

Maat
Order

Hetheru
Power

#2 Shu
Air
Space
Ether

Tefnut
Water
#3

PET

#4 Geb
Earth

Nut
Heaven
#5

#6 Asar
Eternal
Soul

Aset
Wisdom
(Intuition)
#7

TA

#8 Set
Ego

Nebthet #9
Mortality

#10

Heru-ur
Master of
the Earth

Nbthotep
Rest

Iusaasety
Movement

The Tree of Life of Anunian Theology (5,000 B.C.E.). From the book "Anunian Theology" by Muata Ashby ©2002 Sema Institute (305) 378-6253. www.Egyptianyoga.com

THE GOD RA

Ra is the first and foremost Divinity of Anunian Theology (Shetaut Anu). All the other divinities arise from him. He has several important forms of manifestation but the most important thing to remember is that he is a manifestation of Cosmic Heru, "The Most High." Ra is the focal point of Divine consciousness in the primeval ocean that emerges and gives rise to all Creation through his three main forms of manifestation, Khepri-Ra-Tem.

The creation is explained as a series of spheres, or realms, or planes of existence. Due to ignorance or misunderstanding, most human beings are only aware of the physical plane. However, Ra is described as the Lord of the "Hidden Circles." The main symbol of Ra is the circle with the dot at the center, but we are given to understand that there are many circles or spheres. In fact the Neterian Scriptures speak of seven important spheres, the *"seven souls of Ra."* Each sphere represents a level of consciousness in the universe and psycho-spiritual consciousness centers of the human personality.[24] Therefore, Ra is known also as the "Lord of Souls." Ra is also the creator of the pairs of gods and goddesses who represent the elements of nature. Therefore, Ra is also known as the "Lord of Doubles (Dualities)."

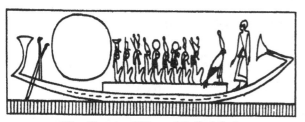

The Boat of Ra with Initiate

As Ra sails in his boat he produces a wake. That wake is vibration and that vibration changes the primeval ocean; it gives it form. But that form needs order so he establishes Maat (order) and sustains Creation. The figure below shows Ra in his boat with his daughter Maat sitting in the bow, breaking through the waters and thus making the way for him. Ra brought with him a Company of Gods and

Goddesses, and through them (the Neteru or cosmic forces of Creation, who are the primeval ocean itself), he manages Creation.

Ra in his boat with Maat at the bow.

The scripture of the Creation explains how nothing existed before Ra came into being. Ra is the fire that acts as a catalyst in the primeval waters and causes them to stir and take shapes.

The Neterian scripture says *"the heart of Ianrutf is glad when Ra sets in the evening."* Ianrutf" means "the place where nothing grows." Thus we are given to understand that Ra is the force that causes "things" to come into existence, i.e. to "grow" and that in the evening the innermost reality, the Ianrutf where Asar (the soul) resides has returned to a state of peace and rest. Therefore, Ra coming forth from the Nun (Primeval Waters) is the opposite of the Ianrutf. Ianrutf is then the original state of the Nun before Ra brought Creation into being. Thus Ra has three states of existence: Khepri (Creative), Ra (Sustaining) and Tem (Rest-contentedness).

Ra brought forth the Creation by bringing into existence two divinities. These in turn brought forth the rest of the gods and goddesses that came into existence. These two important divinities are Shu and Tefnut (air-inner space, and water). They represent the first duality to come into existence. Together with Ra they constitute the first Trinity of Creation composed of Fire (Ra), Air (Shu) and Water-Life Force (Tefnut). So Ra is the opener of the "Path of the Double Lion." (Shu and Tefnut are known as the lion god and goddess also referred to as Akheru (Two lions of the two horizons.))

Thus, Ra is the fire of consciousness that creates and perceives time and space and interacts with that creation. Ra is the source consciousness but as we learn in the story of Ra and Aset, the personality of Ra

---

[24] See the book The Serpent Power by Muata Ashby

is really only the outer manifestation of the Supreme Being. Ra has another aspect which is hidden and which goes under a secret name. This is the transcendental aspect which is beyond time and space, i.e. in the Ianrutf where not even words exist. The task of a spiritual aspirant is to discover the real name of Ra as Aset did.[25]

The God Nun or Nunu

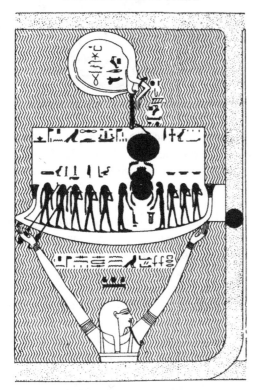

(From the sarcophagus of Seti I)

THE PRIMEVAL WATERS OF CREATION

In the particular scene above, taken from the sarcophagus of Seti I, the personification of the primeval waters of Creation, Nun, pushes the Boat of Atum-Ra, who emerges as Khepri (Scarab) onto the waves. Behind Khepri are the Divinities Geb (Earth), Shu (Space, Air, Ether), Heka (The Divine Creative Word), Hu (Divine sense of taste) and Saa (Divine Understanding). Assisting him are Aset and Nebethet. There are three divinities standing in the bow of the boat with the *aa*, ⬕, doorway symbol on their head. They symbolize the three worlds or planes of creation that are engendered, opened and sustained by Khepri. In the text, it is said that Khepri is the Creator aspect of Asar. Thus, they are in reality one and the same.

---

[25] See the book The Mysteries of Isis by Muata Ashby

This interpretation is supported by the following vignette from the Papyrus of Ani, where the souls of Ra and Asar are shown meeting in the mystical city of Djedu.

Pert m Hru (Book of the Dead) Chap. 4 (Chap. 17) from plate 9 *Souls of Asar and Ra meet in the Djedu of the Duat*.

Nun

Nun is the primeval matter; the stuff from which all matter is created. When physical matter is examined closely it is found to be composed of atoms that have been combined in varied ways to produce compound molecules. However those atoms are all made up of the same material substance. That substance is energy and energy is consciousness and consciousness is The Divine Self. Therefore, the material universe and everything in it is composed of "divine stuff" the Nun. Ra-Khepri is the Divine creative intelligence within the Nun. The gods and goddesses are the will of the creative intelligence that operate throughout every aspect of Creation and who sustain Creation at the behest of the Divine Self.

Nun
(the Primeval Matter)

Again, referring to the vignette of the sarcophagus of Seti I, Khepri pushes the sundisk into the arms of Nut, who is standing on the head of Asar in order for her to receive it. She in turn passes it into the area encircled (encompassed) by the body of Asar himself, i.e. the Duat (Netherworld).

Since the texts which compose the exposition of the Kamitan teachings come from various tombs, papyruses and inscriptions, the depictions of the gods and goddesses do not always seem uniform. This is because the priests and priestesses were describing different aspects of the same teaching. For example, in the boat above there are ten divinities accompanying Khepri, a form of Ra, the Neter, as the Creator. In the previous image of The Boat of Ra with Initiate (previous page above), there are ten divinities including Ra, i.e. nine Neteru (gods and goddesses) and one Neter. The initiate looks on from the bow of the boat. In the boat below we again see nine divinities plus the king, who is Heru.

In Ancient Egyptian mystical philosophy, Creation is explained as an emanation which came from a primeval mass of undifferentiated matter called Nu or Nun. From this mass arose Atum-Ra in the form of Khepri, the Scarab on the Divine Boat. The boat below shows Ra and his main retinue which includes the king himself in the last position, symbolizing his divinity and the fact that he is righteously following the divine path.

See also the section: ***The Garment of Nun***

NEBERDJER

Neberdjer: Amun-Ra-Ptah
(The Transcendental Self and the Sacred Trinity)

There are several Trinities in Ancient Egyptian mythology, each conveying a special message through the symbolic references and relationships of the symbols. The Trinity of Ra-Nut-Geb, representing the three basic principles of physical existence: Spirit (God-Supreme Being), Heaven and Earth, is one of the oldest forms of this concept to be found in the Dynastic period of Ancient Egyptian history. As the evolution of the exposition of the Supreme Being progressed, its elucidation through the medium of theology and mystical philosophy was refined. This refinement, which occurred over a period of 5,000 to 10,000 years, led to the teachings of the Asarian Trinity of Asar, Aset and Heru, and those of Neberdjer: Amun-Ra-Ptah.

In the early history there were no iconographical depictions of Neberdjer. He-She was considered as being transcendent of form and concept. In the late period of Kamitan history the image as encompassing all of the attributes of the other gods and goddesses appeared in the form of a composite all-encompassing divine image containing all attributes of divinity.

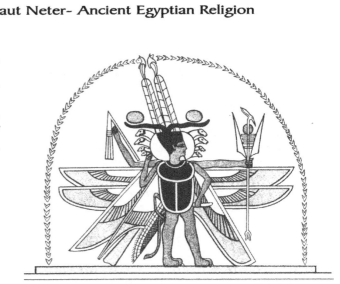

Neberdjer, the All-encompassing Divinity

The Ancient Egyptian Trinity composed of Amun, Ra and Ptah was formally known as:

"Neberdjer: Everything is Amun-Ra-Ptah, three in one."

The following passages from the *Hymns of Amun* sums up the Ancient Egyptian understanding of the Great Trinity concept in creation and that which transcends it.

> 33. *He whose name is hidden is Amun, Ra belongeth to him as His face, and the body is Ptah.*
> 34. *Their cities are established on earth forever, Waset, Anu, Hetkaptah.*

The statement above is another example of a Neterian *Correlative Theological Statement*, a statement that links theological traditions that outwardly appear to be different and separate. In the passages above we not only learn that the three main theological traditions are linked and the organizations of their connection but also that the gods of the Egyptian Trinity of Amun-Ra-Ptah, arise from the nameless Supreme Being known as Neberdjer or Neter Neteru. Therefore, the Trinity is in reality describing one Divinity which expresses in three aspects. Thus, in the Egyptian system of gods and goddesses, we also have the female aspects Amunit-Rait-Sekmet as consorts to Amun-Ra-Ptah, representing their dynamic power of manifestation.

In the creation story involving the Asarian Mysteries, Asar assumes the role of Khepera and Tem, while at the same time giving insight into the nature of Neberdjer:

"Neb-er-djer saith, I am the creator of what hath come into being, and I myself came into

being under the form of the god Khepera, and I came into being in primeval time. I had union with my hand, and I embraced my shadow in a love embrace; I poured seed into my own mouth, and I sent forth from myself issue in the form of the gods Shu and Tefnut." *"I came into being in the form of Khepera, and I was the creator of what came into being, I formed myself out of the primeval matter, and I formed myself in the primeval matter. My name is Asar."*

Neb-er-tcher (Neberdjer)

Neberdjer Speaks:
"I was alone, for the gods and goddesses were not yet born, and I had emitted from myself neither Shu nor Tefnut. I brought into my own mouth, hekau (the divine words of power), and I forthwith came into being under the form of things which were created under the form of Khepera."

These passages above all point to the fact that while the name of the Supreme Being under the different priesthoods appears to be different, these are merely names for different expressions of the same principles and teachings which present additional complementary wisdom about the Divine; therefore, there is no separation, discontinuity or confusion within the theologies. These are again, *Correlative Theological Statements*, here also linking Neberdjer to Asar. More importantly, the last passage reminds us that all of the names and forms are merely outward expressions of the same Supreme Being, *Neb-er-djer,* in its physical manifestation. Neberdjer, as previously discussed, is a name which signifies the all-encompassing meaning of the collective members of the Trinity. Neberdjer includes all male and female aspects of the Trinity, and is therefore to be understood as the androgynous and primordial being from which arose all names and forms, all gods and goddesses, all creation and all opposites in Creation (male and female, hot-cold, etc.) the passages above from the Anunian Theology may be termed *Correlative Theological Statements*. These are statements that correlate the main divinities and unequivocally show them to be manifestations of other divinities within the same tradition and within the other main traditions of Neterian religion. *Correlative Theological Statements* are found in the four main Neterian Traditions (Anunian, Wasetian, Meneferian, Asarian) and they correlate the main divinities of the traditions to each other.

(Papyrus 10,018 –British Museum)

In the creation story involving the Asarian Mysteries,[26] Asar assumes the role of Khepera and Tem:

"I was alone, for the Gods and Goddesses were not yet born, and I had emitted from myself neither Shu nor Tefnut. I brought into my own mouth, hekau, and I forthwith came into being under the form of things which were created under the form of Khepera."

The important passage and iconography above explain and illustrate the majestic vision of tantric philosophy in Neterian spirituality. Far from sexual vulgarity, the teaching reveals secrets about the nature of the Divine Self. In the previous passage we had *I poured seed into my own mouth,* and in the last one we have *I brought into my own mouth, hekau.* This juxtaposition of seed and hekau is a profound understanding of the creative potential of word, thought and consciousness (*Paut* the stuff or matter or substance) out of which Creation is created. It means that Neberdjer impregnated "himself," with word, that is, vibration; at once making him an androgynous being as well as the source matter of "her" own creation. So from the All comes the All. Everything comes from God and is composed of God, so too all is Divine, all exists in the Divine and all is rooted in the Divine.

Neberdjer has a female aspect called *Neberdjert.* Neberdjert may be thought of as a goddess but in reality Neberdjert and Neberdjer are one all-encompassing divinity. This is also a name of the eye of Heru.

---

[26] See the books *The Ausarian Resurrection: The Ancient Egyptian Bible* and The *Mystical Teachings of The Ausarian Resurrection: Initiation Into The Third Level of Shetaut Asar.*

THE MYSTERIES OF ANU

⊐ Atum (Tem)

The sun and the moon were incorporated into Ancient Egyptian worship from the most ancient times. The moon is symbolically associated with Asar, Aset and Djehuti, while the sun is symbolically associated with Ra, Ptah and Amun. According to the ancient Anunian creation story, the Supreme Being took the form of the sun god and arose out of the Primeval Ocean. According to one version, Ra arose in His boat along with the Ennead of gods and goddesses. According to the Menefer story, the Supreme Being arose in the form of a primeval hill or piece of solid land in the form of Atum, Tum or Tem. Thus, the Supreme Being who manifests as the rising sun out of the Primeval Ocean is known by various names. These are: Atum, Tum or Tem, Ra-Tem, Atum-Ra or Asar and Ptah. Atum is also one of the first god symbols to be depicted in human form. The priesthood of Anu developed an elaborate cosmology incorporating the concept of Tem into the creation myth, thereby merging human existence with the Divine. The *Pyramid Texts* of *Pepi II* determine the Company of Gods and Goddesses of Anu to be: Tem, Shu, Tefnut, Geb, Nut, Asar, Aset, Set and Nebethet. In the *Pyramid Texts* of *Pepi II*, the following account is given about the emergence of Atum (or Tem, Tum):

He who was born in the Nu (primeval waters),
before the sky came into being,
before the earth came into being,
before the two supports* came into being,
before the quarrel** took place,
before that fear which arose on account of the Eye of Heru existed...

*(Shu-Tefnut)
**(quarrel between Heru and Set)

One of the most important teachings of Anunian Theology is that if Creation is in reality God, composed of God's body and it will revert back to its original undifferentiated state one day, that means that Creation as ordinary human beings know it is an "illusion." It is not an abiding reality. Illusion

(*rasui*- dream- fancy- illusion). Therefore, the goal of spirituality is to wake up from the dream to discover that which is real, -Maat, and abiding- , *un*.

The Ra Trinity

From left to right: Two forms of Kheperi: Morning Sun (Creator), Ra: Noon Sun (Sustainer of the Day), Tem: Sunset (dissolver of the Day)

The idea of the Primeval Ocean (Nun) and the original primeval spirit which engendered life in it occurs in several world myths. The earliest occurrence of the idea of the primeval waters is found in the Egyptian religion which predates all other known religions of the world in human history. This pre-dynastic (10,000-5,500 B.C.E.), myth speaks of a God who was unborn and undying, and who was the origin of all things. This deity was un-namable, unfathomable, transcendental, gender-less and without form, although encompassing all forms. This being was the God of Light which illumines all things, and thus was associated with the sun, the forms of *Ra* or *Tem*, and with *Heru* who represents *that which is up there*, i.e., the Divine. Tum, Atum, Tem or Temu is an Ancient Egyptian name for the deep and boundless abyss of consciousness from which the phenomenal universe was born. *Khepera (or Khepri)*, the dung beetle, represents the morning sun which is becoming, creating. This form is also associated with the young Heru, *Heru in the Horizon*, also known as *The Sphinx*. Ra ⊙ represents the daytime sun which sustains Creation. The term "Tum" comes from the root *tm* , "to be complete," "fullness" or *temem* , which means "to make an end of." Also Tum is regarded as the evening or setting sun in the western sky, symbolizing the completion, the end of the journey. This is why the initiate wishes to go to the *"beautiful west"* upon completion of the span of life. The burial ground is symbolically placed in the west of the city. The beautiful west is the abode of Asar and Ra.

Sundisk (Symbol of Ra)

The story related in the Papyrus of Nesi-Amsu is that the primeval God laid an egg in the primeval chaotic waters from which the God {him/her} self emerged. This primordial God, emerged out of the waters, emanated as Ra, the Sun, life-engendering principle and Hetheru, the dynamic Life Force, Djehuti, the word or creative medium, and Maat, the principle of cosmic order and regularity, the Company of Gods and Goddesses, as well as human beings and the phenomenal world. So these are all essentially emanations from that same Primeval Ocean. Another myth tells of how the creator masturbated and engendered life through and within Himself by ejaculating on his own hand or into his own mouth. The papyrus of Nesi-Amsu further discusses the emergence:

> "When Atum emerged from Nun, the primordial waters, before the sky and earth were born and before the creation of worm or reptile, he found no place to stand..."

Tum, therefore represents the first emerging thought which contemplated its own existence in the vast ocean of undifferentiated consciousness which was devoid of names and forms, devoid of tangibleness, solidification, coagulation and grossness.[27] All that existed was subtle matter, the Primeval Ocean. The Pyramid Texts continue, explaining how Atum continued the process of creation by emitting the other principles of creation in the form of the gods and goddesses as follows.

> "Tum (Atum) is he who came into being (through Himself) in Anu.
> He took His phallus in His grasp that he might create joy in Himself, emitting the twins Shu (air, dryness, space, ether) and Tefnut (moistness)..."

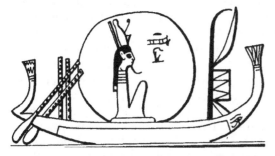

Atum (Tum, Tem) in the Solar Boat wearing the double crown, sitting within the sundisk.

In this manner, the various qualities of matter emanated from Tum and gave form to the Primeval Ocean, and continue to give and sustain its form at every moment. Geb is the son of Shu and Tefnut and represents the solid earth. Nut is the daughter of Shu and Tefnut and represents the sky and the heavens, and is the mother of Asar, Aset, Set and Nebethet as well as Heru-Ur.

In a creation story involving Khepera (Ra in the aspect of the rising sun, the creation of a new day), he says he rose up from Nu and:

> "I found no place there whereon I could stand. I worked a charm upon my heart, I laid a foundation in Maa,[28] and then I made every form. I was one by myself, {since} I had not yet emitted from myself the god Shu, and I had not spit out from myself the goddess Tefnut; there was no other being who worked with me."

From the perspective of this particular mythic teaching, **Tm,** (Tem, Tum, Atum, Atum-Ra), therefore, is the ultimate source and cause of Creation. From Tm (completeness-wholeness) arises Khepri who transforms into Ra and finally, Ra reverts back to the original essence, Tm.

RA AND THE TRINITY OF ANU

In the myth of Ra and Aset, Ra says: *"I am Kheperi in the morning, and Ra at noonday, and Temu in the evening."* Thus we have *Kheper-Ra-Tem,* ⊙◯𓏤𓆑, as the Anunian Triad and hekau. In Chapter 4 of the *Prt m Hru*, the initiate identifies {him/her} self with Tem, symbolizing that {his/her} life as a human being with human consciousness is coming to an end. Instead of an awareness of individuality and human limitation, there is now a new awareness of infinity and immortality, even though the physical body continues to exist and will die in the normal course of time. The initiate will live on as a "living" soul and join with Tem (individual consciousness joins Cosmic Consciousness):

> "I am Tem in rising; I am the only One; I came into being with Nu. I am Ra who rose in the beginning."

This passage is very important because it establishes the mystical transcendence of the initiate who has realized {his/her} "oneness" and union with the Divine. In other papyri, Tem is also identified with

---

[27] Capable of being touched; material; something palpable or concrete.

[28] referring to Maat-truth, righteousness

the young Heru, the solar child) as the early morning sun. Thus, Kheperi-Ra-Temu are forms of the same being and are the object of every initiate's spiritual goal. Being the oldest of the three theologies, the Mysteries of Anu formed a foundation for the unfolding of the teachings of mystical spirituality which followed in the mysteries of Hetkaptah, through Ptah, and the Mysteries of Thebes, through Amun. With each succeeding exposition, the teaching becomes more and more refined until it reaches a high degree of refinement in the Hymns of Amun.

Above: The Ancient Egyptian Creator Supreme Being, Khepri, in the form of the evening sun (Tem), encircled by the divinity *"Asha Hrau,"* the serpent of "Many Faces" (infinity and multiplicity). The Serpent symbolizes the power or Life Force through which Creation is engendered. The Serpent, "Mehen" lives in the primeval ocean out of which Creation arises. There are three symbols at the feet of Ra and next to these are the heads of the serpent. Note the symbol, ◿. It is an Ancient Egyptian determinative used to signify "limb," "flesh," "parts of the body." In mystical terms the meaning is that from the singular essence arise the three aspects, the Trinity, and from these arise the multiplicity of Creation. Thus, Creation is the very flesh or body of God which transforms into a trinity and then manifests in a multiplicity, *asha,* of ways.. From his head is emerging Khepri, the Creator of the universe, who performs the actual act of creation.

It is important to understand that the creation act is not something that happened once long ago. Khepri creates the new day every day. Thus, the implication is that creation is a continuous process which sustains the universe at every moment just as a person sustain their dream world at every moment during a dream.

The scarab (dung beetle of Egypt) is an insect which burrows into the mud caused by the Nile flood waters, and after the muddy waters recede, the beetle comes up with a new body, a new being. The beetle is likened to Ra, the sun in the morning who comes out of the murky waters of the dark night. The scarab uses the dung ball as nourishment for its young. In the same way the sun rises in the morning as a new being. The scarab (energy of transformation) pushes the sun on its journey every day. In the morning, the sun is Kheper, the scarab, at noon it becomes Ra, and in the evening, the setting sun, it is Tem. These different phases, symbolize the one Supreme Being which manifests as a triad of time: past, present and future.

The scarab symbolizes transformation, and here we are transforming ourselves mentally, physically and spiritually into higher beings. In letting go, we are transforming our selves, we are becoming peaceful, becoming true agents of Hetep and coming into harmony with Maat.

As Creator, Khepri congealed the Nun, his own body, into all the forms of Creation. He created not only the universe but also the spiritual teaching that was codified by Djehuti into Medu Neter or the hieroglyphic texts which contain the spiritual philosophy. Above right: forms of the god Khepri (far right) and as Khepr-Ra (left).

Khepri can also be depicted as the ur-uadjit (winged sundisk-below), which exemplifies his characteristic as Creator and all-encompassing divinity over what is created.

Above left: The frog god Ka is a form of Khepri and wears Khepri's headdress. He is known as "Father of the gods." The frog divinities lived in the primeval ocean, the Nun, and just as they emerge from the marshes after rain or the Nile flood, so too they emerged from the Nun when Khepri created Creation. They give life to all beings.

The goddess *Heqet* (above right) gives life to the newly formed human body that has just been fashioned by Khnum. Thus, she is associated with the sources of the Hapi (Nile river), along with Khnum. The Coptic Christians continued the tradition of revering frogs as life-givers.

TEFNUT AND SHU

Tefnut

The Forms of Shu

In the creation story involving the Asarian Mysteries, Asar assumes the role of Khepera and Tem while at the same time assuming the nature of Neberdjer, Shu and Tefnut. Recall the speech of Neberdjer:

"Neb-er-djer saith, I am the creator of what hath come into being, and I myself came into being under the form of the god Khepera, and I came into being in primeval time. I had union with my hand, and I embraced my shadow in a love embrace; I poured seed into my own mouth, and I sent forth from myself issue in the form of the divinities Shu and Tefnut."

In the form of Tefnut, the goddess is the consort of Shu and she represents the life force that is contained in air. She also symbolizes moisture and every form of watery substance as well as the power of water. In these capacities she is directly related to Sekhmet and Bast, as the feline aspect and iconography of the goddess is a typical Kamitan linking technique (*Correlative Theological Statement*) used throughout Kamitan mythology.

Shu is the first-born son of Ra as he emerged in the Boat of Millions of Years, from the Primeval Ocean. He represents air, space and ether. Ra commanded that he separate Geb and Nut, who were in a sexual embrace. Since then, he sustains Nut, the sky, with his upraised arms, and separates her from Geb, the earth, so that Creation may continue to exist, for human interactions cannot occur without space and air. Shu is as well, the king of the gods and goddesses, able to lead aspirants to the Divine.

As stated earlier, Shu represents physical air, dryness, the space between heaven and earth. His symbol is the feather. Tefnut is moisture and her name is derived from the word *tefi* meaning spit. It was stated in the Creation text that Ra spat her out of himself and sneezed Shu. So when Ra created Shu and Tefnut he became from one, three. Recall the statement:

 **"I was One and then I became Three"**

An important attribute of Shu is the Northern Wind. The Northern Wind carries Life Force and this is the same air that goddess Aset used to blow over the body of Asar with her wings in order to bring his body back to life in the Asarian Resurrection myth.

In the Pert M Heru text Chapter 4 it was stated that Shu and Tefnut shared one soul and that this soul is the same as that of Asar and Ra, who also represent the Moon and the Sun respectively. So Shu and Tefnut are dualities actually rooted in oneness, in Ra.

Shu opens the mouth of initiates with the *Seba-Ur* instrument (iron artifact in the shape of the great constellation of the north-pole, symbolizing the unchanging nature of the spirit.[29] The metal, iron, itself is stated to be the metal encasement of the first psycho-spiritual energy center of the Serpent Power of human consciousness (*Sefek ba Ra*).[30] So Tefnut is the Life Force (Sekhem) and Shu is the vehicle of the life

force. With this understanding an aspirant can control (manipulate) air and promote the accumulation of Life Force and thereby promote the raising of the Serpent Power and the "opening of the mouth" (awakening of consciousness). It was also said that the deceased live on the food of Shu, which is the sunlight, i.e. the life force that is to say, Tefnut.

Shu and Tefnut are also known as the *Akerui* (leonine) divinities, also referred to as *Ruti* (the two lions). That is, they are the lion and lioness who guard the Akhet (horizon) which is the entrance to the Netherworld, i.e. they are the boundary between the Netherworld and the Physical World, depending on which perspective is used. The lions are symbolic of the mountains flanking the valley through which the dead and the sun must pass. The Akerui are known as *Sef* & *Duau*, Yesterday & Today, and also *Manu* & *Bakau*, Sunset & Sunrise. Thus the Akerui aspect refers to time and space.[31]

AKHET AND AKHER

Above: Akhet, the horizon, with the sundisk.

From the point of view of creation, Shu and Tefnut are the first physical entities created by Ra and are thus the passageway of the spirit into the realm or plane of matter, time and space. This is why they are associated with the Akerui, who represent yesterday and tomorrow, i.e. the principle of duality.

Above: Akerui, the lion gods of Yesterday and Tomorrow

---

[29] See the book African Origins by Muata Ashby.
[30] See the book The Serpent Power by Muata Ashby.

[31] For more details see the Tree of life audio lecture series Principles of Shu and Tefnut

The sun traverses between the Akerui, i.e. the past and the future. Therefore, always remaining in the eternal present. This is a deeper mystical teaching for every spiritual aspirant to understand, how not to get caught up in the pettiness of life and the tension, and anxiety over what happened in the past and the tension, and anxiety over what is desired in the future. In *Pyramid Texts* 796, 1014 and 1713 it is stated of the righteous soul: *the gates of Aker are opened for you.* The eternal present is the pathway between the physical plane and the astral plane. The past and the future do not exist. Only eternity (the present) is real.

GEB AND NUT

Geb and Nut are the earth and the sky (heavens). They are the children of Shu and Tefnut, and they are also the physical universe in which human interaction takes place. After their father, Shu, separated them, Nut who was pregnant and gave birth to Asar, Aset, Set, Nebethet and Heru Ur. It is from these Neteru that all other Neteru and human beings are descended. Geb is considered as the king of the earth, as well as a beneficial force on behalf of all spiritual aspirants.

When Ra separated Geb and Nut they were in a sexual embrace and the separation occurred in mid intercourse. Geb's penis remained erect coming out of the earth and this monument is called the "Teknu" or "Obelisk ⌐°⌐°⌐. When the separation occurred Asar, Aset, Set, Nebthet and Heru-Ur were born. This is the beginning of the Kamitan New Year which occurred at the summer solstice. At the time of separation which was carried out by Shu at the request of Ra, Geb got into a twisted posture (spinal twist) as well as a bent over posture known in Yoga exercise programs as the

plough posture while Nut remained aloft as the sky, supported by Shu. Geb's "Spinal Twist" posture is specifically mentioned in the scriptures and explicit mention is made of the fact that one of his hands is facing down, touching the earth and the other is raised up towards the sky.[32]

One of Geb's primary symbols is the goose headdress and the crown of Lower Egypt. The avian symbolism signifies the nature of his energy which holds the capacity to rise from a sedentary nature. While Geb is the earth element he also represents the subtle aspect of earth which manifests in the astral plane. All the physical elements that are in the physical plane manifesting as gross objects are also in the astral plane but they manifest as subtler objects. Thought itself is composed of subtle physical elements. These are aspects of Geb. The earth is known as the "Het-Geb" or "House of Geb." This means that he lives in it and when people die and are buried they go to his house to meet him. The region of the cemetery where the tombs are is called "Neter-khert", the "lower divine region" as opposed to Pet, the heavens which is above and the Duat which is beyond, in a different realm.

Geb presides over "divine food" which is composed of minerals, trees, vitamins etc. He is also the buildings that are constructed on earth which are of course composed of earth materials.

When Geb moves it is heard as thunder and felt as earthquakes. Notice that Geb is also the clouds and lightning. These are not Nut. Nut is not the sky per se, but rather the outer space, the heavens. Geb is all that is solid, and physical. One of Geb's titles is "Smam-

---

[32] See the book Egyptian Yoga: Movements of the Gods and Goddesses by Muata Ashby

ur" or "Great Uniter." He can unite the deceased personality to the earth or allow them to go freely to unite with Ra in the heavens. He has the capacity to hold unrighteous souls on earth and not allow them to go forward on their journey beyond the earth realm. The scripture explains that he holds souls with bars and bolts on the doors as if in a jail.

For this reason, in the texts of resurrection the initiate is to ask Geb to "open the jaws, open the eyes, to loosen the leg bandages." The initiate is to declare: "my father is Geb and my mother is Nut." In this manner the initiate identifies with Asar who was the resurrected child of Geb and Nut and in so doing the initiate also achieves the fate of Asar and is freed from the bonds of the earth element.

The initiate is to live on the "Bread of Geb" which is pure nutrients from the earth, those foods made righteously. In order to master the earth element and escape the physical realm Geb must be propitiated through a life of virtue and purity. If this is successful, Geb "loosens the door bold and lets the light of Ra shine on earth." This opening allows the initiate to escape the earth by grabbing hold of the rays of light which are tow ropes hanging from the Boat of Ra. The boat sails over the Neterkhert (lower heavenly region- grave-earthly afterlife region). The soul climbs aboard the boat and joins the ranks of primordial gods and goddesses, the Anunian Paut (Company of Gods and Goddesses) and becomes one with Ra. In order for all of this to occur the aspirant must overcome the fear of death, and must master the earthly desires including food and sex.

In one myth Geb and Nut gave birth to a Divine Egg. From that egg the Benuu bird (Greek - Phoenix) emerged. So Geb is referred to as the "GenGen-Ur" or "Great Cackler." Amun could also appear as the "GenGen-Ur." The Benuu is known as the *new born sun,* *the soul of Ra,* and the *living form of Asar.* These are all *Correlative Theological Statements.* Therefore, Ra is begotten as Asar in the realm of time and space – physical realm, through the earth element (Geb). Therefore, Geb is known as the "Father of His Father" and Asar is actually Ra incarnate and consequently Ra also manifests in the form of Heru, the son of Asar. In essence all the manifestations are in reality Ra.[33]

---

[33] For more details see the Tree of life audio lecture series Principle of Geb

THE DIVINE EGG IN ANCIENT EGYPT

The story related in the Ancient Egyptian *Papyrus of Nesi Amsu* is that the primeval God laid an egg in the primeval *formless* waters from which the God him/herself emerged. This primordial God who emerged out of the waters created or emanated Ra-Tem-Nefertum, the Sun or Life Force, Djehuti, the carrier of the **Divine Word** or creative medium, and Maat, the principle of cosmic order and regularity. The underlying emphasis was on the fact that all of these, including human beings and the phenomenal world, are in reality emanations from that same Primeval Ocean. This means that there is one primordial essence for all things, be they plants, humans, gods and goddesses, etc.

So, in Ancient Egypt the god Ra, the "Great Cackler" emerges from the Egg. Ra is the "Golden Sun" who creates the world as Khepri, the Creator. This teaching is further explained in the Hymns of Amun:

From the Ancient Egyptian Hymns of Amun:

1. He is self-created and as He fashioned Himself, none knows His forms.

2. He became in primeval time; no other being existed; there was no other god before Him; there was no other god with Him to declare His form, all the gods came into being after Him.

3. He had no mother by whom His name was made. He had no father who begat Him, saying, "It is even myself." He shaped His own egg. He mingled His seed with His body to make

*His egg to come into being
within Himself.
4. His unity is Absolute. Amun is One
- One.*

In mystical philosophy God is the Self. The Self is a self-existent being which transcends concepts of creation and created. The Self emerged out of the Self and what emerged is none other than the Self. Creation and the Self are one and the same. God is the undivided principle that assumes the names and forms which human beings call objects and the varied life forms which are in existence. Although the Divine Self is the sustaining force behind all phenomena and all life, many human beings are ignorant of the existence of this force and thus see themselves as the source of their own existence. They are ignorant to the fact that their very existence is sustained by the Higher Self. Through this process of ignorance, human consciousness is fooled into believing that its thoughts and ideas are its own and that its memories and experiences constitute its unique existence. This concept of a unique and separate existence is what constitutes egoism in the human psyche and the separation from Divine Consciousness.

GOD BENUU

Above-top left and right: the Benuu as bird and as god.

Right: Anpu places the mummy in the tomb while the

Benuu and the Ba look on.

The Benuu lives in the "Het-Benben" or "house of the obelisk". The house encloses the Benuu stone or primordial point. It was located in the city of Anu. The Benuu represents the deathless aspect of human existence that experiences death and destruction of the physical aspect of the personality, and then lives on again to reincarnate or take its rightful place on the divine throne. Therefore, in a special Heaku (words of power-chant) of the Pert m Heru, it is said: "I go in as a Hawk and come out as the Benuu," i.e. "resurrected." Ra is the Hawk who goes into Geb and is born through Nut as the Benuu. The Benuu is thus Ra resurrected aspect of Asar.

Benuu from Pert m heru Chap 4 from plate 7

GODDESS NUT

Nut is the mother goddess, and she lifts up all righteous aspirants into heaven, to take their place on her body as a shining spirit (star). One version of the Creation story tells how Ra traverses over Nut's back in his boat (sundisk), and every evening she consumes him and every morning she gives birth to him as the morning sun.   Nut is the heavens and specifically the sky region between the Eastern horizon and the eastern mountain (Bakau) and the Western horizon and the western mountain (Manu). Her symbols are the water container and the sky . She is often depicted as a woman bent forwards over the earth or as a cow with her body studded with stars.

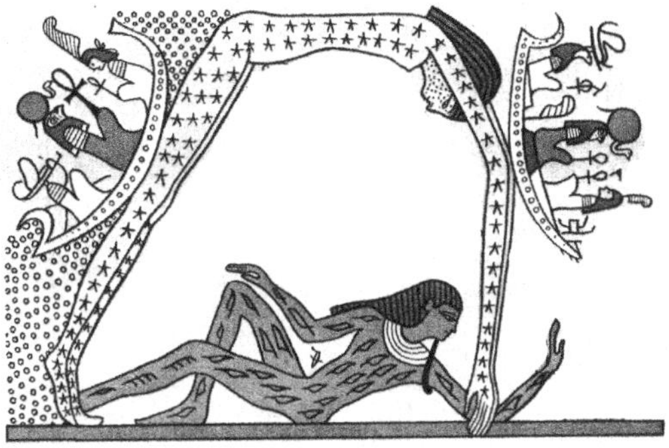

Goddess Nut in the Creation Papyrus

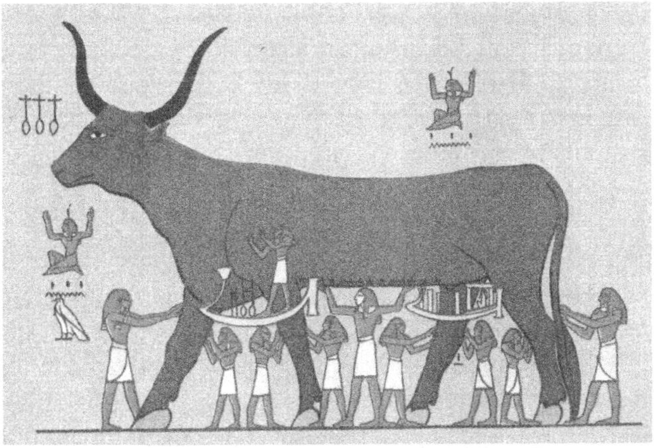

Goddess Nut in the Tomb of Seti I

She is sometimes presented wearing the horns and sundisk headdress just as Hetheru and Aset or with the vulture crown headdress as Mut. Nut's legs and arms are the pillars that hold up the sky, which is her body. Nut's legs and arms also mark the four cardinal points of the compass (north, south, east and west). Ra sails in his boat over her back during the day and when he reaches her head area in the west, she eats him and he sails through her body at night. In the morning she gives birth to him again and he rises as Khepri in his morning boat. (below)

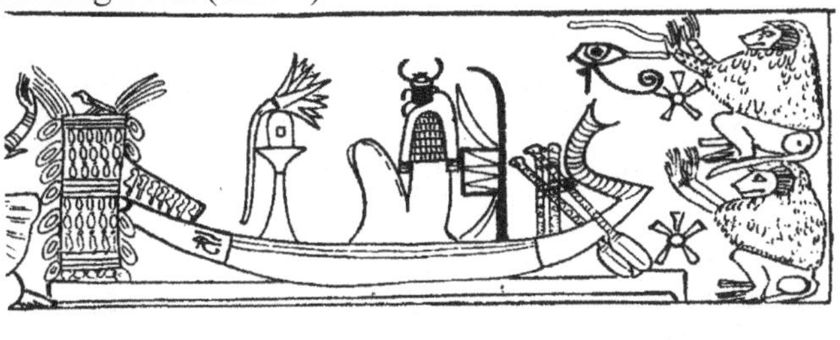

The conception of Goddess Nut is that she has two aspects, the day sky and the night sky. If her image is as sky goddess is reversed and juxtaposed against that given in the scripture we see two Nuts facing each other over two sides of the earth, the day side and the night side, each lasting roughly 12 hours, hence the Kamitan creation of the 24 hours of the day.

Day Nut

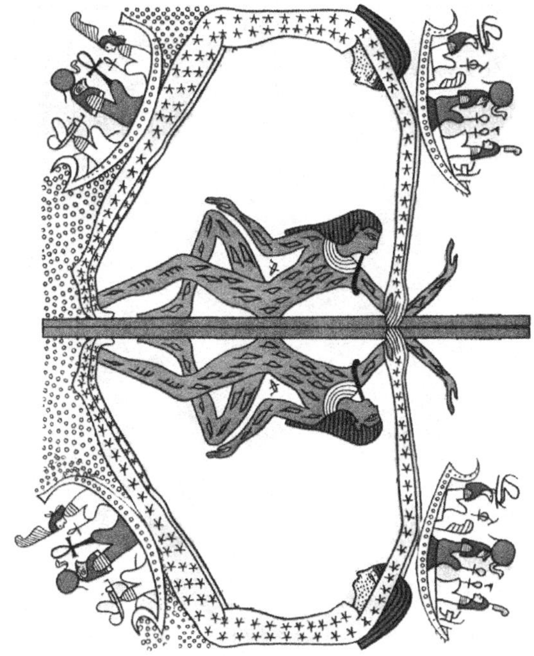

Night Nut

The image above can be viewed diagrammatically and when the movements of the boat of Ra, the position of the goddess and the realms or planes of existence are mapped, out the teaching related to Nut and the other divinities becomes clearer.

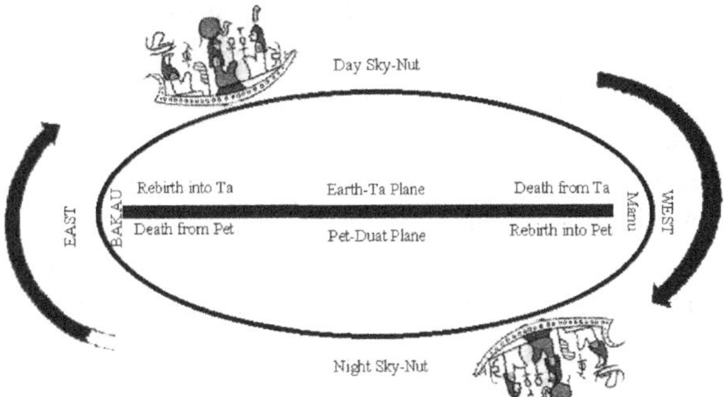

The birth of the morning is actually a death to the night just as a person's dream personality dissolves in order to give way to the daytime personality. Likewise the daytime personality gives way at night. When a human being dies it is merely an expression of being

born into another plane, for sleep is a form of death that human beings experience every day. The death at the end of physical life is simply the same process but without coming back the next morning to the same body as before.

Nut is also the goddess of the sycamore tree, the tree of life, from which she provides food and drink to righteous aspirants.

Nut is thus the protector of the dead. She protects aspirants from their enemies and provides the subtle food for existence in the *Pet* (heavenly) realm. She also allows souls to have movement in the *Pet* plane of existence. She was often depicted as the coffin lid with open arms (see below) ready to embrace the aspirant's body and receive the aspirant's soul to lift it up to heaven so that it might become one of the Akhus, luminous beings –enlightened souls who live in the sky as the stars. See the illustration of the interior of A typical ancient Egyptian coffin showing spiritual texts of the Pert M Heru (Coffin Texts) and the female figure inside, as if receiving and embracing the body of the aspirant. This is goddess Nut. Thus, Nut is the Coffin itself.

In the Pyramid texts it is stated that Nut lifts up righteous aspirants who have been allowed to transcend the earth realm by Geb. She is the door that is opened to aspirants so that they may depart from the earth plane. That is the same door that is closed when the bold of Geb obstructs the movement of an unrighteous aspirant. Nut is the blackness of night and thus her children are also dark in complexion. Asar is referred to as "The Lord of the Perfect Black" and it is said that when Aset was born Nut exclaimed "look at this black child of love."

Nut is the same Divinity manifesting in all of the major forms of the Goddess including: Aset, Nebthet, Taurt, Hetheru and Mut. Nut most importantly represents the subtle principles of physical expansiveness: Infinity. These are the principles to be mastered by a spiritual aspirant. Nut is the power behind the effectiveness of Hekau (words of power) of the Pert m Heru wherein the aspirant states the desire to live in the Duat. This occurs under the dispensation of Goddess Nut for she provides the sustenance for those who live there.[34]

Muntju of Ancient Egypt

The God Ra has an aspect by the name of *Muntu (Montu, Monthu);* this aspect is the expression of war in Kamitan myth. So Muntu is the god of war but not warmongering but the duty of war to protect and uphold Maat. The worship of Muntu was prominent in the 11th Dynasty Period. Muntu is related to Heru-Behded who is the warrior aspect of the god Heru, who is also an aspect of Ra.

Above-Left- The God Montju-Ra of Ancient Egypt. Above-Right Heru-Behded, The Warrior

---

[34] For more details see the Tree of life audio lecture series Principle of Nut.

GOD MEHEN AND GOD ASHA-HRAU

In Ancient Egyptian religion, the lotus of Creation emerges out of the primeval ocean which is stirred by the Mehen Serpent, a gigantic snake whose movements churn the ocean into transforming itself into the various forms of Creation as water turns to ice when it reaches a low enough temperature.

Above: Khepri and Asha-hrau

In Buddhist myth the same conceptualization is given to Buddha as it is derived, like many other concepts, from Hindu theism, specifically that of Brahma, the Creator who sits on a lotus, which also comes out of the primeval ocean, in order to bring Creation into being. So the concept of the Serpent, the churning of the primeval ocean out of which a lotus emerges with a being who sits atop of it are all common to the Neterian, Hindu and Buddhist traditions.

An important example of the Kamitan Caduceus, is Atum-Ra, symbolizing the central shaft, attended on by goddesses Nebethet and Aset.

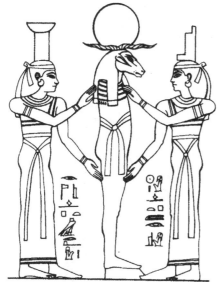

One Ultimate, Absolute Abode, Two Paths Leading To it: Non-Dualism in Ancient Egypt

Essentially, Asar and Ra are actually one being. This is one reason why the moon was chosen as a symbol of Asar. It is written that Ra has the Moon and Sun as his eyes, and either works as a passageway to the deeper transcendental Self, just as the eyes of a human being act as a window into the inner Self. This idea of the oneness of the Supreme Being is stated again directly in the image above which reads: *This[35] is Asar resting in Ra* (left), *Ra resting in Asar* (right). The two great goddesses Nebethet and Aset attend on Atum Ra as he stands on the pedestal of Maat. Once again, the image of the Trinity is given with one male aspect and two female aspects, symbolizing non-duality (one God, one Spirit) and duality (two goddesses), respectively. The concept of two paths is evident in the very decision to present the culmination of the spiritual journey in the form of two chapters wherein the spiritual aspirant can join Ra (Chapter 35) or Asar (Chapter 36). This presentation points to the highly advanced philosophical view that the Ancient Egyptian Sages were putting forth, that the gods and goddesses (neteru) are merely images for worship, and are not to be seen as ultimate or absolute realities in and of themselves. They are to be understood as windows into the transcendent, avenues by which the energies of the mind and body may be channeled towards a higher, spiritual goal in life.

The identification of Asar and Ra is also evident in the vignette above from the Prt M Hru text. It is the "soul of Ra and the soul of Asar meeting in the Duat." The important concept here is that the two most

---

[35] The Creator, *Atum-Ra*

important divinities of Shetaut Neter, Asar and Ra, combine to form Amun. This should not be thought of in a linear or sequential pattern, 1 + 2 = 3. Rather it should be thought of as 2 = 1, that is, god has three aspects and manifests as the Trinity (Asar, Ra, Amun) while still remaining nondual and transcendental. More evidence of this teaching is found in the philosophy of the god Banebdjedut.

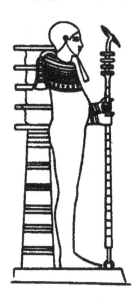

Banebdjedut (above) is a form of Khnum but he is known as the "Soul of Djedu" and "Soul of Ra" and "Life of Ra." He is also known as the "Soul of Geb" and the "Soul of Shu." He is at once the generative, sexual power of the two divinities (Asar and Ra), as Djedu is the ancient sacred city of Asar whose power of resurrection flows from his Djed, that is his pillar with the four horizontal levels that form his backbone. Banebdjedut is the ram god of Lower Egypt, and consort of the fish goddess Hatmehit and the father of Heru-pa-khahart (Greek-Harpocrates, Heru the child).

Banebdjedut as "the one with four faces on one neck." (*Ra-Asar-Shu-Geb*). Banebdjedut symbolizes the fourfold nature of Creation through the four directions of geography and the procreative power that operates in Creation.

He played a role in the contest between Heru and Set for the Egyptian throne when he interceded on behalf of Heru. He advised the gods to consult with Ancient Egyptian goddess Nat (Greek Neith). Banebdjedut was depicted sometimes in anthropomorphic form with a ram's head or as a Ram with horizontal antlers and a vertical cobra as his headdress. The center of his sect was at Djeddu (Greek Mendes). Banebdjedut was identified by the classical Greeks as their gods Priapus and Pan, who were both associated with sexual power and fertility.

Just as the God Heru dwells in goddess Hetheru and the god Asar dwells in goddess Aset, Banebdjedut dwells in Hatmehit. Hatmehit is a fish goddess, associated with the land of Punt in east central Africa, south of Nubia. She is an aspect of Aset and Hetheru and is also referred to as "Divine Mother" and "eye of Ra." She represents the creative matrix of water in which the soul (Banebdjedut) deposits the seed and the offspring is Heru-pa-khahart, Heru the child, "dweller in Djedu." This same Heru-pa-khahart is identified with Heru sa Asar sa Aset (Heru the son of Asar and Aset.)

Goddess Hatmehit

Ra, Nebthotep and *Iusaasety*

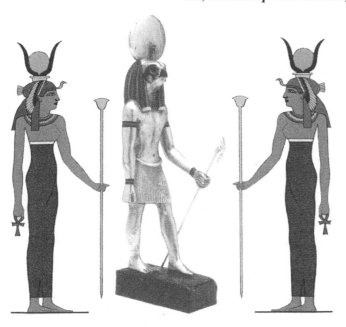

The goddesses *Nebthotep (Nebethetepet)* and *Iusaasety* are important aspects of Anunian Theology and are closely associated with Ra. Together with Ra they form an important Trinity which describes the nature of Creation. Creation is engendered by the primal force of Spirit, the divine fire of the Supreme Being, Ra through Hekau –Word-sound of Power. Time and space are actually relative aspects that come to exist through the change in and motion of objects in space. In other words, time and space is sustained by the coming and going (movement) of elements. Essentially, therefore, Creation consists of truth, the ever-dynamic fire of the spirit which operates through energy- Sekhem that sustains Ankh (life), the elements and the relative motion of objects. However, the Spirit underlies all and therefore it can move nowhere since it is everywhere. Objects in Creation move in and through Spirit and are rooted (dependent) on Spirit for their existence. If objects were to be completely motionless in space there would be no existence. For example, all hearts would be still and no stars would burn. If objects were to be in perpetual motion there would also be no creation because the motion itself would become a constant that would allow no awareness of existence. Awareness is a factor of relative motion. It is an action that the mind performs in time and space. If that action were to cease the world would also cease to exist from the perspective of that mind that has ceased to operate, to move.

The task of the Creator is to balance the principles of **Nebthotep** and **Iusaasety** in order to bring about a universe in which consciousness can perceive it. Therefore, there is motion (Iusaasety) and motionlessness (Nebethotep). Iusaasety may wear a scarab beetle on her head and she may be seen as a counterpart to the sun-god Khepri-*Atum* as the feminine principle in the creation of the universe. The task of a follower of Neterian religion is to find the place wherein there is motionlessness and then to discover that God is to be perceived and experienced there since God exists in the world of motion as well as out of it where there is no motion. These two places are in the same existence but in different dimensions. But the realm of motion distracts the mind and thus God is not easily discerned there. Thus, the art of transcending time and space is the ideal which leads to the ability to perceive the Divine. Then having had that discovery, it can extend into the realm of time and space as well. When that happens a person is considered "enlightened-resurrected-awakened." This program of discovery is accomplished through worship of the divinities, learning about them, embodying their characteristics, mastering their principles and thereby rendering those principles, which are impelled by human ignorance, fueled by the fire of the spirit (Serpent Power-aspect of the Sekhem). Then in such an advanced aspirant the movements of the world as if cease and the rest of Spirit, which moves nowhere, becomes the ever-present reality.

UNITY IN DIVERSITY: ASAR AND ATUM

After the millions of years of differentiated creation, the chaos that existed before creation will return; only the primeval god[36] and Asar will remain steadfast-no longer separated in space and time.

–Ancient Egyptian *Coffin Texts* (CT VII 467-468)

The passage above concisely expresses the powerful teaching that all creation is perishable and that even the gods and goddesses will ultimately dissolve into the primordial state of potential consciousness. Therefore, it behooves a human being to move towards the Divine since that is the only stable truth that exists as an abiding reality. This is known as the Absolute, from which all has emanated and into which all will dissolve. A righteous person has the choice to go to the Djed and abide in Asar, to merge with him, or they can await the time when Ra traverses through the Duat, the eternal journey described earlier, illuminating it as he passes in his Boat. If they choose Ra, they will be picked up and be loaded unto the boat where they will merge with Ra and experience peace, bliss and happiness for all time. The *Book of Amduat* discusses the Duat with the followers of Ra in mind, while the *Prt m Hru* and the *Book of Gates* discusses the Duat with the followers of Asar in mind. If they choose to stay in the Duat, they will lead a life in the astral plane similar to that on earth for a certain period of time but with very important differences. These differences are outlined in Chapter 8 of the Ancient Egyptian *Book of Coming Forth By Day*.

"The God Ra on His Boat." Creation is sustained by the journey of Ra in his boats. Ra possesses two boats: "The Boat of Morning and The Boat of Evening." Ra is seen often traveling with the other major deities in his boat (Djehuti, Hetheru, Maat, etc.). In order to sustain creation, Ra journeys across heaven (cosmos) but must continually defeat the serpent Apep (evil-decay-entropy) in order to do so. Apep attempts to destroy Ra

---

[36] Referring to the Supreme Being in the form of Atum-Ra

(creation) each day. Therefore, the battle against evil (chaos) is a continuous one since it cannot be destroyed. Chaos and Order are integral components of creation. Creation cannot exist without the two. They are complementary opposites; the dissolution of either would mean the dissolution of creation. This signifies the ongoing battle within every human being. The challenge is to maintain a dynamic balance between good and evil (creation and destruction-dissolution). In the myth of the Asarian Resurrection, Set is the character that represents egoism and amorality (chaos), which are in contradiction with Maat. Set and Heru do battle and Heru, the force of good, wins and Set is made to serve Ra by assisting him in his daily journey by fighting Apep to protect the boat and to allow its journey of creation, bringing order out and staving off disorder. So the ego must be controlled and placed in the service of spirit in order to bring about peace, prosperity, life and enlightenment.

Above left: The initiate controls Apep who is in the form of a serpent. Above right: the god Heru controls Apep, who appears as a man (anthropomorphic) underwater.

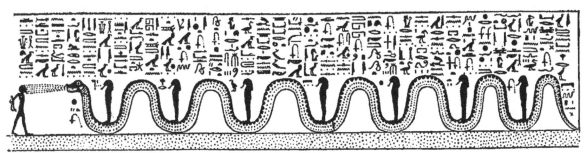

Kheti

There is another great serpent. His name is Kheti. Kheti is a fire-spitting serpent of the Duat. He burns all unrighteous souls who end up in the Duat after death.

OGDOAD OF ANU

Neteru	Male	Neteru	Female
Nu,	Primeval waters	Nut,	Primeval waters
Hehu,	Time	Hehut,	Time
Kekui,	Day (manifest)	Kekuit,	Night (unmanifest)
Kerh,	Potential power	Kerhet,	Potential power

There is a tradition in Anunian Theology (evident in the Pyramid Texts) that includes a teaching related to eight neteru. These eight represent personifications of qualities (differentiations, conditioning) of the primeval ocean of creation, the Nun. They embody the qualities in the form of eight serpent divinities, four being males and four being females. Their names provide insight into the nature of the primeval essence, the substratum of Creation out of which all the gods and goddesses, elements of Creation and indeed human beings originate.

The eight divinities represent basic but fundamental and powerful conceptions related to the essential nature of the primordial constituents of Creation. Notice also that these qualities are expressed in the form of both male and female divinities, recognizing early on that the essence and creative force of the Spirit (God(dess)) is carried out by a wholistic force that while being originally one and non-dual, polarizes itself in order to create an illusion of duality. It is this illusion that allows Creation to appear to exist, that is, for separate objects to appear to be separate from each other and from Creation and thereby be able to interact with each other as separate entities even though in reality they are not, never have and never will be separate. This conception gave way to the more popular conception of the Pauti which included Ra, Shu and Tefnut, Geb and Nut, Asar and Aset, Set and Nebethet and Heru.[37]

---

[37] See the books *Anunian Theology* and *Egyptian Yoga Volume 2: Theban Theology.*

On Previous Page: Ptah and Senusert - Cairo Museum

Shetaut Menefer

INTRODUCTION TO THE NETERU OF MEMPHITE THEOLOGY

Shetaut Menefer

The Mystery Teachings of the Menefer (Memphite) Tradition are related to the Neterus known as Ptah, Sekhmit, Nefertum. The myths and philosophy of these divinities constitutes Memphite Theology.[38] Ptah is the source and support of Creation. He brings Creation into being by willing and thinking it into being. Sekhmet (Sekhmit) is the dynamic aspect or the power of Ptah and Nefer-tem refers to the beautiful (nefer) new life which emerges daily as the new day (tem - relating to Atem-Atom). The main symbol of Nefertum is the Lotus. He is the lotus of Creation which emerges out of the primeval waters (Nu). This is the same lotus upon which Heru sits. Therefore, the names of the characters in the Trinity of Memphis (Ptah-Sekhmet-Nefertum) relate to a profound understanding of the nature of Creation.

The temple of Ptah in Menefer (Memphis) and its related temples espoused the teachings of Creation, human origins and the path to spiritual enlightenment by means of the Supreme Being in the form of the god Ptah and his family, who compose the Memphite Trinity. It tells of how Ptah emerged from a primeval ocean and how he created the universe by his will and the power of thought (mind). The gods and goddesses, who are his thoughts, go to form the elements of nature and the cosmic forces that maintain nature. His spouse, Sekhmit has a powerful temple system of her own that is related to the Memphite teaching. The same is true for his son Nefertum.

Below: The Memphite Cosmogony.

The city of Hetkaptah (Ptah)

The Neters of Creation - The Company of the Gods and Goddesses.
Neter Neteru
Nebertcher - Amun (unseen, hidden, ever present, Supreme Being, beyond duality and description)

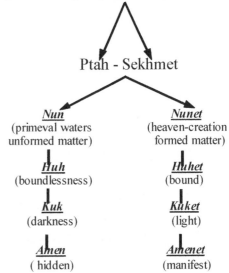

Ptah - Sekhmet

Nun (primeval waters unformed matter)	Nunet (heaven-creation formed matter)
Huh (boundlessness)	Huhet (bound)
Kuk (darkness)	Kuket (light)
Amen (hidden)	Amenet (manifest)

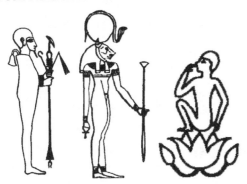

Ptah-Sekhmit-Nefertem

Each Neteru listed above here has specific wisdom related to the nature of self, Creation and the Divine. Following this tradition means studying their mythic significance, their wisdom teaching and their mystical insight. Together, they constitute a wholistic teaching, integrating the philosophy of the tradition and the relationship with the other traditions. These teachings, their understanding and application are to be learned through the process of Shedy. Notice that Amun (Amen) is part of the Company of Gods and Goddesses of Memphite Theology. This constitutes a *Correlative Theological Statement* linking Memphite Theology to Wasetian (Theban Theology). Overleaf-image on a temple column of Nefertem as the child on the lotus.

---

[38] For more details see the Book Memphite Theology by Muata Ashby

Ptah is the third member of the great Ancient Egyptian Trinity. He figures prominently in the Prt m Hru in Chapter 11 of Opening the Mouth (expanding the Mind) ceremony. The name of Ptah is written in hieroglyphic as a human form supporting heaven and standing on earth. In this manner he is iconographically related to Shu, who assumes the same posture in Anunian Theology. The name Ptah is composed of the following parts:

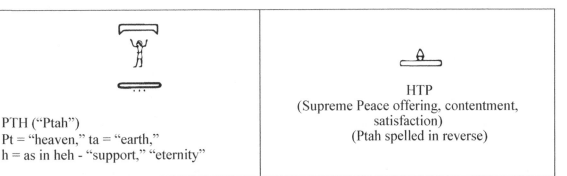

PTH ("Ptah") Pt = "heaven," ta = "earth," h = as in heh - "support," "eternity"	HTP (Supreme Peace offering, contentment, satisfaction) (Ptah spelled in reverse)

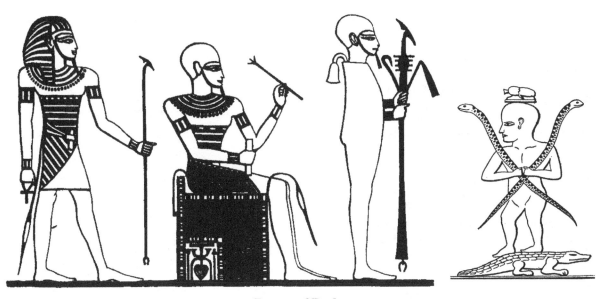

Forms of Ptah

Ptah is known as the *Overlord of the two lands,* referring to "Lower Egypt" and "Upper Egypt," also material existence (manifest) and spiritual (un-manifest). *Htp* (Supreme Peace) is also the name of *Ptah*

(Pth) if written backwards. He is also known as *Hetepi* ⚊🔥〚〛. Thus, Ptah (Neter, God, Heru) is the support of heaven and earth and the supreme abode of peace which transcends the realm of time and space and the pairs of opposites. In this aspect, Ptah is again associated with *Shu,* the God of air and breath, who is therefore, the sustainer of heaven and earth or the soul and the body and Heh, the lord of eternity. Far right: Ptah as the divine dwarf-Pigmy, Lord of the primeval matter and the two serpent goddesses (Uadjit and Nekhebit) of Creation.

Ptah-Sokar-Asar

Above: Ptah the Potter, fashioning the egg of Creation. In this aspect Ptah assumes the position of Creator and the assimilation of the potter function relates him to Khnum as well as to Wasetian (Theban) Theology.

Ptah-Sokar-Asar is the triune divinity, a form of the three divinities Ptah, Sokar (Seker) and Asar, which together epitomize the Ancient Egyptian capacity to mythologically and philosophically blend and equate the forms of the Divine. This shows the underlying concept that all of the divinities are in reality aspects of each other. Otherwise, these iconographical combinations would not be possible. The philosophical and iconographical teaching related to Ptah-Sokar-Asar also constitutes *Correlative Theological Statements* that connect Memphite Theology to Anunian Theology and Asarian Theology.

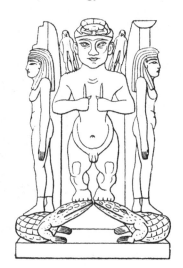

Other Important Forms of Ptah

Ptah Nunu (left) and Ptah Tanen (right).

The third member of the Trinity, Ptah, as the Creator emerging from the primeval waters, Nun, and as the primeval hill, Atum (Tanen).

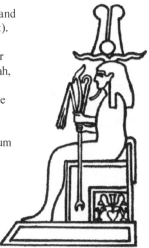

Above Ptah-Asar the divine dwarf with Khepri on his head and with the two goddesses Aset and Nebethet.

"Ptah conceived in His heart (reasoning consciousness) all that would exist and at His utterance (the word - will, power to make manifest), created Nun, the primeval waters (unformed matter-energy).

Then, not having a place to sit Ptah causes Nun to emerge from the primeval waters as the Primeval Hill so that he may have a place to sit. Atom (Atum) then emerges and sits upon Ptah. Then came out of the waters four pairs of gods, the Ogdoad

Sekhmet (Sekhemit)

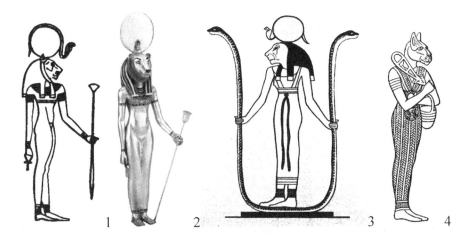

One important element of the goddess is the feline aspect. Sekhmit is a primary form of the feline essence of the Divine. In nature, cats have an inimical relationship with serpents. In Ancient Egyptian mythology, the *Serpent of Darkness* is seen as the embodiment of ignorance and evil which threatens the movement of the Boat of Ra and which prevents the spiritual aspirant from attaining enlightenment. Therefore, the goddess in the form of a cat (Bast-above far right (4)) or the lioness (Tefnut - Sekhmet above left (1, 2, 3)) is seen as the warrior and champion of the gods (Asar and Heru) as well as the aspirant. She is the one who paves the way for spiritual evolution by destroying the evil of ignorance and sinfulness in the human heart. Thus, she is the goddess who controls the Serpent Power as well.[39]

---

[39] See the book Serpent Power by Muata Ashby

Forms of Nefertum

Ptah Nefertum and the Mysticism of the Memphite Trinity

The Egyptian Trinity mythology of *Amun-Ra-Ptah* represents a major philosophical discourse on the composition of nature and the path of Kamitan spirituality. Memphite Theology, based on the god Ptah, is only a third of the entire teaching. Ptah is the Supreme Spirit and he manifests Creation through his consort Sekhmet and their child Nefertum. The Trinity of Memphis (Ptah-Sekhmet-Nefertum) relates to a profound understanding of the nature of Creation. Ptah is the hidden inner essence of creation and the essence of the human soul as well. Like Vishnu, in Hindu myth, Ptah is passive, immobile and detached. He "thinks" Creation into being by his will and has indeed become the Universe, through the actions of the Creator Nefertum. Ptah's thoughts are transformed into "word" (i.e. vibrations), and these cause the Nun (primeval Ocean) to take the varied forms of Creation which are described in detail in the foremost scripture of Memphite Theology, the "Shabaka Stone Inscription."[40] This philosophy means that just as wind and its motion are one and the same, and the ocean and its waves are one and the same, in the same way, the Supreme Self and the objects of the world are one and the same. As in Anunian Theology, according to Memphite Theology, the world is composed of *neteru*. These neterus are divine energy, cosmic forces that constitute all physical phenomena. These neteru have assumed the bodies (forms) of all the objects in the world which appear on the surface to be different and separate from each other, but in reality, the neteru are essentially conditioned aspects of God and therefore God has entered into all forms of existence. Memphite Theology is actually a unique form of the Kamitan religion in that it is highly psychological and philosophical and oriented towards intellectual development leading towards intuitional realization of the nature of Self. In this sense it is no surprise to find that the early followers of Buddhism which was a discipline emphasizing mystical psychology and philosophy, developed an affinity for the city of Memphis and became attached to its temple which promoted the teachings of Memphite Theology, since they have much in common with the Buddhist teachings. The Memphite scripture elucidates on the process of Creation. Ptah thinks and a Creator, Tem, on his lotus, comes into existence and Creation is brought forth.

> *"2- Then, not having a place to sit Ptah causes Nun to emerge from the primeval waters as the Primeval Hill so that he may have a place to sit. Atom then emerges and sits upon Ptah."[41]*

-From the Shabaka Inscription

In order to understand and appreciate the word Nefertum more fully, its definition and function will now be presented. Nefertum means "beautiful completion." In the Ancient Egyptian *Book of Coming Forth By Day* it is said that when an initiate attains resurrection, i.e. Spiritual enlightenment, they are actually becoming Nefertum. In the Creation Myth of the city of Anu (Anunian Theology), Atum or Tem is the divine aspect of the spirit as the first individuated entity to emerge from the primeval ocean. Also, in a separate but related teaching, from the myth of Ra and Aset, Tem is referred to as the third aspect of Ra as follows.

---

[40] *Memphite Theology: The Hidden Properties of Matter,* Muata Ashby 1997

[41] ibid.

In the myth of Ra and Aset, Ra says: *"I am Kheperi in the morning, and Ra at noonday, and Temu in the evening."* It is also a *Correlative Theological Statement* that connects Anunian Theology to Asetian Theology (Mysteries of Goddess Aset (Isis)). Thus we have *Kheper-Ra-Tem,* ⊙◯⚊🐦, as the Anunian Triad. In Chapter 4 of the *Prt m Hru*, the initiate is to identifies {him/her} self with Tem, and to assert:

"I am Tem in rising; I am the only One; I came into being with Nu. I am Ra who rose in the beginning."

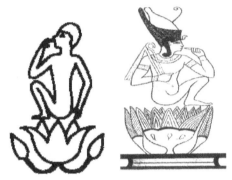

The statement further relates to Tem as Nefertem: the newborn sun, the morning sun, which is symbolized by the divine solar child, who sits on the lotus or is seen emerging from a lotus.

Above- The Shabaka Stone (now with much of its text rubbed off due to mishandling)

The origins of Ptah and the nature and composition of "matter," or what is termed "physical reality," and the concept of "consciousness" were understood and clearly set down in the hieroglyphic texts which date back to 5000 B.C.E in the theological system of Menefer (Memphis), Egypt.

Through the Shabaka Inscription we are to understand that Ptah created the gods and goddesses (Verse 3) through his thought and desire i.e. will, (verse 1-2) and they became the manifested creation. Creation itself is explained as the body that the gods and goddesses, i.e. forms of the spirit, exists in.

The passage above is very important because it establishes the mystical transcendence of the initiate who has realized {his/her} "oneness" and union with the Divine. It is also a *Correlative Theological Statement* that connects Memphite Theology to Anunian Theology. In other papyri, Tem is also identified with the young Heru-pkhard (Harmachis -young Heru, the solar child) as the early morning sun. Thus, Kheperi-Ra-Temu are forms of the same being and are the object of every initiate's spiritual goal. Being the oldest of the three theologies, the Mysteries of Anu (Anunian Theology) formed a foundation for the unfolding of the teachings of mystical spirituality which followed in the mysteries of Hetkaptah (Memphis- Memphite Theology), through Ptah, and the Mysteries of Waset (Thebes- Theban Theology), through Amun.

In the Ancient Egyptian Pyramid Texts there is a very important passage which provides insight into the role of Nefertum and the entire teaching behind the Trinity of Memphite Theology.

"I become Nefertum, the lotus-bloom which is at the nostril of Ra; I will come forth from the horizon every day and the gods and goddesses will be cleansed at the sight of me."

—Ancient Egyptian Pyramid Texts

Thus, we are to understand that in Memphite Theology Ptah is the source, the substratum from which all creation arises. Ptah is the will of the Spirit, giving rise to thought itself and that thought takes form as Sekhmit, Creation itself. The same spirit, Ptah, who enlivens Creation, is the very essence which rises above Creation to complete the cycle of Spirit to matter and then back to Spirit. The Lotus is the quintessential symbol of completion, perfection, transcendence and glory. Thus it is used in Ancient Egyptian and Hindu mythologies as the icon par excellence of spiritual enlightenment.

Therefore, smelling the lotus, and acting as the lotus means moving above the muddy waters of Creation and turning towards the sun which is the symbol of Ra, the Supreme Spirit.

In Chapter 24 of the *Pert M Heru (Book of Coming Forth By Day)*, the role of goddess Hetheru in the process of salvation is specified as the initiate speaks the words which will help {him/her} become as a lotus:

> *"I am the lotus, pure, coming forth out into the day. I am the guardian of the nostril of Ra and keeper of the nose of Hetheru. I make, I come, and I seek after he, that is, Heru. I am pure going out from the field."*

The lotus, the serpent and the sun have been used since ancient times to symbolize the detachment and dispassion that a spiritual aspirant must develop towards the world, that is, turning away from relating to the world from the perception of the limited senses and the conditioned mind, and rather, turning towards the underlying reality and sustainer of Creation, the illuminating transcendental Spirit, as symbolized by the sun. The serpent represents resurrection, as the death of the body is a changing of bodies just as the serpent changes its skin. Its caustic venom is the sunray, which enlivens or destroys. The lotus is a solar symbol, and as such is a wonderful metaphor for the process of spiritual evolution leading to Enlightenment. The lotus emerges everyday out of the murky waters of the pond in order to receive the rays of the morning sun. As it rises up through the murky waters to climb above, its leaves, which have a special coating or texture, promotes the water to run right off of them without a drop sticking or clinging to them. It then opens and blooms to the light of the morning sun. The spiritual aspirant, a follower of the Goddess, seeking to experience the Supreme Spirit, must rise {him/her} self up through the murky waters of egoism and negativity (anger, hatred, greed, and ignorance), eventually to rise above, leaving all remnants behind (i.e. transcending them), as {he/she} blooms to the light of the Self, i.e. attain Enlightenment. Hetheru and Heru form a composite archetype, a savior with all of the complementary qualities of the male and female principles, inseparable, complete and androgynous.

The obvious relationship between Nefertum and Heru and Heru and Khonsu and Asar and Ptah and Ptah and Ra-Tem and Ra-Tem and Nefertum indicate an underlying correlation, a relationship between the divinities from the major theologies, demonstrating that they are all related.

The God Imhotep

Imhotep was perhaps the greatest Sage of Ancient Egypt, who lived in the Old Kingdom Period (5,000-2,500 B.C.E.). He was a legendary figure in his own time because he was a master healer (medical doctor), royal architect, scribe, and Spiritual Philosopher. His writings have not yet been discovered, but some historical records survive that show both Ancient Egyptians and foreigners alike revered him; so much so that he was deified (canonized). In the time when Hippocrates and other ancient Greeks went to study medical science in Ancient Egypt, they revered and worshiped Imhotep under the Greek name Asclepius, as the god of medical science and healing. It must be understood that the string of movies from Hollywood called "the mummy" wherein Sage Imhotep is depicted as an evil mummy are nothing but gross misrepresentations of the truth which history records.

(A)

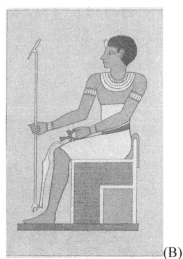

(B)

As a physician, Imhotep is recognized as having started the medical sciences. He is often depicted as a seated bald man (A) who has an open scroll of papyrus on his lap, showing that the medical sciences were codified. Doctors often worked with written records of previous treatments, just as lawyers (priests and priestesses of Maat) worked from precedents that had been recorded on papyrus. Thus, the doctors and lawyers were well versed in reading and writing. After being deified, he was recognized as a god who brought the medical sciences to the world. As a god he is depicted as a seated man with skullcap (B)- like the god Ptah. He holds an *uas* scepter and an ankh. As a god he is recognized as the son of the Kamitan deity Ptah and brother of the Kamitan deity Nefertum. Thus, Imhotep was considered as the god of physicians.

Most people learn about African culture and Ancient Egyptian spirituality through commercialized theme parks such as Bush Gardens, and Hollywood productions such as Tarzan or Cleopatra, documentaries by western scholars or Christian movies about the Old Testament produced in Western countries, which are based on fiction and racial (ethnic) stereotyping or Biblical interpretations. The "mummy" movies created by Hollywood purporting to show the mummy of Sage Imhotep as an unethical, lustful murderer, and movie and television shows such as *Stargate* which depict the Ancient Egyptian gods and goddesses as evil aliens who enslave people and possess their bodies like parasites have no basis in historical fact whatsoever. This shows how the repetitions of untruths become facts over time in the absence of ethics in the entertainment business, and scholarly silence on the issue. This practice denigrates African culture as surely as if a movie denigrating Moses or Jesus of Christianity or Muhammad of Islam were similarly produced. Imhotep was canonized as an African saint at least 3,000 years before the advent of Judaism, and 4,000 years before the advent of Christianity and Islam. He was a Sage, scientist and philosopher as well as a medical doctor. To impugn his name is to denigrate all Africans everywhere, and to disparage the role of African people in the development of humanity. It is an effect of racism and cultural genocide by the western media, that is allowed to continue by the western leaders and academia, who do not speak out against it. It is a continuation of the practice of demonizing an African personality that truly deserves the status of any great spiritual leader that has ever existed before or since, including Jesus, Buddha, Ramakrishna, Confucius, Lao Tze, etc. It is the duty of all who uphold the precepts of righteousness and truth in business to protest such erroneous and malicious, slanderous works in the arts, literature, etc.

Shetaut Amun

INTRODUCTION TO THE NETERU OF THEBAN THEOLOGY

On Previous page: Asar and Ra as Amun- With the goddesses Aset and Nebethet (from the Tomb of Nefertari)

Shetaut Amun[42]

The Mystery Teachings of the Wasetian (Theban) Tradition are related to the Neterus known as Amun, Mut and Khonsu. This temple and its related temples espoused the teachings of creation, human origins and the path to spiritual enlightenment by means of the Supreme Being in the form of the god Amun or Amun-Ra. It tells of how Amun and his family, the Trinity of Amun, Mut and Khonsu, manage the Universe along with his Company of Gods and Goddesses. Though the tradition existed since ancient times the movement became very important in the early part of the New Kingdom Era.

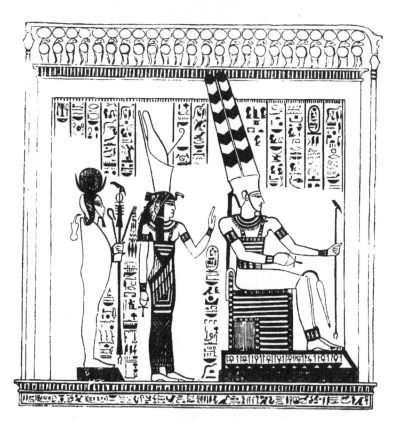

Amun, Mut, Khonsu

The Mystery Teachings of the Wasetian Tradition are related to the Neterus known as Amun, Mu, and Khonsu. Each Neteru listed above here has specific wisdom related to the nature of self, Creation and the Divine. Following this tradition means studying their mythic significance, their wisdom teaching and their mystical insight. Together, they constitute a wholistic teaching, integrating the philosophy of the tradition and the relationship with the other traditions. These teachings, their understanding and application are to be learned through the process of the Shedy disciplines. The main scripture of Wasetian Theology is contained in the *Hymns of Amun* which sum up the Ancient Egyptian understanding of the Trinity concept in creation and that which transcends it.[43]

---

[42] For more details see the Book Egyptian Yoga Vol. 2: Wasetian Theology by Muata Ashby
[43] ibid

AMUN

Amun, the Self, is the "hidden" essence of all things. The Sun (Ra) is the radiant and dynamic outward appearance of the hidden made manifest and also the light of Cosmic Consciousness, the cosmic mind or that through which consciousness projects. In this aspect, Ptah represents the physical world, the solidification or coagulation of the projection of consciousness (Amun) made manifest. These manifestations are reproduced symbolically on earth in the cities of KMT (Egypt), Anu (city of Ra), Waset (city of Amun), and Hetkaptah (city of Ptah). Waset (Weset) or Newt was known to the Greeks as Thebes, who knew it also as Diospolis (heavenly city). Thebes is the city identified in the Old Testament as No (city), No-Amon (city of Amon).

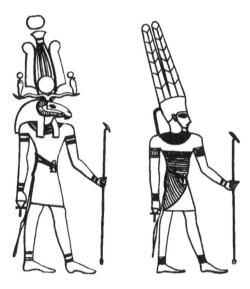

Amun as the Ram headed man (left) and a man with double plumed crown (right).

(The Symbols of Amun)

In the form of Amun-Ra, the evolution of the concept of the Divine takes on an emphasis of the subtle and hidden qualities of divine consciousness. As a ram headed man, the iconography of Amun emphasizes the qualities of the ram (virility, leadership, confrontation and the astrological period of the ram as it relates to the Great Ancient Egyptian Year). The human headed form emphasizes all-encompassing, non-dual divinity as symbolized by the double plumes uniting in one being.

The concept of Amun is a central theme of Ancient Egyptian religion and mystical philosophy. Sages have mythologized the idea of Amun in such a fashion that the study of myths reveals increasingly more profound layers of the mystery of life. The outer layers are shed through intuitive understanding of the philosophical ideas and teachings revealing the core wherein the discovery of the true essence of mystical religious philosophies is found.

The name *Amun* appears in the remotest times of Egyptian history, as the other main divinities, and came to prominence in the ancient city of Waset (Thebes), Egypt. The mysteries of Amun represent a quintessence of Ancient Egyptian philosophy concerning the nature of the un-manifest aspect of all existence and the understanding of human consciousness as a transcendental and immortal witnessing subject. This teaching speaks of God as an un-manifest, nameless, formless, *Being of Light* which is the source of all that is manifest. The formless *Being of Light* later became known as the *Watery Abyss* and Amun. In the Shabaka Inscription, this teaching was espoused with *Ptah* assuming the role of the manifestation of the un-manifest Self, and from him emanate the Neteru in the form of an Ogdoad (eight) of Neteru.

MUT

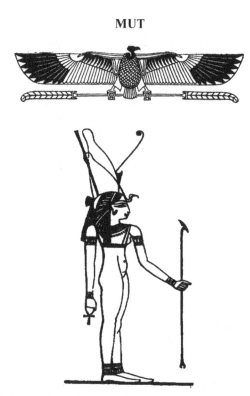

Mut as the vulture goddess and consort of Amun.

The goddess Mut is the counterpart of Amun. She is nature itself, and she exemplifies its capacity to recycle. Her main symbol is the vulture. Just as vultures eat carrion and turn it into life, so too the goddess takes in death, and brings forth new life for the spiritual aspirant. The goddess Mut is the tutelary deity of all Queens. She is their protector and symbol of motherly power. For this reason the queens (especially of the New Kingdom era) wear a crown-headdress that incorporates the vulture motif.

Khonsu

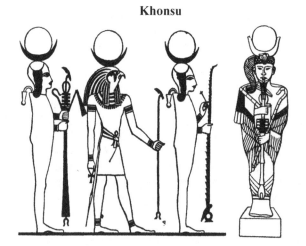

Above: The forms of Khonsu, The Traveler, offspring of Amun and Mut (Amunet).

In short, Amun is the origin and essence of all things and is the innermost reality of all human beings. Amun is the same Life Force essence which manifests through the sun (Ra), therefore, Amun is known as Amun-Ra. Since Amun and his consort Amunet (Mut) are in reality one being who manifests as a duality, encompassing all the pairs of opposites, Amun is also known as *Ka-Mut-F* or the Bull Of His Mother, signifying that the hidden soul within all things has the power to exist and generate life from within itself. Therefore, all life is an expression of the self-existent being, beyond time and space though manifesting as time and space, and all objects in creation.

Amun-Ra in boat with Saa and Heka

Amun-Ra in boat with Company of Gods and Goddesses

Amun is shown in the Books of the Duat[44] holding a serpent-shaped scepter. This serpent was called Kam-at-f ⟨hieroglyphs⟩. One meaning of Kam-at-f is *"He who hath finished His moment."* This serpent, representing creative power, enshrines the soul of Amun. As Amun is neither alive nor dead, the serpent surrounding his soul represents creation and the soul is the source and power which sustains creation. The symbol of Khepri, the scarab ⟨hieroglyph⟩, is associated with Amun. This constitutes a *Correlative Theological Statement*, linking Amun theology with the Anunian.

Amun    Mut

Ka-Mut-F

(A)    (B)    (C)

The depictions of Khonsu above (A-B) show the direct relation of Khonsu to Heru in his Hawk form. Here he is a young falcon-headed man with the lunar disc and crescent combined headdress. He is a protective spirit alongside the king's Ka (astral body).Khonsu as Khonsu-Nefer-Hotep (C) is of particular interest. Khonsu-Nefer-Hotep means Khonsu in beatified peace. He is a god of healing as is attested by the famous "Story of the Princess of Bekten" who was sick and her father sent for a statue of Khonsu to be brought to Syria from Egypt. The statue cured her. He is the god of vegetative growth, ripening fruits, conception and human love. His hawk aspect links him to Heru and to Anunian Theology.

The specific name for the divinity of love is ⟨hieroglyphs⟩ *Ndjm*- the God of Love. This name is a pun on the word for sweetness ⟨hieroglyphs⟩ *ndjm*. It is an acknowledgment that the Divine is the source of joy, pleasure and delightfulness. It is also related to the terms ⟨hieroglyphs⟩ *ndj*- protection and ⟨hieroglyphs⟩ *nedjmmit* - sexual delights. Thus, God is the source of refuge, love, pleasure and joy.

---

[44] *Duat* is the Ancient Egyptian name for the Astral Plane or Netherworld. It also is written as Duat or Duat.

Below: The Trinity of Amun and the Company of Gods and Goddesses of Amun in Waset (Thebes, Egypt)

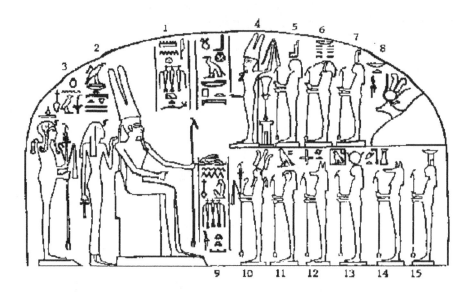

The Company of the Gods and Goddesses of Amun.

1-Amun-Ra
2-Mut
3- Khonsu
4- Min
5- Aset (Isis)
6- Djehuti (Thoth, Hermes)
7- Maat
8- Nbt Ament -Lady of Amenti (aspect of Hathor)
9- Asar (Osiris)
10- Un-Nefer-Khenti-Amenti
11- Heru (Horus) of the two Horizons
12- He of the embalming chamber
13- HetHeru (aspect of Hathor)
14- Governor of the house of the physician
15- Nebthet (Nephthys)

Notice that the Company of Gods and Goddesses of Amun includes Aset, Maat, Heru, Asar and Nebethet. These inclusions constitute a *Correlative Theological Statement*, linking Amun theology with the Anunian (Ra), Asarian (Osiris) and Asetian (Isis) theologies.

As stated earlier, Amun is also known as Ka-Mut-F or the Bull Of His Mother.

Ka	Ka-Mut-F "bull-mother-his own"	Mut

In the form of Kamutf Amun brought the Creation into existence with eight divinities, each symbolizing one of eight complementary (male-female) cosmic principles of Creation, i.e. the opposites of Creation. These divinities were later regarded as the Ogdoad. The specific form which Amun used is Amsu (Min), the ithyphallic form, symbolic of the power to generate, impregnate and create. This occurred in the city known as "Khemnu" or "City of the eight." The gods and goddesses of the ogdoad were:

Cosmic force represented	Goddess	God
Primordial waters Infinity Darkness Hidden Essence	Nunet Hehet Keket Amunet	Nun Heh Kek Amun

In later times the position as the head of the Ogdoad was given to the god Djehuti due to his popularity in the city of Khemenu. Note here that the Ogdoad of Amun is a reworking of the Ogdoad of Ptah. So this same teaching is carried forth through the four traditions. Again, this constitutes another *Correlative Theological Statement*, which links the Neterian traditions, once again showing that behind the apparent multiplicity there is a calculated pantheism underlying the mythic systems that reflects the fundamental teachings and principles in seemingly different divinities.

Below: the God Djehuti (far right) gives life-breath to Asar (far left).

Min (Amsu-Min)

Min (Amsu-Min)

In the *Prt m Hru* (Chap. 4[45]), the initiate is to identify with Amsu-Min and say:

> *"I am Amsu (Min) in his movement. This is true; he has given to me his plumes and they are on my head now. Who is this person that is being spoken about?*
>
> *As for Amsu it is Heru, the **redeemer of his father**. As for his movement it is his birth. As for his plumes on his head they are the actions of goddess Aset and Nebethet. They give of themselves to his person. They will be his protectors."*

Min is the aspect of Amun manifesting as Heru in the form of the victorious savior (vindicator) of his father's (Asar's) honor. The passage *"**redeemer of his father"*** is a *Correlative Theological Statement*, which links the divinity Min (Amun) to Heru, who is one of the central divinities of the Asarian Tradition. Hetheru is his companion and female aspect, whose passion and restorative influence provides healing and strength to allow Heru to continue the struggle against Set. Both of them (Heru and Hetheru) represent the idea of aroused and sublimated sexual energy. In this capacity Amsu-Min (Amun) he is known as "Bull of his mother," i.e. generator of his own coming into being. In the next passage it is explained that the two plumes on the head of Min are Aset and Nebethet. The passage above also shows that Aset and Nebethet are the forces of life and death which manifest the power of Amsu (Heru).

The state of "Heru-Min" consciousness, when Heru is victorious, is the goal of all spiritual efforts. It means being triumphant over ignorance in the form of egoism and the fetters of Set (anger, hatred, greed, lust, selfishness, desire, elation, depression, conceit, etc.). At this stage, there is no possibility for the lower nature to sway the mind of a person. Now the lower self is like a slave to the Higher Self. The freedom from the fetters allows the mind to experience boundless *Sekhem,* Life Force energy-power, and to be at peace, Hetep, ▱. This peace and harmony allows the mind to see beyond the veil of ordinary human consciousness, in effect, to behold the Divine Self, Asar.

In *Prt m Hru* CHAPTER 4[46] *The Wisdom of the Secret Identity of the Gods and Goddesses* texts: verse (11) states that *As for his plumes on his* (Amsu's) ***head, they are the actions of the goddesses Aset and Nebethet.*** Thus, the *Shuti* (the plumes- two goddesses) are the feathers on the crown of Amsu, who is the lord of Maati–absolute and temporal existence.

---

[45] Generally referred to as Chapter 17
[46] Generally referred to as Chapter 17.

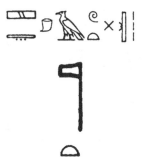

Shetaut Netrit

INTRODUCTION TO THE NETERU OF THE GODDESS PATHS

Below: Goddess Hetheru – from the Tomb of Nefertari

THE GODDESS TRADITION

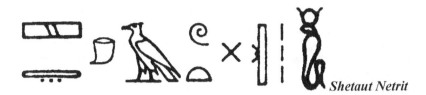

Shetaut Netrit

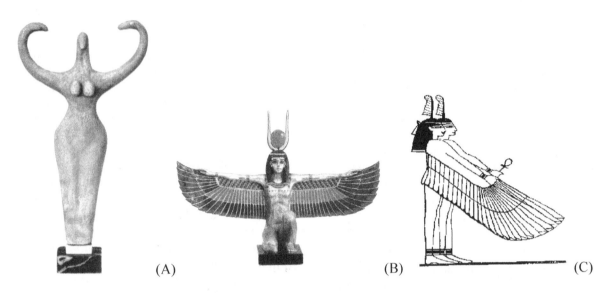

(A) (B) (C)

Above: (A) This predynastic symbol of the female - mother - Goddess, is represented as a winged divinity in the early period and also in the dynastic period of Egypt in the same pose. The wings are symbolic of the Egyptian Sky- Hawk (avian) quality of the goddess. Aset (B) and Maat (C) of the dynastic period Egypt are also female Goddesses represented with wings.

The hieroglyphic sign *Arat* means "Goddess." General, throughout ancient Kamit, the Mystery Teachings of the Goddess Tradition are related to the Divinity in the form of the Goddess. The Goddess is an integral part of all the Neterian traditions but special temples also developed around the worship of certain particular Goddesses who were also regarded as Supreme Beings in their own right with the same prominence as Ra, Amun or Ptah. Thus as in other African religions, the goddess as well as the female gender were respected and elevated as the male divinities. The Goddess was also the author of Creation, giving birth to it as a great Cow. The following are the most important forms of the goddess.[47]

---

[47] See the Books, *The Goddess Path, Mysteries of Isis, Glorious Light Meditation, Memphite Theology* and *Resurrecting Osiris* by Muata Ashby

Aset, Net, Sekhemit, Mut, Hetheru

Mehurt ("The Mighty Full One")

Each Neteru listed above here has specific wisdom related to the nature of self, Creation and the Divine. Following this tradition means studying their mythic significance, their wisdom teaching and their mystical insight. Together, they constitute a wholistic teaching, integrating the philosophy of their tradition and the relationship with the other traditions. These teachings, their understanding and application are to be learned through the process of Shedy.

Net (Anet)

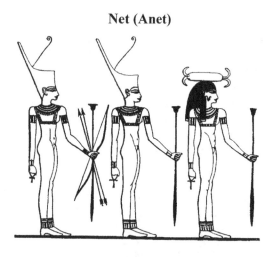

Net is one of the most important divinities of Neterian theology. The seat of her worship in ancient times was Zau (Greek or Arabic= Sais). She is the goddess of creation and war, as well as protection, honor and decisive action. Her attributes are the bow, shield and arrows as well as the weaving spool. She is androgynous (neither male nor female), and was known to watch over Asar's ceremonial bed when

he lay dead, along with Aset and Nebthet. She assisted Djehuti in bringing justice for Heru in the Asarian myth. The goddess Net is the primordial Supreme Divinity with female aspect. She is the ancient form of the goddesses Aset and Hetheru, and her worship extended to the far reaches of antiquity, into the Pre-Dynastic period of Ancient Egyptian history. There are records from both priests and priestesses who served the temples of goddess Net. These show that worship of her was popular, and expressed generally throughout the land of Egypt in ancient times. As we will see, the teachings related to goddess Net are profound and in every way as elevated as those of the Supreme Divinities of Ancient Egypt which portray the male aspect.

In *Pyramid Text* line 606, Net, together with Aset, Nebethet and Serqet, watched over the funerary bed of Asar. Goddess Net gives the bandages and shrouds used for the mummy of the deceased and through these she imparts her protection as well as her blessings in the form of spiritual power.

Sebek

In *Pyramid Text* line 620-627, it is explained that the initiate is Sebek, the god who is the son of Net, and that the initiate rises like the son of Net. In the city of Net, Sebek is recognized as a form of Heru. Thus, the statement above is a *Correlative Theological Statement*, in which the tradition of Net is associated with that of Heru, and Asar. Therefore, there is no conflict in finding that the goddess Aset was ascribed her attributes in the later dynastic period. The following speech of the goddess is also used by goddess Aset.

"I am everything which has been, and which is, and which shall be and there has never been anyone who has uncovered my veil."

Of the goddess it is said that she:

"Created the seed of the gods and goddesses and men and women."

Net is the Goddess of Light, and thus her festival is characterized by the practice of lighting torches and lamps, and in modern times: candles. As light she gave birth to Ra, the sun divinity, who lights up the world. So Net is the:

"Divine Cow who gave birth to Ra."

The statement above is a *Correlative Theological Statement*, in which the tradition of Net is associated with that of Ra (Anunian Theology). Thus, Net is *Mehurt* (Creator cow goddess), the primeval waters from which creation arose.

Her androgynous nature is related in the following epithet:

"Father of all fathers and mother of all mothers."

"Net-Menhit, the Great Lady, Lady of the south, the great cow who gave birth to the sun, who made the seed of the gods and goddesses and men and women, the mother of Ra, the one who raised up Tem in the primeval time,[48] who existed when nothing else had existence and who created that which exists after she came into existence."

The goddess gave birth to the gods and goddesses and to human beings, but she herself was not given birth. She brought herself into existence and gave birth without being impregnated. She was the primeval ocean and she emerged as herself out of herself and all has come forth through and

from her. She is self-existent, and her nature is secret, a *shetat* or mystery to all.

shetat – (deep mysterious nature of the goddess Net)

Net is also referred to as:

"Ua-Netert"
"Divinity One"

Thus, Net encompasses the non-dual, absolute, all-encompassing divinity, i.e., she is Neberdjer. This teaching is further illustrated through the hieroglyphic symbols of her name.

Her symbols are the bow, ⌒, two arrows, ←, the shield, ⊠, and the knitting spool, ꓨ .

The name *Net*, ⌒, or *Anet,* is a play on the word *nt*, ⌒ ,or *ntet*, ⌒⌒, meaning "that which is," "that which exists," i.e. that which is real, true, and abiding. The Kamitan word *nt* - is linked to the root of the Egyptian word for 'weave' - *ntt*. The goddess provides *saa*, 〰, or protection for the spiritual aspirant. She uses a bow and arrow to shoot down the enemies of the righteous (anger, hatred, greed, jealousy, envy, lust, etc.). That is to say, her attributes, solar fire consciousness (rays), all-encompassing divinity, inscrutability, determination, etc. are the arrows she shoots. In her name of *Net hetep,* ✗⌒, the goddess is the abiding supreme peace. The shield represents protection from injury and crossed arrows are neutralization of duality. The shield and arrows are used to put evil spirits to sleep.

---

[48] At the time of Creation.

Net is also known as *Amentet*, the hidden goddess and consort of the god Amen as well as *Rat*, the consort of the god Ra. Thus we are to understand that all the goddess forms are in reality aspects of Net. Thus the epithets of Net constitute *Correlative Theological Statements*, in which the tradition of Net is associated with that of Amun, Aset and Hetheru.

Net is also known as *Mehenit*, [hieroglyphs], the weaving goddess. The material woven by the goddess is used for wrapping the mummy, but she also weaves her own clothing. This clothing is the outer appearance of the physical universe. The objective of spiritual movement within the *Het-Net*, [hieroglyphs], the house of Net (temple of Net, Creation), is to propitiate the goddess to remove her clothing, to unveil herself, so that the initiate may see her true form...absolute existence.

Being the Goddess of Light and having the power to weave the intricate web of Creation wherein all is connected, the goddess allows herself to be disrobed by those who follow the path to her discovery. This path was given in the Temple of Aset, who is a later form of goddess Net.

(above: the god Nun)

The Garment of Nun

The Kamitan term *"Weaving the garment of Nun"* is an allusion to the Ancient Egyptian goddess Net, the progenitor of goddess Aset, with whom the teaching "no mortal man hath ever unveiled me" is also associated. This phrase appears as one of the descriptions of the goddess. She is known as the "weaver" who brought Ra, the light, into being. The garment of Creation is also to be understood as the patchworks, which compose the day-to-day reality of life, that in turn deludes the mind. In fact, Creation is composed of atoms and molecules, which interact and come together to compose elements. However, these atoms are in themselves composed of energy, but the limited mind and senses do not perceive this ocean of energy, which is an aspect of the Nun, the Primeval Ocean. This effect of not perceiving the most subtle essence of Creation is the veil of the

goddess, and therefore, it is the goal of every aspirant to unveil her, that is, to see her true form, the pure light of consciousness devoid of the ignorance. The existence of this veil however, is not the fault of or an effect created by the Goddess. It is the fault of ignorance, which has deluded the mind of the individual. This is true because upon attaining enlightenment, a human being discovers the underlying essence of Creation, beyond the illusions they had made for themselves. This essence is there even now, but the deluded mind cannot perceive it because it is besieged by ignorance that is reinforced with desires, passions, mental agitations (anger, hatred, greed, lust, etc.) and egoism. The various paths of Yoga science act to tear asunder the veil of illusion about the world.

One more important aspect of the goddess "are" the sefek Hetheru (Seven Hathors).

At left: Asar Sokar of Kamit and the Seven Sacred Hetheru Cows

Asar is known as the bull because he impregnates the seven cow goddesses who constitute the seven aspects of Creation. Thus, in Ancient Egypt the bull and seven cows also represent Asar as the bull or power behind the seven-fold Life Force energy centers (the cows) that sustain the soul in time and space. The Seven Hathors are seven aspects of the goddess Hetheru. They act to determine the fate of an individual and were identified by the Greeks as their own goddesses whom they called "the Fates." These goddesses also determine the future and so were propitiated for their prophetic capacities and seven-fold power of manifestation in time and space.

Shetaut Asar

INTRODUCTION TO THE NETERU OF THE ASARIAN MYSTERIES

Shetaut Asar

Asar-Aset-Heru

(Osiris, Isis and Horus)

The tradition and worship of Asar, Aset and Heru was general, throughout ancient Kamit. The centers of this tradition were the city of Abdu containing the Great Temple of Asar, and the city of Pilak containing the Great Temple of Aset.[49] Each Neteru listed above here has specific wisdom related to the nature of self, Creation and the Divine. Following this tradition means studying their mythic significance, their wisdom teaching and their mystical insight. Together, they constitute a wholistic teaching, integrating the philosophy of their own tradition and their relationship with the other traditions. These teachings, their understanding and application are to be learned through the process of Shedy.

Myth of Asar, Aset and Heru

Ra asked Asar and Aset to incarnate to teach human beings and civilize them. Asar and Aset dedicated themselves to the welfare of humanity and sought to spread civilization throughout the earth, even as far as India and China.

During the absence of Asar from his kingdom, his brother Set had no opportunity to make innovations in the state because Aset was extremely vigilant in governing the country, and always upon her guard and watchful for any irregularity or unrighteousness.

Upon Asar's return from touring the world and carrying the teachings of wisdom abroad there was merriment and rejoicing throughout the land. However, one day after Asar's return, through his lack of vigilance, he became intoxicated and slept with Set's wife, Nebethet. Nebethet, as a result of the union with Asar, begot Anpu (below).

Set, who represents the personification of evil forces, plotted in jealousy and anger (the blinding passion that prevents forgiveness) to usurp the throne and conspired to kill Asar. Set secretly got the measurements of Asar and constructed a coffin. Through trickery Set was able to get Asar to "try on" the coffin for size. While Asar was resting in the coffin, Set and his assistants locked it and then dumped it into the Nile river.

The coffin made its way to the coast of Syria where it became embedded in the earth and from it grew a tree with the most pleasant aroma in the form of a Djed. The Djed is the symbol of Asar's Back. It has four horizontal lines in relation to a firmly established, straight column. The Djed

---

[49] For more details see the Book Resurrecting Osiris by Muata Ashby

column is symbolic of the upper energy centers (Hindu-chakras) that relate to the levels of consciousness of the spirit within an individual human being.

The King of Syria was out walking and as he passed by the tree, he immediately fell in love with the pleasant aroma, so he had the tree cut down and brought to his palace. Aset (Auset, Ast), Asar's wife, the personification of the life giving, mother force in creation and in all humans, went to Syria in search of Asar. Her search led her to the palace of the Syrian King where she took a job as the nurse of the King's son. Every evening Aset would put the boy into the "fire" to consume his mortal parts, thereby transforming him into immortality. Fire is symbolic of both physical and mental purification. Most importantly, fire implies wisdom, the light of truth, illumination and energy. Aset, by virtue of her qualities, has the power to bestow immortality through the transformative power of her symbolic essence. Aset then told the king that Asar, her husband, is inside the pillar he made from the tree. He graciously gave her the pillar (DJED) and she returned with it to Kamit (Kmt, Egypt).

Upon her return to Kamit Aset went to the papyrus swamps where she lay over Asar' dead body and fanned him with her wings, infusing him with new life. In this manner Aset revived Asar through her power of love and wisdom, and then they united once more. From their union was conceived a son, Heru (Heru), with the assistance of the gods Djehuti and Amon.

One evening, as Set was hunting in the papyrus swamps, he came upon Aset and Asar. In a rage of passion, he dismembered the body of Asar into several pieces and scattered them throughout the land. In this way it is Set, the brute force of our bodily impulses and desires, that "dismembers" our higher Self. Instead of oneness and unity, we see multiplicity and separateness which give rise to egoistic (selfish) and violent behavior. The Great Mother, Aset, once again sets out to search, now for the pieces of Asar, with the help of Anpu and Nebethet.

After searching all over the world they found all the pieces of Asar' body, except for his phallus which was eaten by a fish. Aset, Anpu and Nebethet re-membered the pieces, all except the phallus which was eaten by the fish. Asar thus regained life in the realm of the dead, the Duat.

Heru, therefore, was born from the union of the spirit of Asar and the life giving power of Aset (Creation). Thus, Heru represents the union of spirit and matter and the renewed life of Asar, his rebirth. When Heru became a young man, Asar returned from the realm of the dead and encouraged him to take up arms (vitality, wisdom, courage, strength of will) and establish truth, justice and righteousness in the world by challenging Set, its current ruler.

The Battle of Heru (Heru) and Set

The battle between Heru and Set took many twists, sometimes one seeming to get the upper hand and sometimes the other, yet neither one gaining a clear advantage in order to decisively win. At one point Aset tried to help Heru by catching Set, but due to the pity and compassion she felt towards him she set him free. In a passionate rage Heru cut off her head and went off by himself in a frustrated state. Even Heru is susceptible to passion which leads to performing deeds that one later regrets. Set found Heru and gouged out Heru' eyes. During this time Heru was overpowered by the evil of Set. He became blinded to truth (as signified by the loss of his eyes) and thus, was unable to do battle (act with MAAT) with Set. His power of sight was later restored by Hetheru (goddess of passionate love, desire and fierce power), who also represents the left Eye of Ra. She is the fire spitting, destructive power of light which dispels the darkness (blindness) of ignorance.

When the conflict resumed, the two contendants went before the court of the Ennead gods (Company of the nine gods who ruled over creation, headed by Ra). Set, promising to end the fight and restore Heru to the throne, invited Heru to spend the night at his house, but Heru soon found out that Set had evil intentions when he (Set) tried to have intercourse with him. The uncontrolled Set also symbolizes unrestricted sexual activity. Juxtaposed against this aspect of Set (uncontrolled sexual potency and desire) is Heru in the form of ithyphallic (erect phallus)

MIN, who represents not only the control of sexual desire, but its sublimation as well. Min symbolizes the power which comes from the sublimation of the sexual energy.

Through more treachery and deceit Set attempted to destroy Heru with the help of the Ennead, by tricking them into believing that Heru was not worthy of the throne. Asar sent a letter pleading with the Ennead to do what was correct. Heru, as the son of Asar, should be the rightful heir to the throne. All but two of them (the Ennead) agreed because Heru, they said, was too young to rule. Asar then sent them a second letter (scroll of papyrus with a message) reminding them that even they cannot escape judgment for their deeds; they too will be judged in the end when they have to finally go to the West (abode of the dead).

This signifies that even the gods cannot escape judgment for their deeds. Since all that exists is only a manifestation of the absolute reality which goes beyond time and space, that which is in the realm of time and space (humans, spirits, gods, angels, neters) are all bound by its laws. Following the receipt of Asar' scroll (letter), Heru was crowned King of Egypt. Set accepted the decision and made peace with Heru. All the gods rejoiced. Thus ends the legend of Asar, Aset, and Heru.

The Resurrection of Asar and his reincarnation in the form of Heru is a symbol for the spiritual resurrection which must occur in the life of every human being. In this manner, the story of the Asarian Trinity of Asar-Aset-Heru and the Egyptian Ennead holds hidden teachings, which when understood and properly practiced, will lead to spiritual enlightenment.

The Neteru of the Asarian Myth as Psycho-spiritual Stages of Human Evolution.

The main characters in the Asarian Resurrection Myth may be seen as Psycho-spiritual stages which every human being must pass through on the journey towards spiritual enlightenment. Beginning with its incarnation as

the soul of Asar, the soul becomes intoxicated and deluded by nature, and the ignorance of reality sets in wherein the base qualities of the mind are experienced. The character of Set exemplifies these qualities. From Set at the lowest level, the psycho-spiritual awareness develops through Anpu-Maat, Heru-Hetheru and Min, until it discovers and unites with the absolute, transcendental reality through Asar-Aset. From this union the divine consciousness manifests in time and space as Heru, the Divine King, who is a reflection of Asar who resides in the Netherworld, who is himself a reflection of Ra in the subtler reality.

Wall Panel of Asar Aset and Heru, now at the Louvre Museum

From a mystical standpoint, the Trinity of Asar-Aset-Heru represents the movement of the Spirit as it manifests in Creation. As we have seen through the story as well as the iconography associated with them, in reality it refers to the deeper principles of human, as well as super-human, existence. Asar becomes the silent Spirit who is the source and support of Creation in his names Asar-Dua, meaning Asar, the Begetter (in the Duat), and Asar-Neb-Heh[50], meaning Asar, Lord of Eternity. Aset is Creation itself. Heru is the dynamic manifestation of the Spirit (of Asar) which moves in and interacts with Creation (Aset). Thus, Asar expresses as Creation (in the form of Aset) as well as the dynamic forces (in the form of Heru) within it. This teaching is also expressed in

---

[50] The term "heh" meaning eternity, relates to the divinity Ptah as the last letter-symbol in his name Pet-Ta-Heh, symbolizes "heh" eternity and sustainer of Creation.

the idea of the Trinity concept and the birth of God into human form (Avatarism). Asar is also an Avatar, a divine incarnation into time and space, the incarnation of the Higher Self, the Soul, into the realm of time and space.

Asar

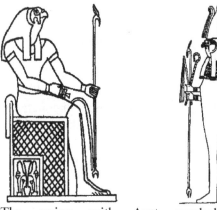

In the Creation myth, Asar is the son of Geb and Nut, who are in turn the offspring of Shu and Tefnut, who are themselves children of Ra. In another Creation myth of Asar, it is said that Asar uttered his own name, *"Asar!!,"* and thereby brought the world and all life within it into existence. This is the process of Divine incarnation whereby the Supreme Being becomes the universe. Asar, *Lord of the Perfect Black,* is the personification of the blackness of the vast un-manifest regions of existence. Asar is the essence of all things, and the very soul of every human being as the Higher Self, who, through ignorance, has become involved in the world, has been slain by its own ego (represented by the god Set), and struggles to regain its original state of perfection. Asar also symbolizes the fragmented ocean of consciousness which has been cut into pieces by the lower self. No longer is there the vast all-encompassing, all-knowing, all-seeing consciousness. The Divine has become limited in association with the human mind, body and senses, due to the desire to experience human feelings and egoistic sentiments. Instead of looking at the universe through the cosmic mind, the Divine now expresses {him/her} self through billions of life forms whose bodies, minds and senses are too limited to see the vastness of Creation.

ASAR SOKAR- KING IN THE NETHERWORLD

Sokar is Asar's title when he is resurrected and he takes his place in the Netherworld as the king. In this aspect he presides over the judgment of the heart of the aspirant.

The union with Aset symbolizes the achievement or striving for spiritual salvation or resurrection while the union with Nebethet symbolizes bondage, suffering and the cycles of birth and death, known as reincarnation.

The User

User is the name of a god who presides over "power" and "dominion" in Creation. Ausares is an alternative spelling for Asar which incorporates the name *Us*. Thus User is an aspect of Asar. This follows the description of the female aspect of User who is Usert – (Goddess Aset). Thus, User is the power of Asar and Usert is the power of Aset; that power is the strength and supremacy over all other powers in Creation, the ability to control and direct.

The name Usert is reflected in the Pharaonic names of King Senusert I (Middle Kingdom Period) *(Greek Sesostris I).* **Senusert means "brother of usert." So the king is related to the power and in a higher sense he is that power in the form of Asar on earth.**

Below - Peraah Senusert I statue – 12ᵗʰ Dynasty

(A)

Plate B: Below - Peraah Senusert I relief – 12ᵗʰ Dynasty

(B)

Aset

Aset, Mistress of Wisdom and Words of Power, Love, Cosmic Consciousness and Intuitional

Wisdom.

In the temple of *Iunet* (Denderah), it is inscribed that Nut gave birth to Aset there, and that upon her birth, Nut exclaimed: *"As"* (behold), *"I have become thy mother."* This was the origin of the name Ast, Aset. The text further states that *"she was a dark-skinned child"* and was called *"Khnemet-ankhet"* or the "living lady of love." Thus, Aset also symbolizes the "blackness" of the vast un-manifest regions of existence, Asar. Her identification is also symbolized in her aspect as *Amentet*,[51] the Duat, itself. Therefore, Amentet (Aset) and the soul of Amentet (Asar) are in reality one and the same. In her aspect as Amentet, Aset represents the subtle substance of nature, the astral plane.

The devotional love of Aset ⇒𝄑𓏺𓂻 *Neter Meri, Beloved One*-Divine Love (universal and transcendental love) was instrumental in discovering and putting the pieces of Asar's dead body back together. The two most important features which Aset encompasses are love and intuitional wisdom. Aset's undying love and devotion to Asar transcended her loss of him twice. Her love also caused the resurrection of her son, Heru, as well. This divine devotion led her to discover the pieces of Asar's dead body. This is the devotion of the initiate which leads him or her to the Divine. All that is needed to attain spiritual enlightenment is a deep, ardent love for the Divine.

In her name, *Rekhat,* Aset also represents *rekh* or wisdom. She is the patroness of all *rekht* or Sages. Aset represents the kind of wisdom which transcends all intellectual knowledge. She is at the same time, Creation, and Amentet, the ultimate hidden reality of that Creation. Thus, it is said that she veils herself and that "no mortal man has unveiled her." The wisdom of Creation or knowing Aset in her full essence means becoming one with her in consciousness. When this unity occurs, one transcends ordinary human consciousness, so in this sense, no worldly human can discover her. The wisdom of Aset refers to that profound understanding of the essence of the Divine which is devoid of any kind of ignorance in reference to the Transcendental Self. This wisdom is the intuitional realization, which comes from pondering the nature of the Divine. Pondering implies repeated reflection and meditation on the

---

[51] This aspect of the goddess will be discussed later.

Divine, trying, with sincerity and humility, to understand and become one with the Divine.

Above: Image From the birthing room of the Temple of Aset, Egypt

The Goddess Aset, Suckling baby Heru

Aset is also a healer. She healed the body of Asar even after it had been dismembered into several pieces. As a goddess she assists all those who pray to her, bestowing health and well being. She manifests in the form of love, motherhood, valor, devotion to God and intuitional realization of the Higher Self, Enlightenment.

Goddess Aset is one of the most important divinities in Neterian religion. Historically, she was coregent with Asar. In later times Aset was especially popular in ancient Greece and Rome as Isis. Much is known about the worship of Aset in Greece and Ancient Egypt and the mysteries of her temple because Plutarch, a Greek initiate of her mysteries, wrote extensively about it. Those writings have been corroborated with the Ancient Egyptian wisdom teachings, myths and titles of the goddess.

The word Aset means wisdom, just as the Greek translation, "Isis" also means wisdom. Specifically, this is the kind of wisdom that puts things together. It can collect the missing pieces for understanding the spiritual philosophy and which allows the initiate to discover the transcendental truth which bestows enlightenment, the great Nehast (Awakening). This is the service she performs for Asar and Heru in the Asarian Resurrection Myth. She resurrects them with her power of Self-knowledge that she gained from becoming one with Ra.[52]

Aset represents the principles of motherhood, marital love, devotion, loyalty, and compassion in terms of worldly affairs. In affairs of mysticism and philosophy she presides over: *dispassion, detachment, obedience, determination-cunning and understanding-intuitional-wisdom*

In order to make her intuitional realization effective, she is known as the *"Lady of Storms"* because one time there was a storm and boats could not come in to port. She quelled the storm through her powers and her act is commemorated on March 5th. In a deeper sense she has the power to calm the waters of consciousness. She does this with the instruments of Hekau (words of power). Her Hekau is powerful so she too is referred to as *Urt-Hekau*, "Great in words of power." In one instance the utterance of her words of power stopped the boat of Ra and so too time and space were stopped. The utterance of her words of power also gave Heru six days of respite when he was battling Set. Those who refuse to accept her (i.e. her wisdom teaching) are given adversity to

---

[52] See the book Mysteries of Isis by Muata Ashby

humble them. Those who accept her receive the boons of prosperity, peace and wisdom.[53]/[54]

Aset and Asar were worshipped by people outside of Kamit, specifically in Asia Minor and Europe (as Isis and Osiris).[55] Asar and Aset were worshipped throughout the ancient world. In the first century B.C.E. Aset was one of the most popular goddesses in the city of Rome. Her temples were filled with altars, statues, obelisks, etc., brought from Egypt, and orders of priestesses were commissioned to perform the "Mysteries of Aset" and other Egyptian miracle plays in the great temples of the Eternal City. From Rome, the cult of Aset spread to Spain, Portugal, Gey, Gaul, Switzerland, and by way of Marseilles, to western North Africa. In a manner similar to which Aset was identified with many other goddesses in Egypt and Nubia, in foreign lands she was given the attributes of other goddesses such as Selene, Demeter, or Ceres, Aphrodite, Juno, Nemesis, Fortuna, Panthea, etc.[56]

In the temple of Aset (above) the path of spirituality (Shetaut Aset), known today as the

Yoga of Wisdom, was taught. It is a spiritual discipline involving the following areas. The aspirant is to purify the body through a vegetarian diet, control the sex urge, and engage in devotional practices and study of the wisdom teachings.[57] **Stage 1: Listening** to the teachings of the myth of the goddess and receiving mystical insights into these.[58] **Stage 2: Reflecting** on those teachings, and living life in accordance with virtue and truth (i.e. practice of the teachings in daily life). **Stage 3: Through Subtle One-pointed mentation,** leading oneself to a meditative union with the Goddess who is the essence of light, which transcends mind, body, time and space.[59]

The Name "Asar" and the name "Aset"

Asar

The goddess, who symbolizes creation itself, the physical universe, supports the incarnation of the soul (Asar). In this way, the physical-Creation (the universe) (Aset) supports the spirit (Asar). This symbol of the goddess herself is the throne, and this is why the throne seat, , is where Asar is shown seated. The name Asar is spelled with the throne symbol, the eye symbol, , and the male determinative, . The eye symbol written in this manner means "to make," "create," "to do" or "engender." Therefore, the mystical symbolism of the name Asar is the essence, which procreates or comes into existence through Aset. Asar has three main important mystical teachings. Asar represents *"Un"* or "existence." That teaching comes from the term "Un-Nefer" or "beautiful-good existence." He also represents *"arit"* or "awareness," "consciousness. This is what the open eye in his name represents. Aset is the "seat" or "abode" where that consciousness resides. Thus, our innermost reality, "Asar", the soul within, is consciousness and existence, i.e. we are not mortal beings or ego beings, but consciousness itself, existing in spirit and not in body, and that is our immortal part; that is the part of us that resurrects. That is the part of us that is Asar. He ultimately represents "Ianrutf" or "region of nothingness." As the "djed" or "Tree of life" which is his backbone, Asar exists in a special region of the Duat (astral plane) where no-things

---

[53] See the book The Asarian Resurrection by Muata Ashby
[54] For more details see the Tree of life audio lecture series Principle of Aset
[55] See the book African Origins by Muata Ashby
[56] For more on the teachings of the Temple of Aset- the Yoga of Wisdom, see the book *The Wisdom of* Aset by Dr. Muata Ashby.

[57] Chanting, singing, prayer.
[58] For more details see the Book *The Wisdom of Isis* by Muata Ashby.
[59] See the book *Initiation Into Egyptian Yoga* by Muata Ashby

exist except him. So we exist beyond thoughts, concepts and egoism. We are pure consciousness, pure existence, pure awareness. This manner of reading of the name of Asar is supported by the myth of Asar and Aset as well as their epithets and their iconographies.

Aset

The symbols of the name of Aset are the throne seat, "as", the phonetic sign for "t", the determinative egg, symbol of motherhood, and the seated female determinative, .

The name Asar is intimately related to the name Aset. Asar and Aset are often referred to as "brother" and "sister." This relates to the idea that they come from the same parent, i.e. the same spiritual source. In ancient times men and women who married were also referred to as brother and sister. This had no relation to his or her parentage. Rather, this epithet relates to the mystical origins of all human beings. Essentially, all men and women are brothers and sisters. Genetically, all human beings originated from one person who lived in Africa 150000 years ago. The common origins of humanity were understood and accepted in Ancient Egypt. Furthermore our true nature is not man and woman but soul, and our parent is the Universal Spirit, from which all souls originate. This teaching was also well understood in Ancient Egyptian philosophy

Through the myth of the Asarian Resurrection, we learn that Asar and Aset are Avatars, divine incarnations, sent to earth to lead souls, incarnating as human beings, towards righteousness, prosperity and spiritual enlightenment. In a higher sense, Asar represents the soul of every human being which comes to earth and must struggle to overcome the lower nature, who is symbolized by Set.

The Asarian Caduceus

The Divinities Asar, Aset and Nebethet constitute an example of the Kamitan Caduceus. The Caduceus is a mystical teaching related to the dormant and hidden Serpent Power that lies within all living beings. The symbol is composed of three aspects, a central shaft and two serpents. If this power were to be harnessed it would bring about the spiritual evolution of the aspirant. It is also known as the staff of Djehuti (Hermes, Asclepius)

and also as the "Serpent Power."[60]

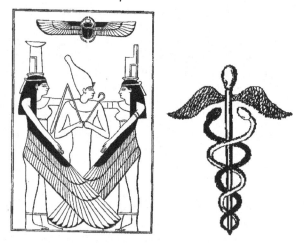

Above: The God Asar embraced by the goddesses Aset and Nebethet.

So the union of Asar with Aset symbolizes the achievement or striving for spiritual salvation or resurrection while the union with Nebethet symbolizes bondage, suffering and the cycles of birth and death, known as reincarnation. But the demise hastened by Nebethet is liberation from the lower nature if her deeper spiritual symbolism is understood.

GOD SET

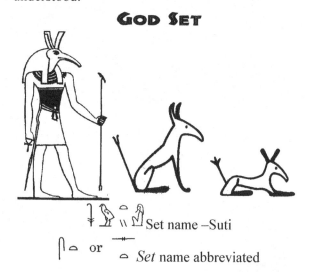

Set name –Suti

or *Set* name abbreviated

The god Set is also extremely important in Neterian religion. He is the younger brother of Asar and Aset and counterpart of Nebethet. Religious dogmatists who regard him as an evil character often misunderstand set. Actually he is the personification of egoism, desire, selfishness and the vises, anger, hatred, greed, lust, jealousy,

---

[60] For more details see the book "Serpent Power" by Muata Ashby

envy, greed, etc. This is the struggle between the Higher and the Lower Self. If the Lower Self (Set) is mastered the project of spiritual enlightenment is more powerful because Set's great power (*Pehti aah* – Set is known as the "one of two fold power") has been added to the divine movement and the obstructions of Set have been lifted from the personality. Notice that the Set animal is a quadruped while Heru, Set's opposite character, is avian. This means that Heru is not earth-bound while Set is earth-bound. This implies that Set represents worldliness while Heru can be on earth but he has the capacity to fly up to the heavens.

 "inj-Set"

The *inj-Set* are the afflictions of Set. The personality is afflicted with these when stricken with unrighteousness. When a human being acts in ways that contradict the natural order of nature, within that person's personality will develop negative qualities of the mind. These are the *afflictions* of Set. Set is the Neteru of egoism and selfishness. The afflictions of Set include: lying, anger, hatred, greed, lust, jealousy, envy, gluttony, dishonesty, hypocrisy, etc. These are the *nshn-Set* - evils of Set. This term is related to *neshsh* {agitation-*nesheshnu*-agitations}. When the mind is agitated it cannot hold on to wisdom and righteous thought processes. So Set (egoism) in the personality leads to an agitated state of mind and that state renders the mind weak and susceptible to vices. Sets vices become attached to a person in the form of special bandages (mummy swathings) that cover the mouth and prevent the "spiritual opening of the mouth" from occurring and must be removed before the spiritual journey can co forward.

saiu Set "The fetters of Set."

In order to be free from the fetters of set one must be free from the afflictions of Set. This is done by propitiating Heru, acting like Heru and vanquishing (subjugating) Set by becoming virtuous and pure of heart. If this happens Set is placed at the front of the boat of Ra to protect it on its journey through time and space (see below). This is what happens in the Asarian Resurrection myth.[61]

Set is the neter who symbolizes the egoistic tendencies of a human being. Set is the aspect of the human mind (heart) with impulses of selfishness, greed, mischievousness, lust, boastfulness, arrogance, vanity, anger, indulgence in sense pleasures, undisciplined, impulsiveness, rudeness, etc. The definition of the name "Set" includes *extroverted, emitting nature, pride and insolence.* Mythologically and historically Set is the opposite principle to Aset. This understanding is derived from ancient Egyptian scripture and it is reflected in the writings of the Greek classical writers and students of the Egyptian Mysteries. According to Plutarch, Set is the name of *one who, full of ignorance and error, tears in pieces and conceals that holy doctrine which the goddess (Aset) collects, compiles, and delivers to those who aspire after the most perfect participation in divine nature.* Egoism produces ignorance and error that block wisdom and experience of the Divine.

The task of sublimating the ego is embodied in the Egyptian story of the battle between Heru and Set, which is a part of the Asarian Resurrection

---

[61] See the book The Asarian Resurrection by Muata Ashby

Mystery.[62] In the myth, Set, who represents egoism in a human being, acting out of greed and jealousy, killed his brother Asar who represents the human soul, and then tore his body to pieces. Due to this act, Heru, the son of Asar who represents spiritual aspiration and righteous action (Maat), engages in a struggle against Set to redeem his father. He must redeem the *Eye,* the center of his power, which Set has stolen. Set as the lower self (ego) is in continuous conflict with Heru, who also represents the rebirth of the soul or Higher Self as an incarnation of his father (Asar). After a long conflict, Heru succeeds in controlling Set by reconstructing the damaged Eye and controlling Set's sexual energy. When this occurs, Heru becomes the ithyphallic *Amsu-Min* or Heru in the aspect of *overthrower of the enemies of his father.*

Set is closely associated with stellar myth in Neterian Theology. *Khepesh* - thigh region of northern sky – is the home of Set. The hippo Goddess *Reret* is the one who confines him with the help of Heru (see below)

The Seven stars of Great Bear constellation are controlled as Reret chains Set with the help of Heru.

The scriptures say: *Heru is Loadstone and Set is Iron.* Loadstone is a magnetic mineral form of black iron oxide and is an important ore of iron. Heru is that magnetic force of spiritual aspiration that attracts seekers and aspirants. Set is the strength within Heru, that an aspirant needs to succeed in the spiritual journey. If the Set principle within the personality holds sway, that force becomes the ruler of the personality and since it is devoid of virtue it leads to unrighteous actions, vices.

If Asar is the King of the righteous, Set is the king of the unrighteous. Set is like the general of the inimical forces, and he has a lieutenant and soldiers. The lieutenant is *Apep* (Greek Apophis) or *Rerek* - another name of the Apep serpent. *Baabaa* is another important servant of Set, who does his unrighteous biddings. *Smaiu* -are the fiends (demons-evil gods and goddesses) of Set.

Set has a form called *Akhakh* - the beast of Set. This may be juxtaposed with the Sefer of Heru which counteracts outweighs and neutralizes Set. While the *Akhakh* has wings it does not fly to the transcendental regions of Heru. Set has another important form, the Black Pig. The *Shai Kam* - black pig of Set – is the form which is beaten by the baboon god for defiling Asar's Hall (see below).[63]

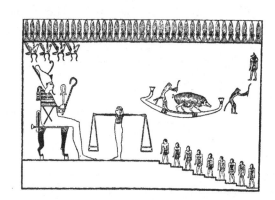

Set is the god of the "Red Land" (desert areas) while Heru is the god of the "Black Land" (Black soil with green fertile vegetation areas-i.e. Kamit itself). So, Set is the neter who presides over the egoistic tendencies of the human being. Set is the aspect of the human mind which is ignorant of its true self and as a result develops impulses of selfishness, greed, mischievousness, lust, boastfulness, arrogance, vanity, anger, indulgence in sense pleasures, undisciplined, impulsiveness, rudeness, etc. The definition of the name Set includes extroverted, emitting nature, pride and insolence. According to Plutarch, Set is the name

---

[62] see the book *Resurrecting Osiris.*

[63] For more details see the Tree of life audio lecture series Principle of Set.

of one who, full of ignorance and error, tears in pieces and conceals that holy doctrine which the goddess (Aset) collects, compiles, and delivers to those who aspire after the most perfect participation in divine nature. Egoism produces ignorance and error, which block wisdom and experience of the Divine.

GODDESS NEBETHET

The name Nebethet means "Mistress of the House" Nebethet is the sister of Asar and Aset. She represents the gross aspect of nature and the natural phase of life called death- Nature, Worldly Consciousness and Death. Nature is what the Spirit impregnates with its life giving essence. Therefore, nature (Nebethet) is the recipient of Asar's seed (spirit). According to natural law, anything that is born must be subject to the laws of nature and ultimately die. In his original form, detached from nature, Asar was timeless, immortal, and untouched by the passions and frailties of human nature. As an incarnation of the Divine, Asar became intoxicated with nature, his own Creation, and associated with it through intercourse with Nebethet. In the myth of the Asarian Resurrection, the sexual union between Nebethet and Asar produced the deity Anpu.

Asar, as a symbol of the human soul, is a stark example of the fate of human existence. His situation embodies the predicament of every individual human being. This is why the Ancient Egyptian Pharaohs and all initiates into the mystery of Asar are referred to as Asar and Heru, and are considered to be the daughter or son of Aset. Every human being assumes the role of Heru, the champion, and once the battle of life is won and the body ceases to function, the initiate now becomes Asar. Just as Asar became intoxicated with his own Creation, so too the human soul becomes involved with nature and thereby produces an astral body (Ka) composed of subtle elements, and from that astral body a physical body is also produced, composed of an aggregate of gross physical elements (water, earth, fire, air), which exist within Shu (ether-space). In this capacity, Nebethet represents the lower nature of matter or the binding, fettering and condensing aspect, which dulls the intellect and intoxicates the mind and senses.

There is deep mystical symbolism in the images and teachings surrounding the Triad of Asar, Aset and Nebethet. In the temples of *Iunet (Denderah), Djebu (Edfu)* and *Pilak (Philae),* there are special sculptured representations of the Mysteries of Asar. These show *The Asar* (initiate) lying on a ritual bed, and Aset and Nebethet, who stand nearby, being referred to as the *"two widows"* of the dead Asar. Aset and Nebethet are depicted as looking exactly alike, the only difference being in their head dresses: Aset ⌡, Nebethet ⌶ or ⌷. However, the symbols of these goddesses are in reality just inverted images of each other. Nebethet means all-encompassing physical domain. Therefore, each is a reflection of the other. So Aset symbolizes the subtle spiritual essence of existence while Nebethet symbolizes the material substance of existence, two aspects of the same reality. Thus, it can be said that both life and death are aspects of the same principle and they are engendered by the same spirit (Asar).

The bodies and facial features of Aset and Nebethet are exactly alike. This likeness which Aset and Nebethet share is important, especially when they are related to Asar. As Asar sits on the throne the two goddesses, Aset and Nebethet, support him. Symbolically, Asar represents the Supreme Soul, the all-encompassing Divinity which transcends time and space. Aset represents wisdom and enlightened higher consciousness. She is the knower of all words of power and has the power to resurrect Asar and Heru. Nebethet represents temporal consciousness or awareness of time and space related to mortal (worldly-physical existence) life and mortal death. This symbolism is evident in the sistrums, which bear the likeness of Aset on one side and of Nebethet on the other, and the writings of Plutarch where he says that Aset represents "generation" while Nebethet represents "chaos and dissolution." Also, in the hieroglyphic texts, Aset is referred to as the "day" and Nebethet as the "night." Aset represents the things that "are" and Nebethet represents the things which will "come into being and then die." Thus, the state of spiritual enlightenment is being referred to here as Aset, and it is this enlightened state of mind which the initiate in the Asarian Mysteries (*Asar Shetaiu*) has as the goal. The Enlightenment of Asar is the ideal state of consciousness in which one is aware of the transient aspects of Creation (Nebethet) as well as the transcendental aspects of Creation (Aset). Aset represents the transcendental aspect of matter, that is, matter when seen through the eyes of wisdom rather than through the illusions produced by the ego. So, an enlightened personality is endowed with dual consciousness. To become one with Asar means to attain the consciousness of Asar, to become aware of the transcendental, infinite and immortal nature (Aset) while also being aware of the temporal and fleeting human nature (Nebethet).

Nebthet

So Nebthet is the goddess of the house just as a woman is the goddess of her home. But Nebthet's house is the world of time and space and mortal existence. She is the one who facilitated the death of Asar and thus propelled him on the path to becoming the "King of the Dead." Along with Aset she is Asar's most devoted supporter and she loves him dearly. In the same manner she lovingly provides mortal bodies and death for all human beings, which is their pathway to spiritual evolution and enlightenment. For without bodies spiritual evolution cannot occur and without death nothing would change or transform. Nebethet is associated with death, decay, darkness, finiteness, mortality and contraction as well as physical love, the voluptuousness of nature, worldly sexual desire and physical existence and physical death. These epithets from the Ancient Egyptian texts are confirmed by the Greek initiate of the Egyptian mysteries, Plutarch. Yet this is not a death that means an end to existence, but rather the death to worldliness, limitation, egoism and ignorance. Thus, in the Pyramid Texts it was said that Nebethet is the *"friend of the deceased."*

Nebethet is also known as the *Neb Khat* "Lady of the Bodies" because she was the *"Fashioner of the (physical) bodies of the gods and goddesses"* that were brought into existence by Ra. Gold is *"the flesh of the gods and goddesses."* Neterian philosophy holds that the gods and goddesses are incarnations of the golden sun. Therefore, gold is a sacred substance and so the images of divinities are either made of gold or covered in it.

As a serpent goddess with her sister Aset, they both form the dual serpents of the Caduceus of Djehuti and Nebethet represents the cooling (lunar) aspect of the Serpent Power while Aset represents the heating (solar) aspect. *sati merti arati nebti Maati* means "the two daughters, goddesses of all righteousness and truth (Aset and Nebthet)." So she is Arat Nebethet as goddess of the cooling aspect of the Serpent Power ("Serpent Goddess of the cooling force"). Both the cooling and heating serpents are necessary in order to balance life. The balancing of the two leads to the full expression of Asar, the soul, through the opposites of Creation. This is one of the main teachings of the Serpent Power spiritual disciplines. The cooling fire calms the ego and settles disputes and regulates the burning fire and vise versa. The cooling fire allows physical love (love manifested in time and space) to develop into burning spiritual love and devotion to God. The conception of the caduceus is also present in the New Kingdom Temple entrance pylons and the single door, which constitutes another example of the Neterian Caduceus concept. In the temple mysteries, when the resurrection of Asar was reenacted, two virgin priestesses assumed the roles of Aset and Nebthet and thus ritually relived the passion and resurrection of Asar. For more on Aset and Nebthet and their relationship to the Maati Goddesses and the Nebti Goddesses see the sections *The Maati Goddesses* and *Uadjit and Nekhebit.*[64]

---

[64] For more details see the Tree of life audio lecture series Principle of Nebethet

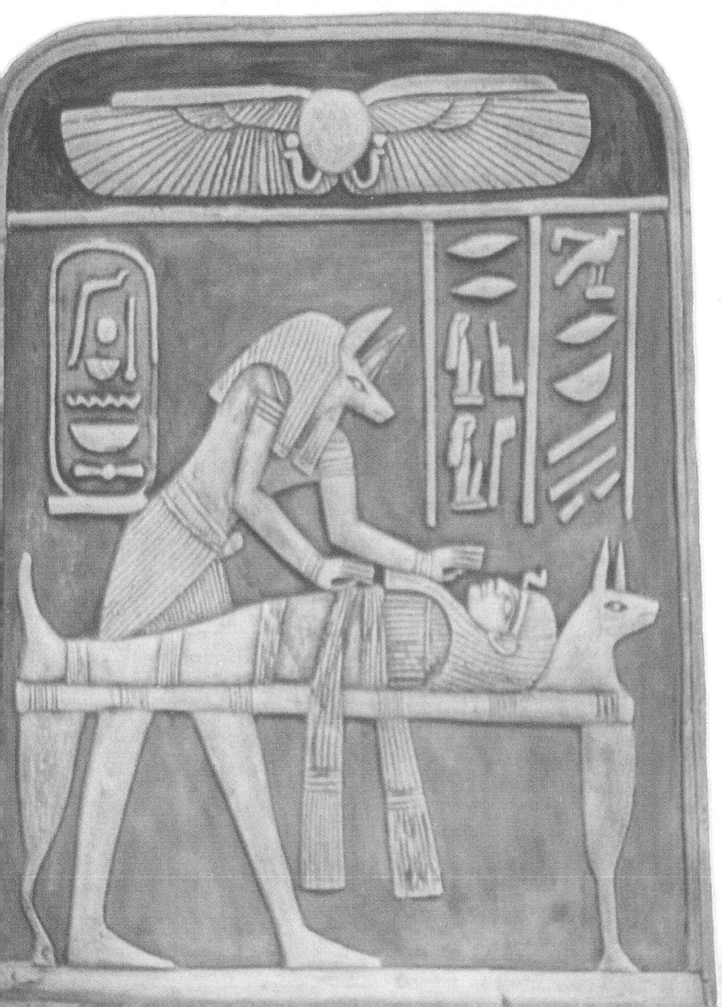

(On previous page: The God Anpu, the Embalmer-Panel from the tomb of Senneden-Thebes-1400 BCE Gray)

GOD ANPU -APUAT

Anpu is the son of Asar and Nebethet. He is the embalmer of the deceased (spiritual aspirant) and symbolizes the guide to the initiate, the trained intellect of the aspirant, who is dead to the wisdom of divine reality and hopes to be resurrected (to discover divine reality). This implies the ability to discipline one's mind and body so as to not get caught up in the illusions or emotions of the mind. Anpu represents disciplined mind and sublimated instinct. When the mind and its wavelike thought vibrations are under control, the way is open to spiritual realization in an atmosphere of peace and harmony. This peace and harmony do not necessarily imply an outer situation of calm. It does imply an inward peace which comes from understanding the implications of the wisdom teachings. Anpu represents the dawn when darkness turns to light. He watches over the balance (scales) in the hall of judgment of the *Prt m Hru* with extreme diligence, and in the aspect of *Apuat*, he is the *Opener of the Ways* who leads souls to the Sekhet Yaru (Greek-*Elysian Fields) in the Great Oasis*. Therefore, his great quality of *discriminative knowledge* allows the aspirant to *diligently* watch the mind in order to promote right thoughts which are divinely inspired (*Shemsu Hor* - follower of Heru), instead of those which are egoistic (Setian) and tending toward nature and its perils (life, death, pain, pleasure, etc.). Anpu, as the son of Nebethet and Asar, is therefore, a combination of gross nature (Nebethet) and the Spirit (Asar).

It is Anpu who lead Asar to the divine abode and it is he who leads the souls to the abode of the Supreme Being in the *Prt m Hru* by constantly urging them to awaken from the dream of the world process and its illusions. Thus, in this aspect, Anpu should be considered as the original *Angel of Death*. The reliefs and hieroglyphs of *Anpu sitting atop the ark containing the inner-parts of Asar* are found at the entrance or purification area of the burial chamber (chest or ark) of the initiate. In the *Prt m Hru*, it is stated that Anpu appointed the *Seven Spirits, the followers of their lord Sepa*, to be protectors of the *dead body of Asar*. Sepa is the name of the chief of the Seven Spirits who guarded Asar, and *seven* is the number of spiritual energy centers in the subtle spiritual body (Serpent Power - Kundalini Chakras). There are also seven cows of Creation, which serve Asar as the "Bull of Creation." So developing discriminative mind allows control over the seven principles, the seven energy-consciousness centers. Anpu is an aspect of Heru, and Heru is the Higher Self. Therefore, the true enlightener of the Self is the Self. In this manner, it is your innermost Self who is enlightening you through your desire to practice spiritual discipline. One more important teaching related to Anpu is that he represents instinct cultivated by reason. As a canine he represents the basic character of mind which revolves around instinctual needs and desires-instinct. Instinct is the level of mind that most people sink to whenever there is some provocation in life, a crisis or some stress. At those times the mental process searches and acts in accordance with the common denominator of situations; is this a friend or a foe? Are you against me or with me? Am I hungry or thirsty? Is this food or is it garbage? Do I like this or do I not like this? Etc. Those who profess dogmatic teachings and repetitive slogans that incite the primal urges in the human mind such as hunger, survival, danger, etc easily manipulate this kind of mind. So such a person may be easily convinced to fight a war if they are told that someone is their enemy and is planning to attack them. That person will follow along without exercising critical thinking or questioning the act they are being asked to take. Anpu represents the victory over such a lower state of mind. This is the triumph of the discriminative intellect that can instantly know truth from untruth. The task of every follower of African religion is to develop such an intellect without which there can be no true spiritual evolution.

The struggle between Heru and Set is the struggle of every human being to control the mind with its erratic desires, longings, unfulfilled expectations and disappointments. This struggle is not avoidable by anyone who is not enlightened. Some people succumb under the weight of the lower self and its desires for fulfillment. This is a pathetic condition which those people have allowed to develop due to their own indulgence in the sensual desires of the body, and also due to their ignorance of their true divine nature which is buried deep within, under the weight of the egoistic thoughts and unconscious ignorant feelings and desires. For more on the Divinities of the Asarian Resurrection Myth see the book *Resurrecting Osiris* by Muata Ashby.

The God Heru and His Forms

The divinity Heru has many forms. Heru represents the rebirth of the spiritual life - aspiration for freedom, the new life of the resurrected soul, the union between spirit (Asar) and creation (Aset). However, unlike Anpu (Anubis), who also represents the union of Spirit and Matter, Heru represents the higher aspect of this union because Aset is the embodiment of intuitional wisdom and truth while Nebethet is the embodiment of nature and the grosser physical elements which are transient. In this aspect Heru represents the subtle spiritual realization of spirit and matter united and seen as one.

BEHDETY OR UR UADJIT

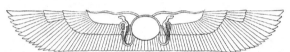

Behudet, Behdety or Ur Uadjit
The Winged Sundisk

The Winged Sundisk is composed of two serpents (Aset and Nebethet), a sundisk symbolizing Ra manifesting as the dual principles (Uadjit -Aset and Nekhebet - Nebthet) and the wings of Heru. This is an important symbol of Heru, meaning "All-Encompassing Divinity." It was decreed by Djehuti that this symbol be used over the doorway of temples.

Heru is the rebirth of the Spirit. This rebirth is not a physical birth from the womb, but a rebirth of higher spiritual aspiration in the mind as the desire for enlightenment. This means that no longer is there just interest in worldly pursuits which are empty and shallow. Instead, there is a burning desire to face and conquer the lower self and regain the original glory and freedom of knowing and becoming one with the Higher Self. Heru regaining the throne of Upper and Lower Egypt symbolizes this. In doing so, he has regained mastership of the higher and the lower states of consciousness. Thus, Heru represents the union and harmonization of spirit and matter, and the renewed life of Asar.

Heru is the God of Light. Before Heru is victorious in the Asarian myth, he is a symbol of the "Dual Nature of Humankind." Heru in this aspect represents the opposite forces that are within each of us, the animal nature (passionate behavior as demonstrated by cutting off Aset's head) and the Divine. Therefore, the real battle is within each of us and not in the outer world of time and space.

Asar-Sokar, Heru and Ra utilize the symbol of the hawk, an animal which is swift and possesses sharpness and clarity of vision. Thus, the symbol of the hawk refers to the quality of a highly developed intellectual capacity to see what is real, true and abiding versus that which is false, fleeting and illusory. It is because of this quality of discriminative intellect that Anpu is considered as an aspect of Heru. The principles of mystical spirituality as represented by Aset, Maat and Djehuti (order, justice, peace, love, contentment, righteous action, study and reflection on the teachings, meditating on the Divine, etc.) lead toward the truth while the egoistic values of society, as represented in the character of Set (greed, hatred, anger, lust, restlessness, etc.), lead to falsehood, pain, suffering, disappointment and frustration.

The picture of Heru-Set (below) shows us that the "enemy" or foe of truth (Maat) is inside each of us. Set, the symbol of evil, is actually a part of Heru that must be conquered and sublimated. In this aspect, Set represents the "beasts" or "demons" we must conquer within ourselves: ignorance, passions, desires, restlessness of the mind, temptation, lust, greed, depression, insecurity, fear and pain. Through the journey of life, a battle rages on between the Higher Self and the lower, and only by living a life of virtue can the "God of Light" inside come alive and vanquish the unrighteous lower nature. This is the underlying theme of the Asarian Resurrection myth and the prerequisite for anyone who wishes to gain the higher benefit of reading the *Prt m Hru* texts.

Hieroglyphic list for the Principal forms of the Divinity Heru

The following list contains only the main forms of Heru to be known by aspirants practicing the Uashu (Worship) as outlined by the Het Aset (Temple of Aset).

1) "Heru" (person, personality)

2) "Heru" – (the Divinity above)

3) "Heru khnti an maa" (Heru foremost blind)

4) "Heru Khnti khat" (Heru foremost of the body)

5) "Heru Sa Ast sa Asar" (Heru son of Isis, son of Osiris)

6) "Heru Sekhemt" (Heru of the Power)

7) "Heru pkhard" (Heru the child)

8) "Heru Ra pkhard" (Heru, Ra as a child)

9) "Heru Bhudet" (Heru the conqueror)

10) "Heru tjemaa" (Heru the thruster, piercer)

11) "Heru Smai Tawi" (Heru Uniter of the two lands)

12) "Heru Nub" (Heru of Gold)

13) "Heru merti" (Heru of the two eyes - seer)

14) Uadjti - Two eyes of Heru (Aset & Nbthet)

15) "Heru Ur" (Heru the great – Heru the King)

16) "Heru-akhuti or Herukhuti" (Heru of the two horizons – Sphinx) (Khepri and Tem combined – beginning to end)

17) , "Heru Ur Uadjit" (Heru the all-encompassing Divinity)

Important Definitions in the forms of Heru

Aton – the Sun – Right eye of Heru

Hera – Face, person, a personality, "Bright face of God"

Heru – "That which is above – the most high"

Heru an mut-f – "Heru the motherless" – form of Heru in his temple at Djebu (Edfu), Egypt.

Heru Behudet (Behudety, the warrior)

The warrior, defender of truth and restorer of righteousness.

Heru Khenti n maa – "Heru the foremost seer"

literally, means Heru the blind one, or when the sun and moon set – meaning that when the eyes (sun and moon) are closed and looking internally, this is the highest vision – i.e. the internal is foremost and not the external. The new moon period is known as the period of rebirth, i.e. the resurrection of the moon. The moon is a symbol of Asar, the dead and resurrected soul.

Heru merti – "Heru of the two eyes" (sun and moon) – also an important form of Amsu-min – associated with Amun.

Heru nub – "Heru the Golden one" – Heru is perfect enlightenment.

Heru pa khard – "Heru as the Divine solar child" – has seven aspects, a reflection of Ra's seven souls (sefek ba Ra). In this form Heru is victorious over animals – (the forces of nature).

From the Meterniche Stele. Heru as a Divine child, master of nature, controller of beasts (evil, unrighteousness, the lower self) and therefore, protector of Asar from the lower forces.

Heru Sekhem – "Heru the lord of the Uadjit" (Serpent Power – two eyes) – the lion  is a symbol of this form of Heru as well as the hawk-headed man.

Heru Ur - "Heru the Elder" – the grown up Heru, this form is the king of upper and lower Egypt, i.e. he is victorious against Set in the battle for the throne. This form of Heru was also associated with Ra and Hetheru as their son.

The Neteru of the Ennead arising from Ra-Atum are Shu, Tefnut, Geb, Nut, Asar, Aset, Set, Nebethet and Heru Ur. Heru-Ur means "Heru the Elder" or "Heru-The Great" and also "Heru of the Future." He represents the perfection of Ra in Creation. In reference to the Asarian Resurrection myth, he represents Heru after he had challenged Set and reestablished order and harmony in the land of Egypt.

Herukhuti: Heru of the two Horizons, the all encompassing one. Heru is the defender.

He represents spiritual aspiration and will power to back up that aspiration to overcome unrighteousness, ignorance and even death. He assisted in the resurrection of his father and through his warrior skills defeated Set, the agent of ignorance and freed the land from injustice. Herukhuti is also a form of the *Hu* (Great Sphinx). The term "two Horizons" refers to Heru's two important forms: Khepri (morning sun, the Creator - beginner) and *Tem* (Atum, Temu), the setting sun (dissolver – demolish – completer).

Heru-sa Asar sa Aset – "Heru the son of Asar and Aset." This is the form of Heru specifically associated with the Asarian Resurrection myth as the son of Aset and Asar (Isis and Osiris).

Heru-shaf-(Heryshaf) God of manliness, bravery, respect-he on his lake-his land"

He is recognized as a form of Heru, as his name

[hieroglyphs] denotes, since it contains the *Her*

[hieroglyphs] spelling (spelling of the name of Heru when

written fully [hieroglyphs] -Heru), he was later identified by the Greeks with the Greek Heracles (Hercules) and the Ancient Egyptian town he came from was called Herakleopolis "town of Heracles." He is known in Neterian myth as the "Ba Asar" and "Ba Ra" or soul of Asar and soul of Ra. He wears the Atef (Crown of Asar). See also "Banebdjedt."

Heru-Smai-Tawi - "Heru the unitor of the two lands."

This form of Heru rises from the Primeval Lotus each year to unite Upper and Lower Egypt with the rule of righteousness and truth.

Panebtawy- Pa-neb-tawy means "The Lord of the Two Lands (Kamit-Egypt)" Heru-ur and his consort, goddess *Tasenetnofret* (aspect of Hetheru) had a child, *Panebtawy*. Panebtawy is the divine child who grows up to be the ruler of Egypt. Therefore, all Pharaohs are recognized as being Panebtawys, i.e. as manifestations of Heru on earth.

Sefer (Image from the Meterniche Stele) The Sefer, or Ancient Egyptian Griffin. In the Story of Hetheru and Djehuti, also known as the story of the Eye of Ra and the Story of the Divine Cow, the role of Divine avenger or the Divinity who enforces the Divine Law, the god Djehuti presents the character of the griffin.

Left- Another example of the Ancient Egyptian Sefer (Griffin). The griffin is a mythological animal encompassing the body of a lion, the head and wings of a hawk (associated with Heru) or an eagle, and the tail of a lion or a serpent. In legends from India, the Far East, and ancient Scythia, griffins were known as the guardians of treasures and mines. In Greek mythology they were the guardians of gold treasures and they drew the carriage or chariot of the sun. In the Ancient Egyptian myth of Hetheru and Djehuti the griffin represents the supreme instrument or power of the Divine. In reality, this is Hetheru's true identity as the Eye of Ra. This is why Djehuti created an elaborate story detailing the hierarchy of creatures and showing how none can escape from the power of the griffin. So in a subtle and indirect way Djehuti taught her about herself throughout the story and at the end of the parable he reveals to her that she has this same power and that she herself is the Eye of Ra which has power over all creatures. Thus, he introduces her to her own higher nature in a clever and artistic manner.

Ur-Uadjit- "The Great Winged Sundisk" is the most powerful form of Heru, all-encompassing Divinity, vanquisher of hippos and crocodiles (important forms of Set).

THE HAWK TRINITY

The Hawk is the primary symbol of Heru and all other divinities are directly linked to him when the hawk iconography is used in depicting them. Ancient Egyptian iconography, the pictographic elements of scripture, can independently provide deep mythological, religious and philosophical teachings by themselves. This is one of the greatest strengths of Neterian scripture and art. This is because the reading process need not be limited to the deciphering of letters, but it can also derive meaning from pictures used in the language (pictures used as letters).

One of the most important iconographies of Kamitan religion involves the Hawk icon. The hawk is an animal which flies high above the earth and whose visual acuity allows it to survey vast regions while being able to focus on minuscule objects. Also, it is able to fly at high speeds. These qualities are what motivated the Ancient Egyptian Sages to use it as a symbol for the basis of the entire system of Anunian mythology which blends the concept of Tem, the singular essence which emerged out of the Primeval Void (Primeval Ocean) with the concept of Heru, the Supreme Divinity. The Hawk theme runs through the myths of Tem as Atum-Ra or Ra-Tem, as well as that of Asar and that of Heru.

The Hawk Trinity: Ra, Sokar and Heru
Left- Ra-Herakhti, Center-Asar Sokar, Right- Heru, son of Asar and Aset, Lord of the Two Lands.

The Hawk motif unites and binds the mythic nature of Ra, Asar and Heru in a very strong way, and we are to understand that we are indeed looking at the same divinity who is manifesting in different aspects and operating in different realms or planes of existence. Ra represents perfection in the heavens or the transcendental, Asar Sokar represents perfection in the

Netherworld and Heru represents perfection in the Physical plane.

The Heru-Set Philosophy

The image below is another rendition the concept of reuniting Heru and Set. The divinities representing Virtue (Heru) and Vice (Set) actually make peace and in so doing foment a "Sema" or union. They tie the lotus and papyrus plants (Upper Egypt-Lower Egypt, Higher Self and Lower Self). In the same manner, the aspirant who wants to overcome the vices needs to engender a movement towards virtue. This allows the personality to be purified and the lower nature is subdued, and then the true essential being (Heru) emerges shining brightly to illuminate the individual and all who come into contact with him or her.

Heru and Set join forces to tie up the symbol of Union (Sema 𓋴). The Sema symbol refers to the Union of Upper Egypt (Lotus) and Lower Egypt (Papyrus) under one ruler, but also at a more subtle level, it refers to the union of one's Higher Self and lower self (Heru and Set), as well as the control of one's breath (Life Force) through the union (control) of the lungs (breathing organs). Further, it refers to the practice and understanding of the mysteries of the mind. By developing intuitive vision, the dualistic understanding of oneself and creation is transformed into the vision of union (Sema). The character of Heru and Set are an integral part of the *Pert Em Heru*.

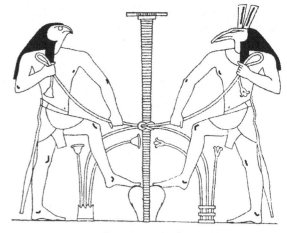

"Sema Heru-Set"

The central and most popular character within Ancient Egyptian Religion of Asar is Heru, who is an incarnation of his father, Asar. Asar is killed by his brother Set who, out of greed and demoniac (Setian) tendency, craved to be the ruler of Egypt. With the help of Djehuti, the God of mind, Aset, the great mother and Hetheru, his consort, Heru prevailed in the battle against Set for the rulership of Kamit (Egypt). Heru's struggle symbolizes the struggle of every human being to regain rulership of the Higher Self and to subdue the lower self.

The most pressing issue after the resurrection of Asar in the Asarian Resurrection Myth is the succession of the throne of Ancient Egypt. Set killed Asar to steal the throne and then Heru grows up to challenge Set for the throne. Their battle is recounted

in at least three versions of the myth. The battle itself is recounted and illustrated at the temple of Heru in Egypt. The following are images of that battle.

At right: Heru spears Set who is manifesting in the form of an unruly hippopotamus.

The black pig and the eating of pork are shunned in Neterian Philosophy. Because of the character and constitution (energies) of the pig, it is a symbol of what is negative for the psychic and physical personality of a spiritual aspirant. One account of the battle says that it lasted three days and that Set was finally controlled with a spear and chains (Set was stabbed 10 times- and *ten* is the sacred number of the god Heru).

In another scene Set manifests as a crocodile that is subdued by Heru.

Above: Heru and Set are occasionally shown purifying the king. This means that both aspects, when balanced, constitute a positive and necessary factor of spiritual evolution.

In the third scene Set manifests as a black pig who tries to get into the Hall of Asar and is driven away by baboons who are beating him and forcing him out. The picture above shows Heru controlling the Set-crocodile with chains.

At right: (also known as "He who has two faces") Set and Heru are depicted as two aspects of the same personality. Much like the Chinese Tao philosophy. Like the Yin and Yang teaching of the Tao, the teachings of Heru-Set shows that good and evil are aspects of the same personality and they are inseparable and necessary for the evolution of Creation and human development. That struggle in the personality is to recognize the two characteristics and then control these by mastering their principles. This is done by purifying the personality and then propitiating their nature and finally assimilating their essence and becoming one with them. That is the Kamitan way of Shetaut Neter. This iconography and its accompanying teaching show the highly philosophical notion that there is no such thing as good and evil in the higher sense. Rather there is ignorance that causes one to act in a demoniac fashion or wisdom, which causes one to act with divine intent.

Images of Heru:

HERU-SET

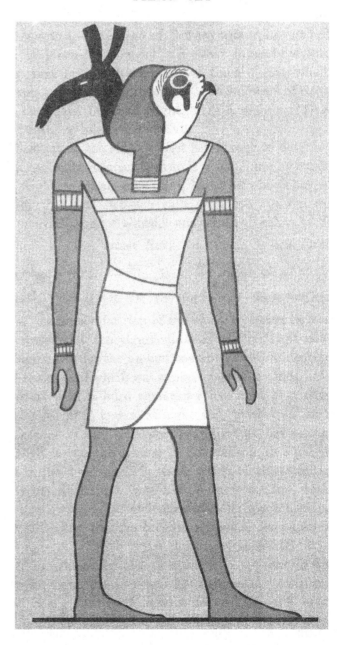

Shetaut Aton

INTRODUCTION TO THE NETERU OF ATON THEOLOGY

The hieroglyphic sign above means "Aton," the sundisk. Atonism is the philosophy of devotional love to the Supreme Spirit by recognizing its dynamic aspect of the sun through which it sustains and enlivens all Creation, pervading and also manifesting as Creation. Therefore, Atonism is the art of discovering the Supreme Being everywhere and in all things. The main proponents of Atonism were the Sage king Akhenaton, his mother Queen *Ti* and the priest *Ai*. Atonism, like the other traditions within Neterianism, existed since the beginning of Kamitan history but was not emphasized until Akhenaton elevated it to the status of state religion. The teachings of Atonism, their understanding and application are to be learned through the process of Uashu Shedy, the yoga of Devotional Love towards the Divine and also through Rekh Shedy, the disciplines of wisdom Yoga.[65]

Left: Akhenaton, his wife Nefertiti and their daughters, make offerings to Aton.

The following passages of the Atonian scriptures provide insight into the nature of Aton and the philosophy of Atonism.

---

[65] See the Audio series *Essence of Atonism* by Muata Ashby

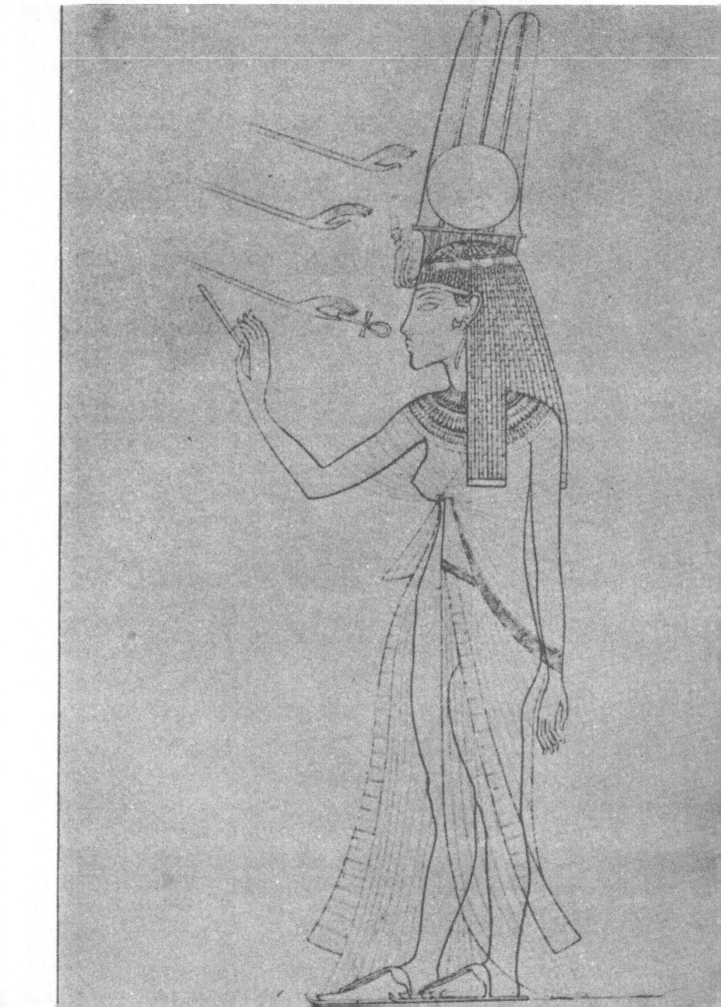

On previous page: Wall relief of Queen Ti adoring the Aton, which extends life-giving rays

From the Hymns to Aton

> One God, like whom there is no other. Thou didst create the earth by thy heart (or will), thou alone existing, men and women, cattle, beasts of every kind that are upon the earth, and that move upon feet (or legs), all the creatures that are in the sky and that fly with their wings, [and] the deserts of Syria and Kush (Nubia), and the Land of Egypt.

> Thou settest every person in his place. Thou providest their daily food, every man having the portion allotted to him; [thou] dost compute the duration of his life. Their tongues are different in speech, their characteristics (or forms), and likewise their skins (in color), giving distinguishing marks to the dwellers in foreign lands... Thou makest the life of all remote lands.

> Oh thou Lord of every land, thou shinest upon them...

> Thou hast made millions of creations from thy One self (viz.) towns and cities, villages, fields, roads and rivers. Every eye (i.e., all men and women) beholdeth thee confronting it (the objects of the world).

These statements by Akhenaton in his Hymns to Aton follow the transcendental and tantric philosophy that originated in the *Pyramid* and *Coffin Texts*. Nature itself and all objects including people are a manifestations of the Divine.

The image below is a depiction of the Sage-king Akhnaton in the form of a sphinx offering Maat to the Aton. This is one of the most traditional forms of religious iconography in Ancient Egypt which can be found on several temples and scriptures. It is the highest declaration of any king or queen to say that they upheld Maat and in so doing they are worthy to attain higher consciousness. The use of the Sphinx shows that Akhnaton saw the Aton teaching as an extension of the same solar philosophy of Anunian Theology, as the Herumakhet (Sphinx) has been shown to be one, if not the most important and oldest, symbol of solar spirituality in Ancient Kamit. Therefore, contrary to the view of most Egyptologists and Religionists conclusions that Akhnaton was the first to institute a particular form of religion, previously unknown in Ancient Egypt which they describe as "monotheism," Akhnaton innovated nothing. He simply expressed a teaching that was already present in Egypt, but which had become dormant until its advocacy was elevated by his mother and his mother's spiritual preceptor.

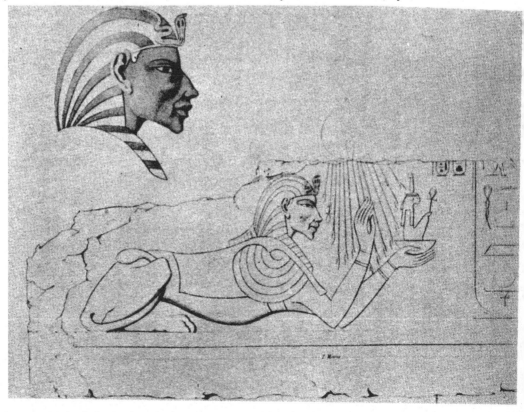

Akhnaton as a Sphinx

The opening verses of the Hymn to Aton by Akhnaton (Amenhotep IV {Greek- Amenophis}) provide insight into the ancient nature of Aton worship and how it is tied to the divinity Ra as well as the oldest form of worship known in Kamit, that of *Heru-Akhuti (Herumakhet - the Great Sphinx)*. Note that adorations are made to the *living Heru-Akhuti* (verse 1) and Akhnaton refers to being one with Ra (verse 3) through living by Maat (righteousness) – (verse 3 and 4). Thus, Aton worship is, in the New Kingdom Period (1580-1075 B.C.E.), a form of renaissance of Ra worship (5,500 B.C.E.), who is a form of *Heru-Akhuti* worship that goes back to the inception of Ancient Egyptian culture and spirituality (10,000 B.C.E.). Therefore, the concept of one God which he highlighted was present in Neterian spirituality from the earliest times.

<h3 style="text-align:center">Hymn To Aton by Akhenaton</h3>

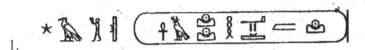

1.

1.1. Dua Ankh Herakhuti Hai m Akhet

1.2. Adorations to the living Heru Akhuti whose body manifests through the sundisk (Aton)

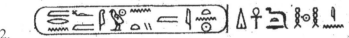

2.

2.1. m ren f m shu nty m Aton rdy Ankh djeta heh in

2.2. through the name his through Shu who is in the Aton. Giving life forever and eternity by

3.

3.1. suten ankh m Maat neb tawi nefer kheperu Ra wa n Ra

3.2. the king living through Maat, lord of the two lands, beautiful creations of Ra, One with Ra

4.

4.1. sa ankh m Maat neb Kau Akhen Aton Maakheru

4.2. son living through Maat, lord of risings Akhu-n-Aton, true of speech

5.

5.1. aha-f rdy ankh djeta heh chaa k nefer pa Aton

5.2. standing (raising) up living forever and eternal risings, beauteous this Aton

6.

6.1. ankh neb heh iu k tih n tj anti

6.2. living lord of eternity, it is you shining and vitalizing as you rise

7.

7.1. Usur tjn meritu k ur tjen aa ti shtyut

7.2. In power to shoot down your loving rays which are great and magnanimous

THE GOD KHNUM AND THE TRINITY OF KHNUM

Khnum fashions a human body and Djehuti assigns years and Aset nurtures it (complete scene).

Khnum, Anqit, Sati

The God Khnum 🏺𝔏𝔐 is the Ram headed man who is an aspect of Amun. In Khnum mythology Khnum is Creator of the bodies of human beings and he creates his creations on a potters wheel. Mostly he fashions human beings out of clay. The god Djehuti stands behind him, counting notches in the spine of a palm frond. The notches signify the amount of years that the body is predestined to last. We are reminded here that Djehuti is the main god who records the results of the balance of the heart in the Hall of Maati. His hands are Shai and Rennutt. The hands of Djehuti (God of reason-intellect) are "Shai" which means "destiny" and "Rennutt" which means "Fortune and Harvest (reaping)." So whatever the result of the balance was at the time of our previous death and judgment, this has provided our fate in this new incarnation. Khnum is the god of the southern district of Kamit where the waters of the Nile enter Egypt from northern Nubia. He was also regarded as a Nubian Divinity as much as a Kamitan one. In this way he was Creator to both. Khnum controls the flow of the waters. In the story called the *Seven Year Famine*, he withheld the flow of the Hapi (Nile) because the people forgot to worship and propitiate his blessings with offerings and righteous worship. This story also alludes to the deeper understanding that just as the Nile is the spine of Egypt at its base, the subtle flow of life-sustaining energy that is dormant at the base of the spine also requires devotion and worship of the Divine in order for it to be awakened and flowing upward to the Delta region, the crown of the head.[66]

As *Asar* has two goddesses to attend on him, *Khnum* also has two goddesses who help him do the work of Creation. Goddess *Anqit* 〰⏗ is a Nubian goddess and she is the sister of *Sati*. "Anqit" means to embrace, to bring in, hold in, i.e to contract inwards. Her name also means fertility. Goddess Sati- 𓏏𓂝 or 𓏏𓂝 is the wife of Khnum. Her name means "to shoot out," i.e. to expand outwards. She is the sister of Anqit. Thus, Khnum is the controller of the flow of the Hapi, the life giving and sustaining waters of life and he is assisted in controlling Creation through the means of expansion or contraction, in other words, the quality of opposites in Creation, their growth or increase or their reduction or decrease as well as the combinations of these two principles. Therefore, Khnum regulates Creation through the two goddesses. Khnum, Sati and Anqit also form another example of the caduceus teaching of Ancient Egypt and are closely associated with Asar, Aset and Nebthet. As Khnum is related to Asar, and Anqit is to Nebethet, Sati is connected with Aset. Thus, Khnum Anqit and Sati constitute a manifestation of the same Trinity system and caduceus iconography that can be seen throughout other Neterian traditions.

---

[66] For more details on this story see the audio lecture related to this teaching by Muata Ashby -Call the Sema Institute. Also see the

book *The Serpent Power* by Muata Ashby

On Previous page:: Djehuti measures the universe with the divine cloth at the behest of Ra to establish what the dimensions of Creation will be. Bottom: Djehuti touches the mouth of Asar (Seti) with the Ankh, giving him the life force that comes from the caduceus he holds in his left hand.

THE GOD DJEHUTI AND THE COMPANY OF GODS AND GODDESSES OF KHEMENU

Pauti Khmn Anu
"Company of Eight Gods and Goddesses of Anu"

The God Djehuti and the Company of Gods and Goddesses of Khemenu are related to Anunian Theology. Therefore, they are viewed as an adjunct tradition in the same way as the Asarian Tradition although the Khemenu[67] Tradition was not as popular as the Asarian Tradition or the Anunian until the late period of Kamitan history. Firstly, the god Djehuti along with the goddess Maat deserve a special place of prominence because they emerged along with Ra in his Divine Boat of Creation the first time he surfaced out of the Primeval Waters.

Eye of Djehuti

Secondly, Djehuti is referred to as the *"heart and tongue of Ra."* This means that he was the mind (intellect) and mouthpiece (performer of actions) of Ra, his viceroy and minister. He transmitted to the world of time and space, the desires of Ra and carried out his bidding on earth. He is therefore regarded as the *Lord of Words* and the *Wheigher of Words* in the great Hall of Maati where the heart of the deceased is weighed against the standard, the feather of Maat (right and truth).

The city Khmnu (city of the eight) became the seat of the worship of Djehuti and the Company of Eight Gods and Goddesses of Anu became the Company of Djehuti. Djehuti had a Divine Boat wherein he sat, a man with the head of an Ibis bird , with a Crescent Moon headdress, along with his second popular form of manifestation, the baboon. (see below) The Baboon form is often seen offering the left eye of Heru, (which is the same left eye of Ra). He is also known as the "Healer of the Eye" and the "Pacifier" of the combatants, i.e. Heru and Set. One more important quality of Djehuti is that he is the controller of the caduceus, the staff with two serpents which is the *"Staff of Life"* or wand that promotes spiritual awakening.

Below: The Ancient Egyptian god Djehuti holds the caduceus (from the Temple of Seti I, Abdu, Egypt).

The two aforementioned forms of *Djehuti* are composite (ibis headed man), or zoomorphic (baboon). Djehuti has an anthropomorphic form, *Yaah-Djehuti*. In this form he is the god of the moon, i.e. the mind. In this form he appears as a mummy bearing the crescent moon (increasing intellect) on his head, and holds the symbols, *nekaku* -flail (discipline and command), *heka*-shepherd's crook (royalty-leadership), *djed* (Asarian higher consciousness), *ankh* (life force), *uas* -capacity to allow the living higher consciousness to flow), *hensekti*, side lock (youth), *menat* (female creative power).

---

[67] Hermopolis of the Greeks

Yaah-Djehuti

and reason follows the practice of studying, questioning, reflecting and inquiring into the nature of truth. In Neterian myth Set, the lower self, refuses to abide by the decree of wisdom but he is eventually sublimated through his own humiliation and ignorance. In the end, when the aspirant is aligned with all the divine forces, the lower self can no longer struggle. The overwhelming force of the Divine pushes the lower self into a position of service rather than of mastership; this is its rightful place.

Two of Djehuti's most important titles are , *"Djehuti Thrice Great,"* and , *"Lord of the words of power."* The Greek-Hermetic philosophers of the time period between 300 B.C.E. and 500 A.C.E. adopted the title *"Hermes Thrice Greatest"* as the name for the originator of the Hermetic teachings, thus openly acknowledging their Kamitan (African) origins.

Above: from papyrus Nebseni, the oldest known rendition of Djehuti depicted as a baboon watching the balance of the heart.

Forms of Djehuti

Djehuti is the symbol of right reason, the link to the Higher Self. When the determination to pursue the Divine arises, the struggle becomes a holy war against ignorance and illusion within one's consciousness. If this process is not understood as a struggle to overcome anger, hatred, greed, bigotry, jealousy, etc., within one's self, the energy of the struggle becomes directed to the world outside of oneself in the form of political, religious, social, ethnic, gender, etc., conflicts.

The struggle between Heru and Set does not end with either destroying the other. Heru pursues the path of reason seeking counsel with the wisdom of Djehuti. Wisdom follows the exercise of reasoning in peace,

The God Djehuti has two principal forms of manifestation, the Ibis and the Baboon. Both of these animals symbolize intelligence and perseverance. The Ibis with its long beak can feel deep into the muddy waters to discover tasty morsels-symbolizing acute intellectual capacity to see through the mucky waters of life and time and space in order to grasp fragments of truth that brighten the intelligence.

The baboon is intelligent but also meek. In the myth of Hetheru and Djehuti, He came to her in the form of a baboon to teach her the wisdom that leads to spiritual freedom and awakening. Baboons are known to have been well trained in Ancient Egypt. They performed many tasks like harvesting fruits for farmers and even clearing off tables at restaurants. In the form of a baboon, Djehuti fixes the eye of Ra, i.e Hetheru (Hetheru and the right eye of Ra are identical). Thereby she became enlightened and freed from all sorrows and ignorance.[68]

DJEHUTI AND THE HERMETIC PHILOSOPHY

Djehuti, as Lord of Words of Power, was known as the creator of Medu Neter ⟨hieroglyphs⟩ (Ancient Egyptian hieroglyphic writing). As such he is the supreme exponent of the philosophy of the Shetaut Neter and thus he is said to have written the books of the Pertmheru himself with his fingers and his beak (as his pen). According to Clement Alexandrinus[69] in his *Stromata* VI, Hermes (Djehuti) was also the author of 42 books dealing with laws, gods and goddesses, education of the priests and priestesses, worship and services of the gods and goddesses (sacrifices, offerings, etc.), history, geography and hieroglyphs, astronomy and astrology, religious compositions and medical science.

In the very late period of Ancient Kamitan history, when the Greeks conquered Egypt, the Greek philosophers began to study and translate the Ancient Egyptian texts and a new genre of literature that was ascribed to Hermes, whom they equated with Djehuti, was commenced. The ancient Egyptian term ⟨hieroglyphs⟩ *Djehuti aahu- "Djehuti three times great"* became *"Thrice Greatest Hermes"* to the Greeks of the Hermetic period. Though a compilation labeled as 42 has not been discovered, the writings of the "Hermetic Texts" coupled with the earlier hieroglyphic medu neter texts certainly cover the range of subjects mentioned by Clement.

Above: Divine boat of Djehuti.

As all other major divinities Djehuti has a Divine Boat. In this boat he moves through Creation establishing the teachings he codified in the Medu Neter.

Above: mask of Djehuti.

As a character in the mysteries, the priests who reenacted the part of Djehuti used a mask in order to enhance the experience of adopting the character, feeling and wisdom of Djehuti.

---

[68] See the book *The Glorious Light Meditation* by Muata Ashby
[69] Clement of Alexandria (150?-?220), Greek church father. His full name was Titus Flavius Clemens. He studied in Alexandria, Egypt, where he founded a school that became a center of learning. Several writings have survived, including his Hortatory Address to the Greeks, the Paedagogue, the treatise Who Is the Rich Man That Shall Be Saved?, and the Hypotyposes. Christian truth is joined to Greek philosophy for Clement, but his work paves the way for specifically Christian doctrine. Random House Encyclopedia

Chapter 3: Goddess Maat and Maat Philosophy

"Those who live today will die tomorrow, those who die tomorrow will be born again;
Those who live Maat will not die."

Goddess Maat

WHO IS MAAT?

Even though the figure of goddess Maat is not usually seen in the *Rau Prt m Hru*, her presence is perhaps the most strongly felt of all. Her name is mentioned more than any other goddess and indeed, she is said to be an aspect of the all-goddess, Aset. Therefore, in order to understand the *Prt m Hru*, we must have a working knowledge of the goddess and her philosophy. When Ra emerged in his Boat for the first time and creation came into being, he was standing on the pedestal of Maat. Thus the Creator, Ra, lives by Maat and has established Creation on Maat. So who is Maat? She is the divinity who manages the order of Creation. She is the fulcrum upon which the entire Creation and the Law of Cause and Effect or *Ari*, functions. Maat represents the very order which constitutes creation. Therefore, it is said that Ra created the universe by putting Maat in the place of chaos. So creation itself is Maat. Creation without order is chaos (*an-Maat*). Maat is a profound teaching in reference to the nature of creation and the manner in which human conduct should be cultivated. It refers to a deep understanding of Divinity and the manner in which virtuous qualities can be developed in the human heart so as to come closer to the Divine.

Maat is a philosophy, a spiritual symbol as well as a cosmic energy or force which pervades the entire universe. She is the symbolic embodiment of world order, justice, righteousness, correctness, harmony and peace. She is also known by her headdress composed of a feather which symbolizes the qualities just mentioned. She is a form of the Goddess Aset, who represents wisdom and Maat further represents spiritual awakening through balance and equanimity.

In Ancient Egypt, the judges and all those connected with the judicial system were initiated into the teachings of Maat. Thus, those who would discharge the laws and regulations of society were well trained in the ethical and spiritual-mystical values of life, fairness, justice and the responsibility to serve and promote harmony in society as well as the possibility for spiritual development in an atmosphere of freedom and peace, for only when there is justice and fairness in society can there be an abiding harmony and peace. Harmony and peace are necessary for the pursuit of true happiness and inner fulfillment in life.

Maat signifies *that which is straight*. Two of the symbols of Maat are the ostrich feather ($\int$) and the pedestal ($\rule{0.5cm}{0.4pt}$) upon which God stands. The Supreme Being, in the form of the god *Atum, Asar*, and *Ptah*, are often depicted standing on the pedestal.

Maat is the daughter of Ra, the high God, thus in a hymn to Ra we find:

The land of Manu (the West) *receives thee with satisfaction, and the goddess Maat embraces thee both at morning and at evening, the god Djehuti and the goddess Maat have written down thy daily course for thee every day...*

On previous page: Goddess Maat. Caption reads: *Maat, daughter of Ra, Mistress, chief of the land.*

Another Hymn in the Papyrus of Qenna (Kenna) provides deeper insight into Maat. Qenna says:

> *I have come to thee, O Lord of the Gods, Temu-Heru-khuti, whom Maat directeth... Amen-Ra rests upon Maat... Ra lives by Maat... Asar carries along the earth in His train by Maat...*

Maat is the daughter of Ra, and she was with him on his celestial boat when he first emerged from the primeval waters along with his Company of Gods and Goddesses. She is also known as the *Eye of Ra, Lady of heaven, Queen of the earth, Mistress of the Netherworld and the lady of the gods and goddesses.* Maat also has a dual form called *Maati*. In her capacity of God, Maat is *Shes Maat* which means *ceaselessness and regularity* of the course of the sun (i.e. the universe). In the form of Maati, she represents the South and the North which symbolize Upper and Lower Egypt as well as the Higher Self and lower self. Maat is the personification of justice and righteousness upon which God has created the universe, and Maat is also the essence of God and creation. Therefore, it is Maat who judges the soul when it arrives in the judgment hall of Maat. Sometimes Maat herself becomes the scales upon which the heart of the initiate is judged. Maat judges the heart (unconscious mind) of the initiate in an attempt to determine to what extent the heart has lived in accordance with Maat or truth, correctness, reality, genuineness, uprightness, righteousness, justice, steadfastness and the unalterable nature of creation.

Ra in his boat with Maat at the bow.

In Neterian iconography, the features, actions, clothing, posture and positioning of the gods and goddesses is as important as the scriptural information about them as far as discerning the teaching that the divinity imparts. In this case the positioning of Maat at the bow or front of the boat of Ra means that she goes first as the boat moves. Essentially, she opens the waters and creates order as the boat passes. Ra comes after. Therefore, in order for there to be spirit there must be order first. Thus, the study of Maat philosophy is primary in the process of spiritual evolution, for without order there can be no real and powerful study and practice or understanding of true spirituality.

The Maati Goddesses

The Two Maati goddesses preside over the judgment of the heart in the Prt m Hru

Who are the Maati goddesses? In the segment above we introduced the idea of opposites in creation. The Hall of Maat, known as the hall of judgment for the heart, is presided over by two goddesses known as *Maati.*

The goddesses Aset and Nebethet have a special relationship to the Maati goddesses. The Ancient Egyptian texts reveal that these two goddesses are none other than Aset and Nebethet. As stated earlier, Aset and Nebethet are depicted as looking exactly alike, the only difference being in their headdresses: Aset 𓊨, Nebethet 𓉁 or 𓉐. However, the essential meaning of their symbols is inverted, that is, the goddesses are in reality just inverted images of each other. Thus, they are complementary goddess principles which operate to manifest life-death-life or the cycle of birth-death-rebirth known as reincarnation.

Sati merti arati nebti Maati
"The two daughters, goddesses {Aset and Nebethet} of all righteousness and truth."

Aset and Nebethet are also known as *Rekhti,* the two goddesses. They manifest in the Judgment hall of Maat in the *Egyptian Book of Coming Forth By Day* as *Maati* or the double Maat goddesses who watch over the weighing of the heart of the initiate (*The Asar*) in their name as *Sati merti arati nebti Maati.* Aset and Nebethet are the basis of the judgment of the soul and the criterion that decides its fate in life as well as after death.

As far as the teachings related to the Maat goddesses are concerned, it has been well established through the attributes assigned to them in myths and the usage of the terms related to them such as ***Maat-Aset*** (place of righteousness) that Maat is an aspect of

Aset. As for the dual form of Maat, one Maati goddess represents the truth of the transcendent, the higher truth and the other represents the truth of the lower, the time and space, temporal and relative physical world. From the Asarian myth and other texts related to Aset we learn that she is the goddess of **rekh** (wisdom) and the resurrection **Nehast** (of Asar) and eternal life (which is the higher truth) and Nebthet is the goddess of Death and reincarnation into the world of time and space (which is lower truth). As **Rekhti** the two goddesses of knowledge manifest as Aset and Nebthet. In their form as **Maati-Nebty,** the Maati goddesses are identified with the Nebty goddesses (Uadjit and Nekhebit). The Nebty goddesses (Uadjit and Nekhebit) follow the same pattern: Uadjit (fire of life) and Nekhebit (death and reincarnation-renewal). Further, the same goddesses represent Lower Kamit (north-Uadjit) and Upper Kamit (south-Nekhebit). Moreover, the title **Nebt Neteru nebu** *"mistress of all the gods and goddesses",* is shared by Maat, Aset and Uadjit. When the attributes presented in the myths for the goddesses are all thus compared it is obvious that they represent the same principle but within different traditions of the Kamitan religion and the variations refer to nuances related to the given specific teachings being presented or the city or temple (school) in which the particular form of the tradition is being expressed. Thus, according to scripture, the singular manifestations of the goddesses Maat, Aset and Uadjit are all correlated and their dual manifestations are also correlated. Lastly, any confusion about the relationship between the Maati goddesses and Aset and Nebethet should be removed by the following passages from the **Prt m Hru** CHAPTER 4[70] *The Wisdom of the Secret Identity of the Gods and Goddesses* texts: (11) **As for his plumes on his** (Amsu[71]) **head, they are the actions of the goddesses Aset and Nebethet.**

The **Shuti** are the feathers on the crown of Amsu, who is the lord of Maati–absolute and temporal existence and are also the same two goddesses. (41) **As for those guardians, the judges, they are baboons[72] and their names are Aset and Nebethet.** Here Aset and Nebthet are being directly named as the judges (Maati goddesses).

So the Maati goddesses are not just related to the principle of duality and law within the limited confines of Maat philosophy or in the Hall of Maat only. Such a narrow interpretation is not supported by the scripture nor by the mythic attributes assigned to the goddesses and their usage. Rather, the principle of duality and the concept of the transcendental (absolute) and the temporal (relative) are themes that permeate all the traditions (varying religious schools) of Shetaut Neter religion and spring from the same source, as all of the Neteru spring from the single source (Neter).

Many people think of the philosophy of Karma as a concept that originated in India. The following text shows that it is a concept that was well understood earlier in Kamit and is very much in harmony with what is today referred to as Karma. In Ancient Egyptian philosophy the word for karma is Ari, meaning "action" which attaches to a person and leads them to their fate even beyond death. The Kamitan teachings to Merikara and the *Pert M Hru* illuminate this teaching in detail. *(Highlighted text is by Ashby)*

Instructions of Merikara

(14) The Court that judges the wretch,
You know they are not lenient,
On the day of judging the miserable,
In the hour of doing their task.
It is painful when the accuser has knowledge,
Do not trust in length of years,
They view a lifetime in an hour!
When a man remains over after death,
His Ari (deeds, actions) are set beside him as treasure,
And being yonder lasts forever.
A fool is who does what they reprove!
He who reaches them without having done wrong
Will exist there like a god,
Free-striding like the lords forever!

—Instructions of Merikara

The writings of Merikara confirm the understanding of a subtle aspect of action which follows one after death. This "residue" is judged and the destiny is administered thereby. This signifies that a person is the author of {his/her} own fate, i.e. karmic fortune (Shai and Rennutt). This teaching also conveys the relativity of time and space, as the "judges" exist in a different plane than the worldly, physical state and the passage of time is different for them. Thus, this

---

[70] Generally referred to as Chapter 17.
[71] Form of Amun, Min
[72] The baboon is usually the symbol of the god Djehuti because it is noticed to be a smart animal. Sometimes Djehuti presides over the judgment of the heart of the Asar in the form of a baboon and here the goddesses are identified with that principle as well as the concept of judgment which a primary attribute of the Maati goddesses. Therefore, the Maati goddesses and Aset and Nebthet are one and the same.

passage also contains a reference that shows the Neterian comprehension of the relativity of time in different planes of existence, advanced metaphysics.[73] The next aspect of Ari (karma) is contained in the ancient Egyptian Judgment Scene.

Ammit

Above- Vignette A- from Chapter 33 of Papyrus Ani: The Judgment scene from the Pert m Heru Text of Ancient Egypt showing the God Djehuti and the Goddess Ammit.

Ammit is an important goddess of the Pert m Heru texts. Ammit means "Great Death." She is a composite beast combining one third hippopotamus, one third lion and one third crocodile. She is the symbolic devourer of unrighteous souls. The Judgment scene above shows how a person's own actions are judged and how this leads a person to their fate, either to move on and discover the Divine and become one with the Divine or to suffer due to negative actions of the past (eat one's own heart) or to reincarnate. Above: Djehuti records the result while the Ammit monster, the Devourer of the unjust, awaits the answer.

The Papyrus of Ani dates back to the 18th Dynasty of the Dynastic Period in Ancient Egypt (1800-1500 B.C.E.). It denotes a philosophy related to the Asarian Resurrection theology that has been traced back to the Pre-Dynastic Age and which constitutes one of the central teachings of Ancient Egyptian religion, the Maat principle. The following detailed description of the Ancient Egyptian Judgment scene provides deeper insight into the workings of the Kamitan system of Ari.

The Judgment of the Soul.

See the Vignette B (full scene) from Chapter 33 of Papyrus Ani: The Judgment scene from the Pert m Heru Text of Ancient Egypt. (below)

Ani and his wife enter the judgment hall. Left to Right: Meskhent and Rennutt, The Ba (the soul, as human-headed hawk), Shai (standing), Meskhent (again-this time as birthing block {above Shai}), Anpu, Djehuti, Ammit.

Text: Ani addresses his heart. At top, the gods and goddesses presiding are (right to left: Ra, Atum, Shu, Tefnut, Geb, Nut, Nebethet and Aset, Heru Ur, Hetheru, Saa and Hu. Far left, Ani enters the hall of Judgment. His heart (conscience) is being weighed by Anpu (Anubis) while the Divine principals Shai, Rennutt and Meskhent look on. Ani's soul and his destiny also look on while Anubis measures Ani's heart (unconscious mind containing the impressions or "residues") against the feather of Maat (i.e. the principles of the 42 precepts of Maat…truth, righteousness, etc.). At far right Djehuti records the result while the Ammit monster, the devourer of the unjust, awaits the answer. The hands of Djehuti (God of Reason) are "Shai" which means "destiny" and "Rennutt" which means "Fortune and Harvest." The implication is that we reap (harvest) the result of our state of mind (heart). Our state of mind, including our subconscious feelings and desires, is weighed against cosmic order, Maat. If found to be at peace (Hetep) and therefore in accord with cosmic order (Maat) it will be allowed to join with the cosmos (Asar). Otherwise it will suffer the fate as dictated by its own contents (mental state of unrest due to lingering desires), which will lead it to Ammit who will devour the ego-personality. That soul will experience torments from demons until it learns its lessons through the process of trial and error, and then pursues an authentic process of mystical practice to become strong enough through wisdom to know itself (become Enlightened). Demons may be understood as negative cosmic energies which the personality has allowed itself to indulge in, in the form of mental anguish and torments people put themselves through, due to their own ignorance. Self-torment may be regret over some action or inaction while alive or a reluctance to leave the physical realm because of a lingering desire to experience more earthly pleasure. This is also termed "eating one's own heart." (see 42 precepts of Maat)

Therefore, one controls one's own fate according to one's own level of wisdom or reasoning capacity.[74]

---

[3] *Mysticism of the Mahabharata* by Swami Jyotirmayananda

[74] *The Ancient Egyptian Book of the Dead* by Dr. Muata Ashby 2000

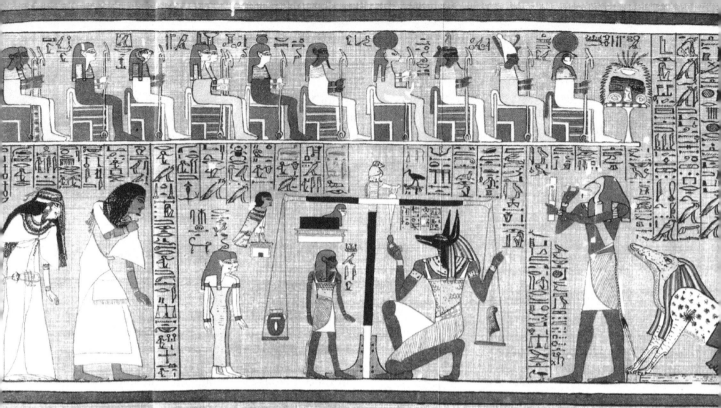

This scene is actually a pictorial (iconographical) representation of the philosophy of Ari or Karma and *Uhm Ankh* or reincarnation.

The Ancient Egyptian myth known as The Story of Sa-Asar succinctly and powerfully illustrates the concept of Ari (action-Karma). It describes the fate of the soul after death in accordance with the actions of the person while alive on earth. Sa-Asar means son of Asar. He was a child god, son of Asar, an aspect of Heru, who brought essential spiritual teachings to the world.

"A man and a woman wanted to have a child, but could not conceive so the woman, named Mehusekhe, went to a temple to sleep there in the hope that a god or goddess would come to her and tell her what to do. A spirit came to her in a dream and told her to go to the place where her husband was, and to eat from a melon vine and embrace her husband in love, and that she would then conceive a child. She became pregnant and her husband, Setna, was very happy. In a dream, the spirit came to Setna and told him the child would be a boy and he is to be named "Sa-Asar," and that he will do great wonders in the land of Egypt. When the child was born Setna named him Sa-Asar, and he grew up and was always mature for his years. When Sa-Asar was a boy of 10, he was already respected as an enlightened Sage. One day he and his father were looking at two funerals. One funeral was for a rich man, who had many mourners, attendants, and offerings to the gods and goddesses. The other

funeral was for a poor man, who had no one to mourn him and no offerings for the gods and goddesses to be placed in his tomb. The father exclaimed, "When my time comes, may my funeral be like the one of the rich man." Sa-Asar looked at his father, and said, "Oh no father I hope you die like the poor man." Setna looked at Sa-Asar with surprise. Then Sa-Asar asked "Would you like me to show you the fate of these two souls?" Sa-Asar led his father to the Netherworld and his father saw that the rich man was judged by the gods and goddesses and was found to be unrighteous, having committed more evil deeds than virtuous deeds so his fate was to suffer. The poor man had led a virtuous life so all of the offerings of the rich man were accrued to the poor man, and the poor man was led into the presence of Asar, the Supreme Self, who was seated on his throne, with the goddesses Aset and Nebethet behind him and the gods and goddesses at his sides. Setna saw the evil rich man suffering. Others were reaching up to grasp at food that was dangling over them by a rope while under them, certain gods and goddesses were digging a pit so that they could not reach high enough. Still others were twining ropes while at the other end of the rope there were donkeys eating the rope. "Tell me Sa-Asar," Setna asked in amazement, "What is the meaning of these things I see? What happens to the people as they are judged?" Sa-Asar answered, "Those who are twining are the people who on earth labor everyday but their labors are fruitless for themselves because they do not perform the right actions, but the fruits of their actions benefit others. Those who are reaching up to get their food in vain are those who in life on earth have their life before them, but do not make use of it. Those who are found to have more misdeeds than good deeds are made to suffer. Those who have an equal amount of misdeeds and good deeds are sent to be servants of Sokar-Asar.[75] Those who are found to have more virtuous deeds than misdeeds are allowed to be among the gods and goddesses as one of them, and their Ba flies up to be among the glorified spirits."[76]

The sophisticated nature of the Kamitan understanding and exposition of the philosophy of Ari (karma) incorporates the intermeshing of the myth, iconography and philosophy related to the divinities and their interactions. These yield a powerful mystical system which became the basis of Kamitan culture and civilization.[77] This myth also allows us to understand that the higher, inner philosophy about offerings and externalities related to the burial are not important. What is important is to cleanse the heart through righteous actions and virtuous living so as to experience the fate of enlightenment and not suffering.

Image below: The Blind Maat Offering by the king Seti (Waset (Thebes)).

The blind Maat is a special form of the Goddess Maat. The offering of blind Maat is an extremely important ritual displayed in papyruses and carved on the temples because it symbolizes the legitimacy of the ruler to aspire to divine consciousness. Maat is the prerequisite to all spiritual evolution. Without righteousness in life no order and peace can be possible. The first responsibility of the king, i.e. anyone who aspires to become one with the gods and

goddesses, is to uphold Maat objectively, without egoistic bias, i.e. "blind."

> *"There are two roads traveled by humankind, those who seek to live Maat, and those who seek to satisfy their animal passions."*
> —Ancient Egyptian Proverb

SUMMARY OF THE PHILOSOPHY OF ARI (KARMA) IN ANCIENT EGYPT BASED ON THE KAMITAN TEXT

Ari
"Action," "to do something," "things done"

Arit Maat
Work rightly, lead life of integrity, in accordance with Maatian principles.

Ari em hetep.
Work contentedly, with peace and contentment, without egoistic desire or expectations.

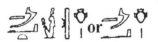

Maat Ab
Thus attain Purity of Heart

Maakheru
Become true of Speech, Spiritually enlightened.

Arit Heru
Receive the Eye of Heru, perfected action, the Eucharist, the act of becoming one with the Divine (the highest action).

---

5 Also Sokkar
6 *The Egyptian Book of the Dead*, Muata Ashby
7 For more details on the Philosophy of Ari see the Book *Egyptian Book of the Dead,* by Muata Ashby

In Kamitan Philosophy action Ari is integrally related to the process of reincarnation.

Meskhent

Above (left): the goddesses Rennutt and Meskhent, right- Shai (From the Papyrus of Ani-see Chapter 33)

Along with her associates, the goddesses *Shai*, *Rennutt* and *Meskhent*, the goddess Maat encompasses the Ancient Egyptian teachings of *Ari* (karma) and reincarnation or the destiny of every individual based on past actions, thoughts and feelings. These divinities have an essential role to play in the judgment scene of the *Prt m Hru*. Understanding their principles leads the aspirant to become free of the cycle of reincarnation and human suffering and to discover supreme bliss and immortality. If a person is ignorant about their higher essential nature, they will only have knowledge of lower human existence. At the time of death their soul will wander and experience either heavenly or hellish conditions in much the same way as one experiences good and bad dreams. Spiritual enlightenment means discovering your essential nature as one with the Supreme Self, and when this is achieved, there is no more hell or heaven; there is a resurrection in consciousness. This is what the goddess urges every aspirant to

achieve through study, reflection and meditation on her teachings, and it is the central theme in the *Asarian Resurrection* myth.[78]

Rennutt goddess

Shai- god of destiny[79]

The hands of Djehuti (God of wisdom) are the God "Shai" which means "destiny" and the Goddess "Rennutt" which means "Fortune and Harvest." The implication is that we reap (harvest) the result of our actions (destiny) according to our level of wisdom. Djehuti, one's own wisdom capacity through higher intellectual understanding, bestows control over one's Shai (Fortune) and Rennutt (reaping one's fortune) and therefore one's Meskhent (Destiny - Karma). Therefore, one's karmic destiny depends on one's reasoning capacity, i.e. *intellect*.

Above: Rennutt as nurse to the pharaoh and the divine child.

Underlying the principles of Shai and Rennutt is goddess "Meskhent." She is the one who determines where the next birth (karmic fate) of the soul will take place. Therefore, the teachings of Ari (Karma) and reincarnation are an integral part of Kamitan Philosophy.

---

[78] For more details see the Book *The Wisdom of Maati* for more on Maat philosophy.

[79] The concept of Shai has two prominent manifestations, male (Shai) and female (Shait)   *Shait*- goddess of destiny.

Chapter 4: Other Important Gods and Goddesses of the Neterian Religion

The Neteru of Kamit, Their Symbolism and Functions

"Neteru"

(gods and goddesses, cosmic forces, energies)

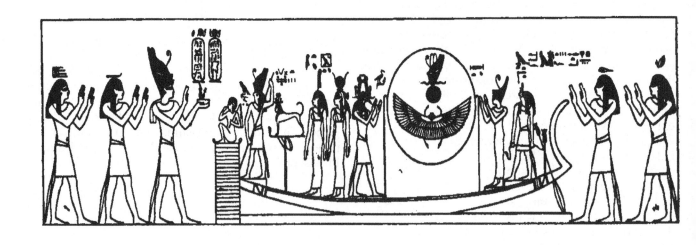

GOD/GODDESS HAPI

Asar-Hapi

Above top: The divinity Hapi represents the androgynous Life Force which sustains all life and manifests as the Nile River. In ancient times as well as modern times life and prosperity, feast or famine in North East Africa was and is dependent on the existence of the Nile. The iconography of Hapi is the man's body with large female breasts. These symbolize not only the burgeoning sustenance of mother Tefnut, who symbolizes the power of water, but also there is a teaching whereby Hapi sustains and unifies the duality (symbolized by two streams and two breasts) of life in the form of Upper and Lower Egypt. Metaphysically speaking, Hapi sustains the body as well as the spirit which inhabits it and make civilization possible. Above: the Hapi - Nile gods joining Upper and Lower Egypt with the Sema symbol. Below: Asar is in his shrine with Aset and Nebethet receiving tribute from the Hapi goddesses *Meres*-goddess of the south (top right) and *Merha* goddess of the north (bottom right).

The god Asar is one of the most popular and important divinities in Neterian Religion. His appeal, as that of Heru, crossed over the main Neterian spiritual traditions and in the later times Asar (Osiris) was worshipped in his form of *Asar-Hapi* (the sacred bull) as *Serapis* in ancient Greece and Rome. The word Serapis comes from Ser (Greek) = Asar (Egyptian) and *apis* (Greek) = *Hapi* (Egyptian). This manifestation (*Asar-Hapi*) originates in Ancient Egyptian Anunian theology but he also manifests in Ancient Egyptian Memphite Theology very prominently. In the Hymn to Asar of the *Prt m Hru* it is said that Asar is *"the hidden soul."* That is, he is the soul of Creation and the soul that resurrects after death. He is one of the primordial divinities of the Company of Gods and Goddesses of Ra but his main teaching is contained in the Asarian Resurrection myth.[80]

---

[80] See the book The Asarian Resurrection by Muata Ashby

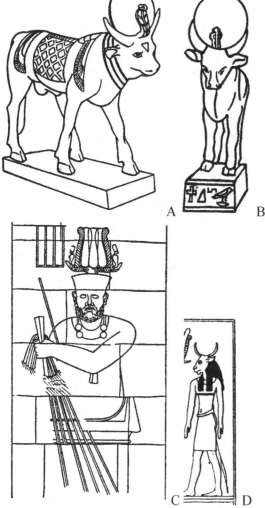

Above A: Hapi- (Greek-Apis) bull of Menefer – Memphis. B: Nem-ur (Greek-Mnevis) bull of Anu. C: Serapis (relief from Meroe), D-Asar Hapi (from Per m Hru)

Asar's main titles are *Un-Nefer*, which means beautiful existence or openness; *her-Abdu*, which means "Lord (ruler) of Abdu" (city of Asar-center of his worship and abode of the blessed); *Khenti Amenti*, which means "foremost of Amenta (region of the Duat plane of existence). He is also *Neb Tawi* -King of Egypt, and when he died and was resurrected he became *Sokar*, the *"King of the Dead."* In the capacity as King of the Dead he is the ultimate judge not only of human beings but also of the gods and goddesses that emerged from Ra-Atum in the beginning of Creation and all other divinities and demons that arose later. Asar's deepest abode is in the *Ianrutf* section of the Duat. *Ianrutf* means "the place where nothing grows", where there is purity.

In the following segments from Chapter 23 of the Ancient Egyptian *Book of Coming Forth By Day*, the initiate, having understood his oneness, and having identified with God in the form of Asar, exclaims the following:

> *"I am yesterday, today and tomorrow. I have the power to be born a second time. I am the source from which the gods arise."*

In CHAPTER 4[81] The Wisdom of the Secret Identity of the Gods and goddesses it is stated:

1. *I am yesterday, I know tomorrow! Who is this person that is being spoken about?*
2. *As for the word "today," it refers to Asar. As for the word "yesterday," it refers to Ra*

Thus we are given to understand that Asar is a reflection of Ra, his incarnation on earth and that knowing the nature and essence of Asar bestows all knowing and spiritual enlightenment.

Asar's main symbol is the Djed Pillar, an artifact that represents his backbone and the four upper psycho-spiritual consciousness centers of the *Sefek ba Ra* which when awakened lead to spiritual evolution and emancipation.[82] This Djed pillar (above) is also to be known as the *khet n Ankh* (lit. "Tree of Life") as it is cut from the trunk of the tree that grew from his coffin (below right) when he was killed by Set. The image below comes from the Temple of Hetheru. In it the tree is growing out of the coffin of Asar.[83]

---

[81] Generally referred to as Chapter 17.
[82] See the book The Serpent Power by Muata Ashby.
[83] For more details see the Tree of life audio lecture series: Principle

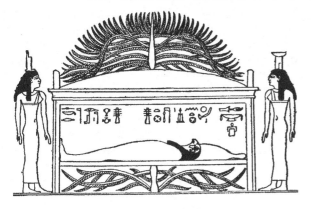

The Pillar of Asar

Above: Aset receiving pillar from king (temple of Abdu, Egypt). The Pillar of Asar is an important artifact and spiritual philosophy of Neterian religion. It relates to the raising of the backbone of Asar, which was struck down by the evil actions of Set. Thus, the raising of the pillar signifies the raising of the four upper psycho-spiritual consciousness centers. This process is presided over by goddess Aset. So Aset (wisdom-intuitional realization of truth) vanquishes Set (egoism and vice), which has killed and dismembered Asar (the soul) in order to allow it to resurrect and live for eternity. This is a temple ceremony carried out by the priests and the priestesses who assume the characters of Asar and Aset, and other characters of the Asarian Resurrection Myth.

Shesmu, is a God or a Demon, depending on his particular function. He is closely associated with the God Asar as his servant. As a God he presides over the Wine Press, (Oils) and as a

Demon he carries out the function of Slaughterer of the damned.

The precious oils were used in the embalming process, medicinal purposes and other beneficial uses. But the same wine press used to make wine for nourishment could be used to destroy evildoers and it could also be used to process the blood of gods into blood-wine for Asar to drink. So he is known as *"Lord of the Blood."*[84] Thus it is given to understand, by Shesmu's dual aspects that the very objects of the world that can bring pleasure and health can also be misused and can actually become sources of pain and self-destruction. Wine can aid digestion but if taken in large quantities it can cause damage to the organs as well as produce dullness of character. So he is also known as *"slaughterer of souls."* As Lord of The Blood he nourishes Asar[85] with the blood of the gods and goddesses; he cooks them and serves them up so that the initiate may gain their powers and insight into their nature. Shesmu is depicted as a man (anthropomorphic), or a lion-headed man (composite) or as a hawk (zoomorphic). The Decans are star groups into which the night sky was divided. Each group of stars appeared for ten days annually. On the list of Decans at the temple of Hetheru at *Iunet* (Dendera), Shesmu is shown as a man on a boat holding an *uas* scepter with a uraeus on top of his head, between two stars (see above). The connection between blood and wine relates to his helper god or punishing demon aspects and it was also related to the wine consumed by the ancient Egyptians as well as the setting sun by its color: red. The Ancient Egyptians DID NOT drink blood wine made of blood. Red wine was metaphorically related as blood due to the similarity of the color red. White wine appeared in the Middle Kingdom period, and was prefered by the Greeks. The red wine - or blood – was what Shesmu offers the pharaohs and that teaching existed since the time of the Pyramid Texts wherein Shesmu assists the Asar (Pharaoh, initiate)

of Asar.

[84] PERT M HRU CHAPTER 8[84]
[85] the divinity as well as all initiates who identify with Asar.

to traverse the Duat (Astral Plane) to reach the abode of the blessed (enlightened spirits).

The Eyes of Ra and Heru

There are several Ancient Egyptian myths relating to the *"Eye."* One tells that the Eye (individual soul) left Ra (the Divine Self) and went into Creation and was lost. Ra sent Djehuti (wisdom) to find the Eye and bring it back. It was through the *magic* (wisdom teachings) of the god Djehuti that the Eye realized who it was and agreed to return to Ra. Upon its return, however, it found that Ra had replaced it with another. In order to pacify it, Ra placed it on his *brow* in the form of a *Uraeus serpent, where it could rule the world.* One variation to the story holds that the Eye left Ra and went to Nubia in the form of a lioness (Hetheru, in her aspect as destroyer of evil and unrighteousness). When Ra heard this, he sent the Nubian god *Ari-Hems-Nefer,* a form of Shu, and Djehuti to bring the Eye back. They took the form of baboons (symbol of wisdom) and soon found the Eye near the *Mountain of the Sunrise*, where Asar was born. The Eye refused to leave because it had learned to enjoy its new existence. It was destroying those who had committed sins (plotted against Ra) while on earth. Djehuti worked his magic on the Eye and brought it back to Ra. Another variation of the story holds that Ra sent *Shu* and *Tefnut* in search of the Eye. The Eye resisted, and in the struggle, shed tears, and from the tears grew men. This is a clever play on words because the Kamitan word for "tears," *Remtu,* , (that fell from the eyes of Ra) and the word for "men," Remtj or Remtju, 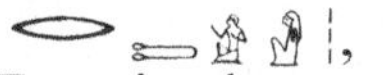, have similar sounds in Ancient Egyptian language. This play on words sustains the idea that human beings came forth, figuratively speaking, out of the sorrow of God as he saw souls leaving him and becoming human beings, i.e. forgetting their true nature. The implication is that the tears (physical substance) of Ra and his rapture (feeling-passion) become vessels (bodies-watery encasements) for the souls to exist in the embodied state, i.e. as human beings.

The relationship of "tears" to "men" symbolizes the idea that humankind is the expression of the desire of the Divine Self to have experiences in the realm of time and space. Further, "tears" are a symbol of human experience. It implies that human experience is a sorrowful condition because consciousness has degraded itself from freedom to the level of gross, limited human experience in the form of an individual ego as opposed to its expansive, limitless Self. This contraction in consciousness is what allows the ego to emerge as an individual and distinct personality out of "nowhere," just as a dream personality emerges out of "nowhere." Instead of knowing itself as the immutable soul, the soul sees the ego and the limited world of time and space as the reality. This development would be like the ocean forgetting that it is the ocean and believing itself to be one of the waves amongst other waves, separate from the ocean. Therefore, instead of seeing itself as encompassing all the waves, it is concerned with its transient experience, as an individual wave, and with comparing itself to other waves.

The Eye with its own body

Life is "sorrowful" from the standpoint of wisdom because even conditions that appear to be pleasurable are in reality setting the individual up for disappointment and frustration later on, because no seemingly positive situation can last indefinitely. Also, the pursuit of worldly pleasure and pain sets up mental impressions that will survive the death of the body and lead the soul to further incarnations in search of fulfillment. Therefore, the Sages say that *all life is painful to the wise.* This is why Kamitan Yoga philosophy emphasizes going beyond both pleasure *and* pain in order to transcend the bondage to time and space. This can be accomplished by turning away from the world which is illusory and seeking to discover the Higher Self.

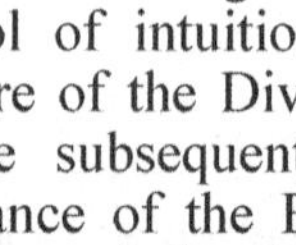

The Left Eye of Heru and Ra

Through the story of the Eye, very important mystical teachings are being conveyed. The Eye, *Udjat,* is a symbol of intuitional vision. Also, it represents the desire of the Divine to go into itself (Creation) and the subsequent forgetfulness that ensues. The resistance of the Eye to return to the divine abode is a symbol of the predicament of ordinary people who, through ignorance and intense desire, detest the idea of even considering the spiritual values of life because their hearts (minds) are consumed with ignorance and passion. They are consumed with the desire to experience the pleasures of material existence. Ra sent the Eye (soul-consciousness) into Creation. Consciousness then became "lost" in Creation, symbolizing the souls of human beings and all life forms, forgetting their true nature. The Eye, lost in Creation, is the human soul which is caught up in the cycle of birth-death-birth (reincarnation) due to forgetfulness and distraction (ignorance of its true nature). The Supreme Being (Ra) sent out the messenger of wisdom (Djehuti) in the forms of *Medu Neter* (ancient scriptures of wisdom) and *Sbai* (spiritual preceptor) to instruct the Eye in reference to its true nature. Having "remembered" who it was in reality, the Eye then returned to its rightful place.

The Right Eye of Heru and Ra

The teaching of the Eye is to be found in the story of Heru and Set where Set (ego) tore out Heru's Eye. It is Djehuti who restored the Eye through the power of magic (wisdom teaching). In this context, the whole teaching of wisdom which Djehuti applies (*Hekau*) to the Eye causes it to remember its essential nature and its glory as the Eye of Heru - *Arit Heru*. Upon its return, the Eye provided Heru with the strength of will he needed to overthrow Set. This story mythologizes the journey of the human soul and its eventual redemption wherein it achieves the sublimation of the ego and attains *Self-realization*.

In this aspect, the plight of the Eye and its subsequent restoration through the teachings of Djehuti in the *Udja Hetheru* text as the transmitter of wisdom, embodies the principle of the *Sba-Sbat* (teacher-disciple) relationship though which spiritual knowledge is transmitted. We saw this same principle in the initiation of Heru by Aset, in the *Asar Uhem Ankh* (Asarian Resurrection) text. Djehuti is the master teacher who initiates the aspirant on the spiritual path of wisdom. In teaching others, the priest or priestess assumes the role of Djehuti. Djehuti is the *Spiritual Preceptor* of the Eye.

When Heru's Eye (the moon) was torn out and thrown away by Set, the god Djehuti who presides as the moon found it and turned it into the Moon. When the parts of the Eye of Heru are added up, it gives the answer 63/64 which approximate the whole number 1. One is the number which symbolizes oneness, completeness, wholeness, all sight, all knowing, the Supreme Being, The Absolute. As long as the soul is involved in creation

(matter), there will remain some small separation between the individual Ba (soul) and the Universal Ba, the ONE. In order to become completely unified, merged into infinity, the individual soul of the enlightened person dissolves into the Universal soul at the time of death; this is complete Oneness with the divine. The missing part of the Eye of Heru, 1/64, is added by Djehuti through his magic, i.e. the magic of purified intellect which comes about through understanding the Hekau (words of power-hieroglyphic texts). Purified intellect opens up the capacity of Saa (understanding) which does not occur through information. Saa is the capacity to make sense of something after the information has been processed and a person's experiences have allowed them to realize what the truth is.

The Eye is therefore, the quintessential symbol of the creative power of the Divine. Also, it is the cardinal principle of power which can be directed against evil and unrighteousness, primarily in the form of demoniac qualities in nature or in human beings. This is why the Eye symbol was used so profusely in ancient times and why the Eye symbols were used on coffins to signify awakened consciousness which will not be defeated by death. In ancient times the mummy was placed in the coffin, lying on the left side and as if looking out through the two eyes of the coffin. The mystical symbolism is that attaining the transcendental and unitary qualities of the two eyes, a human being thus attains the capacity to transcend death, i.e. to look out on eternity.

Ra is known as *Arit ua*- or one eyed one. This means that there is a dual aspect to the eye philosophy but there is also a non-dual aspect. When the two eyes are combined, that is, harmonized through following the mystic teaching (Shetaut Neter) the third eye, at the center of the forehead, emerges, and with it comes spiritual enlightenment. The *Arit Ra*- is also the Eye of Ra manifesting as the midday sun. Ritually, the *Arit Heru Arat Hetep* - Eye of Heru is the goddess Hetheru and also it is the special offering, the eucharist that resurrects the body of Asar, that is made whole and brought back to life through Heru, that is, attaining the Heru nature in the form of Heru-Ur.

For more on the Neterian Eucharist see the book *Egyptian Book of the Dead* by Muata Ashby.

Amentat

Ament means "hidden." It is a specific reference to the female form of the astral plane or Netherworld known as *Amenta* or the Duat. Aset was known as the dark-skinned daughter of Nut. Like Asar, her husband, who was known as the "Lord of the Perfect Black," Aset was the Mistress of the Netherworld known as Amentet (Amentat). Thus, Aset also symbolizes the "blackness" of the vast unmanifest regions of existence. Her identification is also symbolized in her aspect as *Amentet,* the Duat, itself. Therefore, Amentet (Aset) and the soul of Amentet (Amen-Asar) are intimately related. Upon further reflection into the mythology, it becomes obvious that since Asar is the Duat, and since the goddess Amentet, the goddess, is also Ament or the realm of Asar, they are in reality one and the same (both the realms and the deities).

Aset and Asar together form the hidden recesses of Creation. In essence they are the source of Creation and are therefore both simultaneously considered to be the source of the Life Force which courses through Creation.

SEKHMET-BAST-RA

Sekhmet-Bast-Ra, The All - Goddess

Another important form of the Goddess is known as *Sekhmet-Bast-Ra.* Sekhmet-Bast-Ra is a composite depiction of the Goddess encompassing the female head, lioness head, and vulture head, symbolizing all of the attributes of the goddesses as well as the attributes of the gods. Sekhmet-Bast-Ra is similar to the concept of Neberdjer, but in this form with a female aspect. This is recognition that all things in Creation are not absolutely female or male. All of Creation is a combination of male and female elements. Therefore, since Creation is androgynous, so too Divinity and the human soul are also androgynous. This understanding is reflected in the following instruction from Aset to Heru in the Asarian Resurrection, verse 125:

> Heru asked: "O Divine Mother, how are male and female souls produced?" Aset answered: "Souls, Heru, son, are of the self same nature in themselves, in that they are from one and the same place where the Creator modeled them; nor male nor female are they. Sex (i.e. gender) is a thing of bodies, not of souls."

ARAT (ART, AART, ARATI)[86]

Arat (The Serpent Form of The Goddess)

The Serpent form of the Goddess represents several important teachings related to the Life Force energy (Sekhem) permeating Creation. Emanating from the Divine Self, it enlivens and sustains all of Creation. It also refers to the internal Life Force energy which lies dormant within every human being. This Life Force energy is known in modern times as Arat Sekhem, the Serpent Power or Kundalini.

---

[86] For more on the teachings of the Serpent Power and the spiritual disciplines related to its development for the purpose of promoting spiritual evolution, see the book *The Serpent Power* by Dr. Muata Ashby.

Art **(Goddess)**

The symbol of the serpent is used to depict the serpent power because it is the perfect metaphor to represent the serpentine mode of movement which characterizes the Serpent Power energy. In the teaching of the Temple of Aset from Ancient Egypt, the Serpent Power (Arat) was symbolized as the image of a serpent with three and a half coils.

UADJIT AND NEKHEBIT

Uadjit (Uatchet) and Nekhebit are the goddesses of Lower and Upper Egypt respectively. Uadjit is often depicted as a serpent while Nekhebit is often depicted as a vulture. However, both can be depicted as two divine eyes *Uadjti* –the Two eyes of Heru (Aset & Nbthet), or serpent goddesses and both may be depicted with the vulture headdress but each wears the crown of the district of Egypt that they represent (North-Lower or South-Upper) They are regarded as the serpents of the Caduceus of Djehuti and consequently they are aspects of Aset and Nebethet and the Maati goddesses. Both were present at the birth of Heru. Uadjit represents the burning fire of the Life Force and Nekhebit represents the cooling restorative aspect. As a vulture, who eats carrion and turns it into life again, Nekhebit also consumes waste and brings forth new life from it. Therefore those living in the south of Egypt venerated her. Those living in the north of Egypt venerated Uadjit. The Peraah wears a crown containing both the Nebti goddesses (Uadjit and Nekhebit) as a symbol of representing both the lower and upper regions into one unified country.

Shetau

The Turtle divinity is called *Shetau* and is a revered divinity for its ability to project its limbs and have entry into the world and then to be able to withdraw its limbs back into its own nature. The spelling for the name of the turtle god is *Shetau*. This contains the spelling for *Sheta* or *Shetau* - hidden - difficult to understand - mystery -hard to get through, which is the root for the term *Shetau Neter* (the Hidden Divinity – Ancient Egyptian Religion.

Nehebkau – is a male serpent divinity. His name means "he who harnesses the Kas (powers)." The Ka is an element of the personality, the astral body (mind) that engenders and sustains the physical body.[87] He receives his name because he swallowed seven serpents and assimilated their strength making him invulnerable to Hekau (words of power), fire or water. He can counteract venomous bites and promote health. Nehebkau receives the aspirants in the Netherworld and provides a meal. Thus, initiates often propitiate him to assist in their protection as they move on their spiritual journey in the Netherworld. Nehebkau can only be controlled by *Atum* who can press a point with his finger on the spine of Nehebkau. The Pyramid Texts say he is the son of the goddess Serqet.

---

[87] See the book *Egyptian Mysteries Volume 1* by Muata Ashby

Netjer-Anhk, "The Living God" who gives Life Force which leads to resurrection. Netjer-Anhk is a form of the male serpent. He is a beneficent force who conveys life and health.

SEKHMIT AND THE THE FELINE ASPECT

Bast

Bastet (Bast) - Cat-headed sun goddess.

She is represented with a woman's body and cat head. She plays the sistrum and was the daughter of Ra. Though peace loving she was also a fierce destroyer of pests. Her son's name is *Mihos*, a lion god. In ancient times she had a strong following and clergy. As goddess of all cats she was revered in her form as the domestic cat. So all cats were respected and protected as forms of the goddess and for their beneficent qualities, catching vermin and destroying inimical forces. As other animals, cats have special gifts, or rather, exceptional and unique energies (ways of being) that are fascinating and which allow them to carry on successfully in the world. These qualities are desirable for the spiritual aspirant. Cats are part wild, and stealthy hunters; they have exceptional hearing and superb eyesight. They can hear a mouse without seeing it, but they could see it with 1/6th the light needed by a human being. Aspirants should develop these qualities when dealing with the world and the inimical forces within that try to drag the mind down into worldly thinking and desires.

Mafdet

The Leopard Goddess Mafdet cutting the head of the Demon serpent Apep.

The Leopard Goddess Mafdet was associated with Sekhmit, the Eye of Ra and with Hetheru. Cats have an inimical relationship with snakes so they assist to protect human lives. She is the embodiment of the destructive force that can be unleashed on the negative impetus, symbolized by the serpent demon Apep. Mafdet is also identified with the execution blade itself.

Above left- Sem Priest making an offering.

Above right- Ancient Egyptian Sem Priestess.

The Sem (officiating) priest(ess) wear a leopard skin, as a symbol of the power to dispel the evil of death and to open the mouth (mind) of the initiate.

Khatru

The *Khatru* (above) is an ichneumon animal. It is a sacred animal because it also has an inimical relationship with serpents. Thus, it is an enemy of Apep just as the cat.

The Ant fish and the Abd fish of the Boat of Ra

In the creation story, these are two fish that guide the boat of Ra on its journey.

Sobek

Sobek (Sebek) is a crocodile god. He is the son of Net. He assisted Asar in his time of need and he represents the harnessing of the potential power of the lower nature. Specifically, he represents the power that lurks within the waters. He is that power which can rise up at any moment and kill or pull one under to one's destruction, if it is misused and misunderstood or it can be used for positive goals if sublimated and cultivated. As the use of the crocodile symbolism implies the characteristics of its class of being, Sobek involves the qualities of patience, stealthiness, the ability to hold the breath for extended periods of time, the ability to go without food for extended periods of time the ability to remain dormant (withdrawn, at rest) for long periods and then to burst forth as lightning, out of the water, to achieve the desired goal- catching their prey. The crocodile deity is associated with the second psycho-spiritual energy consciousness center.

The divinities Nebethet, Sobek, Serqet, and Apep may often appear to be placid, peaceful and perhaps even loving sources of pleasure and sweetness. But there is another side, a side that leads to pain, suffering and death. These are the people, objects and situations in life that appear to be sources of joy but which are in reality sources of suffering. The error is not in the divinities but in people who interact with them (their cosmic principle) out of ignorance.

Serqet

Serqet or Selket, a scorpion goddess, assisted the goddess Aset when she was running away from Set in the Asarian Resurrection Myth.[88] She is a goddess of protectiveness, a guardian against the evil of egoism and vice. She protects Aset (wisdom) by warding off (stinging) the ego. She poisons its illusions and imaginations. Think about a scorpion's power to inflict pain. Also think about its power of protection. In the story of Aset, Asar, and Heru, there is a part where after Asar is killed by Set, Djehuti, the messenger of wisdom of Ra, the Supreme Being, sends seven scorpions to guard Aset on her journey out of Egypt and away from Set who was trying to kill her and Heru. Mostly, we know of scorpions as dangerous creatures or hurtful creatures, something like snakes, however, there is another side to all these stories, and once we become acquainted with the deeper meanings behind the symbolic forms used in myths, we can then begin to discover the inner dimensions of the meditations and exercises of the mysteries.

The Goddess Selket assisted Aset in her time of sorrow over the death of Heru and Asar. She protected Aset and Heru from the evil of Set and was the voice of reason in the time of mental anguish. Actually, the scorpion symbol is a "water-scorpion," an insect that resembles the land-based scorpion. The water-scorpion is a predatory insect that grabs its victims and sucks out their bodily fluids. People

---

[88] See the book The Asarian Resurrection by Muata Ashby

157

should handle it carefully as its bite is painful. A water scorpion can hang upside down perfectly still for hours just waiting. It has a snorkel used for breathing so it can breathe and hunt at the same time. The symbolism of the water-scorpion brings out the special abilities necessary to access the goddess's power. An aspirant must be able to remain still for long periods and then be able to remain submerged in the waters of the Duat, higher plane, while the physical personality remains "breathing" in the physical world, as if through the snorkel of mind. This practice enables an aspirant to become immersed in the larger world of expanded consciousness and thereby discover the higher aspects of the spiritual personality.

Sesheta

Goddess Sesheta is the cosmic force that presides over the faculty of writing that is bringing ideas (cognition-thought) to a concrete form supported by the association with scripture and language. Chapter 19[89] verse 3 of the Pert m Heru text, *The Chapter of The Tree of Life: Breathing Air and Possessing Water in the Duat* provides insight into the nature of Sesheta.

3. Asar_____ maakheru is opening up in Djed[90]. Asar_____

---

[89] The translation for this chapter was based primarily on the Papyrus of Auf-Ankh and the *Papyrus of Ea* and is commonly referred to as #57. It is included here as representative of a genre of teachings found in similar chapters, specifically: Chapter 58: "Breathing Air and Possessing Water in Netherworld (Duat)"; Chapter 59 "Drinking Water in the Netherworld"; Chapter 60 "Another Chapter for the Same Purpose"; Chapter 61 "Another Chapter for the Same Purpose"; Chapter 62 "Another Chapter for the Same Purpose"; Chapter 63 "Drinking Water and Not Drying Up by Fire."

[90] The Pillar of Asar, metaphysically, the upper psycho-spiritual consciousness centers which awaken when a person becomes enlightened.

maakheru's nostrils are opening up in Djedu[91] in Hetep[92] the dwelling place in Anu, the house that was constructed by Sesheta, on which Khnum[93] is standing.

The brief text above signifies that through the discipline of writing the capacities of harmonization of the opposites (Hetep) and the psycho-spiritual consciousness centers (Djedu) are accessed (opened). One of the most important disciplines of the Kamitan priests and priestesses is to transcribe the medu neter. In ancient times this was done partly to maintain the texts themselves as papyrus paper has a finite life. However, there was another reason; to develop the mind, study the teachings and engender the development of higher consciousness through continuous study and reflection on the teaching.

Djehuti and Sesheta write the history and name of Rameses 2 on the tree of life.

Sesheta is the goddess of writing and counterpart of Djehuti. She is a divinity of priests and priestesses and scribes. She is also the presiding deity over the seven psycho-spiritual consciousness centers of spiritual enlightenment of the Serpent Power. She is also associated with the sacred *Persea Tree* on which the names of the kings were written at the time of coronation. She was the *"Recorder of Deeds," "Mistress of Books,"* and *"Reckoner of*

---

[91] The city of the Djed Pillar of Asar.

[92] Supreme Peace.

[93] The god who created human beings on his potter's wheel, "The Fashioner of Men and Women." Also, this word means "union."

time." The Persea Tree was associated with the goddess in the feline form who resided in the city of Anu (Heliopolis of the Greeks) and slew the demon serpent *Apepi,* who was the enemy of Ra and also of all souls. The terms *"Shetat"* or *"Seshetat"* are the secret rituals in the cults of the Egyptian Gods. Sesheta's writing of the mysteries creates a dwelling place for the initiate, a place wherein the opening of eternity is possible. In this house, constructed by the words of wisdom and the transformative power they have the Pillar (Seven psycho-spiritual centers of the subtle spine) of Asar is opened and the Creative force, Khnum (the god of the base of geographical Ancient Egypt), opens the floodgates of the subtle Nile, i.e. the flow of the Serpent Power out of the "house" (the energy center at the base of the spine) is opened. She is depicted as a woman with a headdress that is also the hieroglyph of her name, which is a stylized seven (or nine) pointed lotus flower on a standard that is held by a headband, all of which is beneath a set of horns that are down-turned. As her name is phonetically related to Sushen, "lotus," she is the scribe of the spirit. She also wears the leopard skin garment characteristic of *sem* priests and priestesses.

THE GODS OF THE SENSES

Above-Relief showing the gods of the senses (from the Temple of Heru at Djebu (Edfu))

Gods of the Senses

The senses are seen as instruments of the personality, used for perceiving information which in turn is transferred to the mind. The gods of the senses are, from left to right, *Saa* (touch, feeling and understanding) and *Hu* (taste and divine sustenance), *Maa* (sight) and *Sedjem* (hearing). *Hu* and *Saa* were known to serve as bearers of the Eye of Heru (enlightened consciousness). They were also considered to be the tongue and heart of *Asar-Ptah* (the Self). Thus, they represent the vehicles through

which human souls can experience and understand the teachings of moral and spiritual wisdom about the Self, i.e. the faculties of speech and intuitional understanding. When the senses adore the Divine Self as opposed to worldly objects and desires the personality is able to turn away from distractions in the world of time and space and the path is only then open for the spiritual evolution and success in the spiritual disciplines. In the scene below the senses turn "inwards" towards the boat of Khepri and not towards Creation. They assist the pharaoh (initiate - third from the left) to make the proper offering and thereby attain the higher consciousness.

The Sekhet Yaru and the Watcher, Herald and Gatekeeper gods

More advanced souls traverse to the Sekhet Yaru. This is the paradise for the worshipers of Asar, also known as the "House of Asar." It is the realm of heavenly enjoyments. All creation is a manifestation of the spirit in a sevenfold manner. The Sekhet Yaru is composed of seven sections known as *Arits* or "Mansions." They may be thought of as rooms within rooms or dimensions within dimensions or planes of existence within successively higher planes of existence. They relate to the seven energy centers of the subtle body of each individual human being as well as the seven Hetheru Cows, which are sired by Asar. Thus, the Spirit (Asar) engenders the seven aspects of Creation (the cows).

Watcher, Herald and Gatekeeper gods

Each Arit has a gate, and each gate has three attendants, a watcher, a herald and a gatekeeper. As an aspiring soul approaches the gate, the watcher takes notice, the herald announces that person's name and if the person knows the higher mystical truth, the gatekeeper allows entry. This teaching degraded in later times to the point where some people began to think that by simply memorizing the names of the attendants, they would be allowed access. Rather, one must know the higher mystical truth which unites one with the dweller within the abode of the house, that is, one must know and be ready to experience one's identity with Asar.

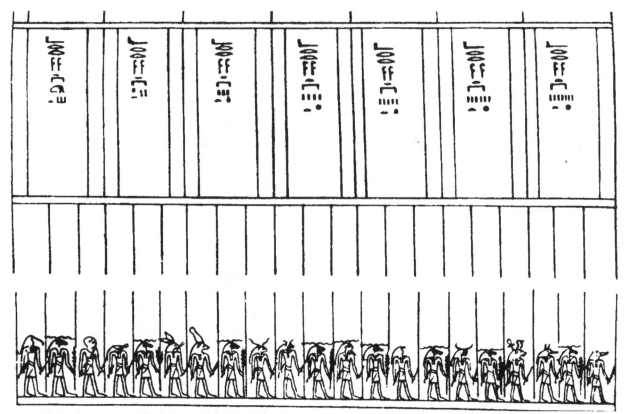

Above: Watcher, Herald and Gatekeeper gods in the seven Aats

Thus, throughout our study we have discovered the numbers 1, 3, 7, 14, 21 and 42. These numbers are important to the understanding of the abode of Asar. They include the number of entrances to the house, which are seven, the number of *Aats* or regions of the Duat, which are fourteen, and the number of principles to be transcended in order to gain entry at any entrance, three. The number 42 is a multiple of 7, and the number of precepts of Maat, as well as the body parts of Asar and the nomes (original cities of Ancient Egypt). The supreme abode being entered into is the One, singular, supreme and transcendental essence, Asar himself. Asar is the singular divinity, the one, expressing as the seven openings, each of which manifest through three modes or a trinity or triad of existence. In total, there are seven watcher, herald and gatekeeper trinities to be transcended because there are three personalities at each gate of the seven entrances, totaling 21 principles. However, this need not be a daunting task since all that is necessary is to understand the principle of the trinity itself. When this is accomplished, all trinities are transcended easily. This trinity may be likened to the teaching that is derived from the Kamitan teaching related to *Neberdjer: Amun-Ra-Ptah,* that is, the Absolute who manifests as the seer, the instrument of seeing and that which is seen.

The Watcher is that aspect which sees (seer) and takes notice, the witness. The Herald is the instrument of acknowledging what has been seen. The Gatekeeper is the element which is seen, and which needs to be satisfied that the aspirant is worthy of gaining entry. The Gatekeeper receives information from the Watcher, who takes notice of those approaching, and then, depending on the determination of the Herald who announces whether or not the person whom the Watcher has seen is authorized (worthy) to enter or not, takes the appropriate action. Each aspect of the trinity (Watcher, Herald and Gatekeeper) should be seen not as independent personalities, but as aspects of one, having the sense of sight, speech and organs of action (hands to open the gate). Knowing the truth about the singular being whose gate they are protecting, allows or legitimizes one to gain entry into the house. It is like going to the mansion of an important person, if one were to tell the guard at the gate that they personally know the person who lives there, once this is verified, that person will be allowed entry without obstruction. Thus, by uniting the trinity into its underlying basic singularity, one enters into the abode of Asar, who is beyond the trinity.

The Four Sons of Heru and the Four Protection Goddesses

Above: Heru and his four sons, who are all armed with knives, stand before Asar and Asar-Hapi (Serapis-bull form of Asar). They are presenting the defeated body of Set, here represented as a man with the head of the Set-animal. The four gods are identified with the *Auf-afdu* - four gods who do battle against evil of Set

Vignette for Chapter 15, Auf-Ankh, the initiate propitiates to the heart while adoring the four sons of Heru.

The four sons of Heru are a prominent aspect of Heruian philosophy. They represent four important aspects of physical existence that when harnessed become a formidable and overwhelming power to overcome the vicissitudes of life especially when confronting the vices of the ego within. The following passages from the Pert m Heru text[94] provide insights into the nature of the Sons of Heru and their position in relation to him and the aspirant in the course of the struggle for spiritual evolution and liberation from Set (ego consciousness).

The four sons of Heru are support/protector divinities. They assist in promoting health and stamina of body and mind for the struggle against the forces of chaos, unrighteousness and decay.

Mseti,   Hapy,   Duamutf,   Kebsenuf

At the time of death the organs presided over by each divinity were placed in a jar and then the jars were kept in a chest for safekeeping. The four sons of Heru also represent the four directions of the compass, i.e. physical existence.

Mseti is the protector of the liver. He is presented anthropomorphically, with a man's (human) head whereas the other sons are presented zoomorphically. Mseti represents the South direction.

Hapi is the protector of the lungs and the flow of air and life force. He is presented with the head of a baboon, which is a relation to the god Djehuti who also has a baboon aspect. In this aspect he is the quintessential spiritual preceptor to the goddess Hetheru in the Myth of Hetheru and Djehuti.[95] Hapy represents the North direction.

Duamutf is the protector of the stomach. He is presented with the head of a jackal which is a relation to the god Anpu, the divinity of right reasoning. Duamutf represents the West direction.

Kebsenuf is the protector of the intestines. He is presented with the head of a falcon which is a relation to the god Heru, the divinity of irresistible force and spiritual redemption who tirelessly persists onward to success. In the same way, Kebsenuf promotes stamina and strength through efficient assimilation. Kebsenuf represents the East direction.

The four sons of Heru are identified with the *Souls of Pe and Nekhen,* Followers of Heru. They are also identified with the cardinal points in circular movement: Mseti (West-facing south), Hapy (East-facing North), Duamutf (North-facing West), and Kebsenuf (South-facing East). The text of Pepi I (Pyramid Texts) states that the spiritual aspirant is to ***"become one of the four gods-(i.e. a son of Heru)"***:

---

[94] CHAPTER 4 The Wisdom of the Secret Identity of the Gods and goddesses (Generally referred to as Chapter 17)

[95] See the book Theater and The performing Arts in the Ancient Egyptian Mysteries by Muata Ashby

In the Pert M Heru Text there are references to the Shemsu Heru. The four sons of Heru are recognized as the foremost Shemsu Heru in the Dynastic Period and were the most widely recorded ichnographically. But they are associated with another group. That group is composed of the four plus another three. Together they are known as the "Seven Sages." The Followers of Heru are also associated with the **Shebtiu** or "builder gods" –divinities who assist in building temples. So they were keepers of the traditions of the temple and upholders of the ancient traditions for future generations.

The following passages from the Prt M Hru Chapter 4[96] *The Wisdom of the Secret Identity of the Gods and Goddesses* provide further insight into the nature of the sons of Heru and the identity of other lesser-known divinities.

21- *They are Mseti, Hapy, Duamutf, and Kebsenuf.[97] Homage to you Lords of Maat, divine beings behind Asar, givers of purity, the cutting away of wrongdoing to those who are within the following of Hetep-Sech-us[98]. Grant ye to me that I may come into your presence. Destroy all wrongs for me just as you did for those seven[99] Akhus in the following of their Lord Sepa[100]. Lord Anpu made a place for them on the day when they came to thee. Who are these persons that are speaking about Asar?*

22- *As to these all, Maat and Djehuti, they are with Isdesba[101] Lord of Amentet. As to the divine beings behind Asar, they are again Mseti, Hapy, Duamutf, and Kebsenuf. They are behind the Chepesh[102] in the northern heavens. As to the givers of cutting away of unrighteousness within the followers of goddess Hetep-Sech-us, it is the god Sebek who is within the primeval waters. As to goddess Hetep-Sech-us, she is the Eye of Ra. Another way to understand this is: She is the ever-present fire in the following of Asar and she makes the souls of his enemies to burn. As to the impurities, they are under the control of Asar who makes offerings to all the gods and goddesses and who is maak-heru since coming down from {his/her} mother. As to those seven divine, glorious spirits, they are: Mseti, Hapy, Duamutf, Kebsenuf, Maa-itf,[103] Cherybqef,[104] and Herukhenty-maa[105]. They were set up by the god Anpu as protectors of the mummy of Asar. Another way to understand this is: they were set up behind the cleansing place of Asar. Another way to understand this is: the seven spirits are 1-Nedjhnedjh,[106] 2-Iaqeduqedu,[107] 3-Yanerdinefb-f Khentyh-h-f,[108] 4-Aqherimyunut-f,[109] 5-Dsher-maa-immyhetinesu,[110] 6-Ubensherperemtechtech,[111] and 7-Maaemgerhinnefemheru.[112]*

The Four Goddesses of Protection

The four sons of Heru are complemented by three goddesses. The goddesses are Nebethet, Aset, Net and Serqet.

Sons of Heru	Complement	Goddesses of the House of Life
Mseti	⇔	Aset (A)
Hapy	⇔	Nebthet (B)
Duamutf	⇔	Net (C)
Kebsenuf	⇔	Selket (D)

---

[96] Generally referred to as Chapter 17.

[97] The four sons of Heru, his foremost followers.

[98] The serpent goddess as the Eye of Ra in her aspect as destroyer of the enemies of Asar and whose purifying effect allows spiritual aspirants to enter Ianrutf.

[99] The god Anpu (Anubis) appointed seven spirits to follow and protect the initiate.

[100] Centipede god who has the power to prevent snake bites.

[101] A protector god in the Company of Gods and Goddesses of Djehuti.

[102] Big Dipper, common name applied to a conspicuous constellation in the northern celestial hemisphere, near the North Pole. It was known to the ancient Greeks as the Bear and the Wagon and to the Romans as Ursa Major (the Great Bear) and Septentriones (Seven Plowing Oxen). The seven brightest stars of the constellation form the easily identified outline of a giant dipper. To the Hindus, it represents the seven Rishis, or holy ancient Sages. "Big Dipper," Microsoft (R) Encarta. Copyright (c) 1994 Microsoft Corporation. Copyright (c) 1994 Funk & Wagnall's Corporation. See the gloss to this verse, also see "Opening of the Mouth" Chapter 11 and its Gloss.

[103] He who sees his father.

[104] He who is under the moringa tree.

[105] Heru the foremost seer.

[106] The Protector.

[107] The One who revolves.

[108] One who does not give to him a flame to he who is foremost in the eternal fire.

[109] The one who goes into him at the appointed time.

[110] The red eyed one who is in the house of red clothing.

[111] The one who shines going forth as after coming back.

[112] One who can see at night and what will be brought to him during the day.

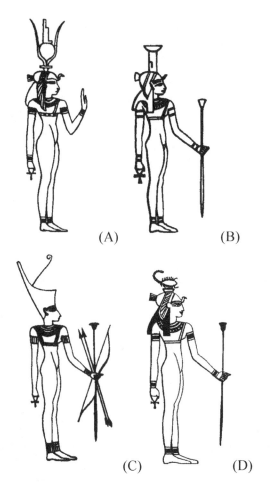

(A)   (B)

(C)   (D)

As to these all, Maat and Djehuti, they are with Isdesba[114] Lord of Amentet. As to the divine beings behind Asar, they are again Mseti, Hapy, Duamutf, and Kebsenuf. They are behind the Chepesh[115] in the northern heavens.

From Prt M Hru Chap. 4, V. 22

Together, the four gods and four goddesses promote the health and efficient operation of the organs so that the personality may enjoy physical health and be able to gain positive experiences in the realm of time and space.

The Chepesh has important mystical symbolism. Mythically it represents the foreleg of the god Set which was torn out and thrown into the heavens by the god Heru during their epic battle. A similar teaching occurs in the later Babylonian epic of Gilgemesh[116\117] when the *"foreleg of the Bull of Heaven"* is ripped out and thrown at the goddess Ishtar, who was the goddess or Queen of Heaven in Mesopotamia. It symbolizes the male generative capacity and is one of the offerings of Hetep given in Chapter 36[118] of the Pert M Heru (Egyptian Book of the Dead). Its cosmic and mystical implications provide us with insight into Kamitan philosophy as well as ancient history. The Akhemu Seku and Akhemu Urdu are celestial bodies but also divinities that bring further insight into the nature of the Divine and the philosophy of Shetaut Neter through Neterian Astronomy.

Akhemu Seku - never setting stars – imperishable

Akhemu Urdu - never resting stars – setting

Opening of the Mouth with the Imperishable Stars and Celestial Divinities

In the Hermetic Texts, which are the later development in Ancient Egyptian scripture, Hermes, the Greek name ascribed to the Ancient Egyptian god Djehuti, states to his pupil Asclepius (Egyptian Imhotep) that: *"Did you know, O Asclepius, that Egypt is made in the image of heaven?"*[113] The Ancient Egyptian Pyramid Texts and the Pert M Heru (Book of Enlightenment) texts contain more references to stellar mysticism. The stellar symbolism of Ancient Egypt relates to the passage of time but also to mystical awakening and spiritual realization.

Ishtar was an aspect of the Ancient Egyptian goddesses Net and Hetheru. Ishtar was the chief goddess of the Babylonians and the Assyrians and the

[114] A protector god in the Company of Gods and Goddesses of Djehuti.

[115] Big Dipper, common name applied to a conspicuous constellation in the northern celestial hemisphere, near the North Pole. It was known to the ancient Greeks as the Bear and the Wagon and to the Romans as Ursa Major (the Great Bear) and Septentriones (Seven Plowing Oxen). The seven brightest stars of the constellation form the easily identified outline of a giant dipper. To the Hindus, it represents the seven Rishis, or holy ancient Sages. "Big Dipper," Microsoft (R) Encarta. Copyright (c) 1994 Microsoft Corporation. Copyright (c) 1994 Funk & Wagnall's Corporation.

[116] Col. V. 1, 161

[117] **Gilgamesh,** legendary king of Babylonia, hero of an epic poem written on clay tablets, found in the ruins of Nineveh; epic has affinities with Old Testament, contains story of the flood. Excerpted from *Compton's Interactive Encyclopedia.* Copyright (c) 1994, 1995

[118] usually referred to as #30B

[113] *Hermetica,* Asclepius III, Solos Press ed., p. 136

counterpart of the Phoenician goddess, Astarte. Astarte, like the Kamitan goddess Hetheru, was represented by a crescent, symbolic of the moon and the horns of a cow. The name appeared as Athtar in Arabia, Astar in Abyssinia (now Ethiopia), and Ashtart in Canaan and Israel. Like the Ancient Egyptian goddess Net, the prototype for all the androgynous Creatoress-War Goddesses of Nubia and Arabia, the sex of the divinity also varied: Athtar and Astar were male deities. Ishtar of Erech (in Babylonia) was a goddess worshiped in connection with the evening star, but Ishtar of Akkad (also in Babylonia) was a god identified with the morning star.[119] Like Net of Ancient Egypt, Ishtar was the Great Goddess, Great Mother, and the goddess of fertility and the queen of heaven. Like Net of Ancient Egypt, she was depicted as a goddess of hunting and war and was depicted with sword, bow, and quiver of arrows. Among the Babylonians, Ishtar was distinctly the Mother Goddess and was portrayed either naked and with prominent breasts, or like Aset of Ancient Egypt, as a mother with a child at her breast. She also corresponded to the Greek Aphrodite, the "Great Mother," goddess of fertility, love and war,[120] who was also known to the Greeks as Hathor (Hetheru of Kamit).[121]

Also, in ancient times the Chepesh symbol represented the "Northern path" of spiritual evolution. Since the constellation of the Ursa Major ("Great Bear" or "Big Dipper"), known to the Ancient Egyptians as "Meskhetiu," contains **seven** stars and occupied the location referred to as the "Pole Star." As it occupies the pole position it does not move, while all the other stars in the sky circle around it. This constellation, whose symbol is the foreleg, ⌐◣, was thus referred to as "the imperishables" in the earlier Pyramid Texts: *"He (the king-enlightened initiate) climbs to the sky among the imperishable stars."[122]*

The stars in the heavens are also considered as souls that have passed on from the earthly plane. Those souls who remain as unchanging are the *Shepsu,* ⬚𓀭𓏏𓏭 noble, enlightened beings who

have now become spirit-divinities (𓄿⊙𓃀𓏭⎹ *Akhu*). Those who are changing, who rise and fall as the earth turns on its axis and who fall out of view only to rise again on the other horizon are the *Ankhu*, the living, because they will reincarnate, to live again on earth. Goddess Nut, who is the sky itself, lifts up those souls who have been resurrected as Asar and they join her in the sky to light the way for mortal human beings.

PHARAOH – THE DIVINE RULER

The Pharaoh is regarded as a divinity but not in the sense of an ordinary god or goddess. He or She is actually a human being but also the heir to a divine inheritance, entrusted with the management of the physical realm. This is one of the oldest traditions of Kushite-Kamitan-Neterian (Secular-religious) culture. The Pharaoh is entrusted with power to rule over the land and provide for the needs of the people with the blessing of the Divine and with the permission of the Divine. Men or women could hold the power of Pharaonic rulership. The succession of rulership descends through the line of divinities leading to the Pharaoh. Ra was the first king after he created the world. Then Shu took over and after him Geb became king. Then Geb gave rulership to his son Asar. Asar was murdered by Set and Set became king until he was challenged by Heru-ur. Heru-ur vanquished Set and became king. Heru-ur and his consort, goddess *Tasenetnofret* (aspect of Hetheru) had a child, *Panebtawy.* Panebtawy means "The Lord of the Two Lands." Panebtawy is the divine child who grows up to be the ruler of Egypt. Therefore, all Pharaohs are recognized as being Panebtawys, i.e. as manifestations of Heru on earth. So when the ruler is alive on earth he or she is referred to as *Panebtawy* (Heru-lord of the earth). When the ruler dies they are referred to as Asar (resurrected) and their own heir takes over as the new Panebtawy, i.e. Heru-Ur. Asar assimilates into Geb and Ra in the form of the *Benuu*. So the soul reverts back to its original essence from the earth to the heavens.

---

[119] "Ishtar," Microsoft (R) Encarta. Copyright (c) 1994 Microsoft Corporation. Copyright (c) 1994 Funk & Wagnall's Corporation.

[120] Excerpted from *Compton's Interactive Encyclopedia.* Copyright (c) 1994, 1995 Compton's NewMedia, Inc. All Rights Reserved

[121] see the book *From Egypt to Greece* by Muata Ashby

[122] Pyramid Texts 1120-23. *Egyptian Mysteries,* Lucie Lamy

On previous page: Queen Nefertiti in warrior pose

One striking form of symbolism that is seen from the beginning to the end of the Ancient Egyptian history is the Sphinx/Pharaonic Leonine headdress.

(A-C)

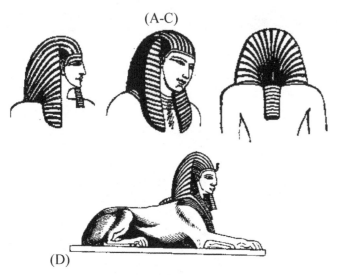

(D)

Above (A-C) - The Heru-m-akhet (Sphinx) Pharaonic headdress.[123]

Above (D)- Drawing of the Sphinx from a sculpture in Egypt

The Great Sphinx of Ancient Egypt-shows the predynastic Pharaonic headdress popularized in later classical Dynastic times. It imitates the leonine mane and the lion power of Herukhuti (Ra as Heru of the two horizons).

The crown of Lower Egypt (Nile delta region) left, and the Crown of Upper Egypt (the south) come together as one crown that combines the two lands into one sovereignty.

Heru presides over the totality of life, the unity over the opposites of Creation and the human consciousness (Heru-virtue, Set-vice). This form was also associated with Ra and Hetheru as their son.

The Pharaonic crown of Egypt indicates the rulership of the two lands of Egypt, i.e. the north and the south. The north has the red crown and the south has the white crown. A study of the esoteric nature of color provides insight into the choice of color for the crown of the pharaoh.

The color spectrum ranges, in order, from violet, through blue, green, yellow, and orange, to red.[124] The colors red and white hold special mystical significance, and this is why we see so many Ancient Egyptian couples represented by them, with the men painted reddish-brown and the women painted yellow or fully white. In color therapy, an art practiced in modern times as well as in Ancient Egypt,[125] the color red is understood as being an agitating or exciting (stimulating) color to the mind. White, on the other hand was considered in Ancient Egypt as soothing,[126] as the red male Hippo was considered violent, mischievous and destructive while the female was considered calm and helpful. Blue is considered as being soothing and relaxing to the mind. Mystically, red and white complement each other, as red symbolizes sexual potency or virility, and white, having the capacity to reflect all colors,[127] symbolizes pregnancy and potential. This is why the Kamitan Peraahs (Pharaohs)[128] wear the double crown, consisting of red and white elements.

There were two periods of development in the Pharaonic system of rule in northeast Africa. The first developed prior to 10,000 B.C.E. as attested by the headdress of the Great Sphinx and the legend of Asar as related in the Asarian Resurrection myth and supported by the history of Manetho (Ancient Egyptian priest-historian of the Late Period), and Diodorus. The second period is the late Pre-Dynastic Period (prior to 5000 B.C.E.). As introduced earlier, there is evidence that the Pharaonic system of rule (kings and queens as spiritual leaders-head of religion) emerged in the Pre-Dynastic Period. In Egypt the Pharaonic system developed into an empire when the "two lands" (Upper and Lower Egypt) were consolidated and later the empire encompassed, the lands now known as Asia Minor, Lower Europe and India. Egypt had 42 monarchies (referred to as nomarchs since they ruled over nomes or municipalities), but what made the Pharaonic rule

---

[123] These illustrations appeared in the book _The Ancient Egyptians: Their Life and Customs_-Sir J. Garner Wilkinson 1854 A.C.E.

[124] _Compton's Interactive Encyclopedia._ Copyright (c) 1994, 1995
[125] Copyright © 1995 Helicon Publishing Ltd Webster Encyclopedia
[126] Gods and Symbols of Ancient Egypt by Manfred Lurker
[127] _Compton's Interactive Encyclopedia._ Copyright (c) 1994, 1995
[128] The term "Pharaoh" is a biblical (Hebrew-Jewish) translation oh the original Ancient Egyptian word "Per-aah".

different is that it was rulership that united all of the separate nomes under one ruler, an Emperor (Pharaoh).

So the Peraah (Pharaoh) might be a man or woman and was not just a king or queen, but also an emperor. When we speak of a breakdown in the Pharaonic rule in the times when Egypt was not completely overpowered, we are only speaking of the loss of Pharaonic rule as an empire and not necessarily a total crash of the society. It would be as if the President of a country lost power temporarily over some sections of the country but the governors of the cities or states remained in power, and later cooperated to bring back order by pooling resources such as personnel and material in order to rebuild the central government. This is what happened during the invasions of the Hyksos as well as the Assyrians and Persians. This was the state of

affairs during the "intermediate" periods between the Old and Middle Kingdom Periods and between the Middle and New Kingdoms. The Ancient Egyptians were not strong enough to overcome the second Assyrian invasion, and there was never a second opportunity to overthrow them since Alexander the Great defeated them and took their place. There was still not enough strength to overcome the Greeks, but also there was lesser imperative, since they upheld the Egyptian culture and religion. Thus the Egyptian culture remained relatively intact under the Greeks as compared to the conditions imposed by the Persians and Assyrians. These conditions would not remain the same under the control by the Roman-Christians and the later Arab-Muslims who came from Asia Minor, conquered Egypt and actively sought to stamp out the old religion. Nubia was the last place, in ancient times, where the Neterian religion was practiced, to generally convert to Judaism, Christianity and Islam. Today, the Nubians living in southern Egypt consider themselves ethnically as Nubian, and at the same time nationally as Egyptian, and spiritually as Muslim.

Uas and Uaset

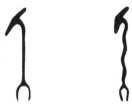

Three of the most important symbols which Ptah is associated with are the *Uas, Ankh* and the Djed.

The *Uas* scepter, ⌇ , is a symbol of "power" and "dominion" which many of the gods and pharaohs may be seen holding. It is composed of a straight shaft with the head of a mythical animal associated with the God *Set* (Seth), who represents egoism, evil and ignorance as well as raw power and brute strength.

The *Uas* or *Was* symbol represents the energy which engenders life. When this energy is controlled by the ignorant ego, evil, negative activity, restlessness, agitation and unrest are the result. When the same energy is sublimated and controlled, divine work can be accomplished in a most effective and exalted manner. Thus, any being who holds the *Was* is in control of the source and power of the Soul. It means having dominion over one's desires and passions, and being free from delusion and ignorance as to one's true nature. In a historical, political or exoteric sense, this implies being the pharaoh who resides in Waset. However, the esoteric symbolism implies that the possessor of the *Uas* is in communion with the Supreme Ruler of *Waset,* who is none other than Amun, the Divine Self. Thus, the *Was* scepter was the emblem of Waset as well as the head ornament of the goddess of the city itself, who was also known as *Waset.* Thus, *Uas* or *Was* may be considered as having a male aspect and a female aspect but in the deeper sense it represents a form of power.

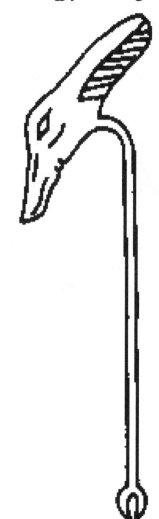

Chapter 5: Instruments of the Gods and Goddesses: Headdresses, Scepters and Weapons for Spiritual Enlightenment

Most Important Headdresses of the Ancient Egyptian Deities

The headdress of the neteru offer a visible emblem of what the particular divinity symbolizes or represents. The Neteru (divinities) all represent certain powers of Creation, which emanate from the Supreme Being. If their powers are understood and propitiated and worshipped, those powers can be caused to serve the petitioner. The Headdress denotes the main principle manifested in the divinity. So the headdress is a way of knowing identity as well as the nature of the divinities but also if the headdress is adopted, that is placed on ones head, one is adopting the nature and essence of the divinity. Here is a list of the most common headdresses or crowns of the deities of Ancient Kamit:

Amentet –Personification of the Western Horizon and the divine abode of elevated souls. She wears a standard upon which Heru sits . Goddess Hetheru is sometimes represented with this standard.

Amun- Divinity usually depicted as a man (anthropomorphic) wearing a headdress that has two tall plumes rising from a short crown. The sundisk may be added in between the plumes, denoting his form as Amun-Ra. The god Heru may also be seen wearing the headdress of Amun, thus, relating him to Wasetian (Theban) theology. The plumes represent Aset and Nebethet, the Maati goddesses, and Uadjit and Nekhebet. Thus, this is another form of the Neterian caduceus and the mystical trinity, like Asar, Aset and Nebethet or Ra and Nebethotep and Iusaasety.

Anqit -The goddess Anqit is often seen wearing a tall headdress of ostrich feathers or reeds. This headdress denotes a Nubian origin and the meaning of her name is "to surround."

Asar- (Osiris) is generally depicted as a black or green skin colored man wearing the *atef* crown on his head . The *Atef* crown unites the plumes of Amun, the sundisk, the crown of Upper Egypt and the ram horns of Khnum. Thus it is an all-encompassing crown uniting the ancient tradition of Kamit into one personification. The Atef crown was worn by his father Geb and also Ra.

Aset- (Isis) The goddess Aset wears the headdress of the throne . This is the divine throne, the abode of the king and in a higher sense the abode of Asar, the soul and divine consciousness. She may also be seen wearing the cow horns and also she may be seen with the vulture headdress. Thus she is an aspect of Hetheru and Mut respectively.

Atum –The god Atum is usually depicted as a human man (anthropomorphic) wearing the double crown of Upper and Lower Egypt , *Pschent,* which symbolizes rulership over the entire empire and in a higher sense, over the duality of Creation. The god Heru may also be seen wearing the headdress of Amun. The Pharaoh (king) also may be seen wearing this crown as ruler of the "two lands" (Upper and Lower Kamit).

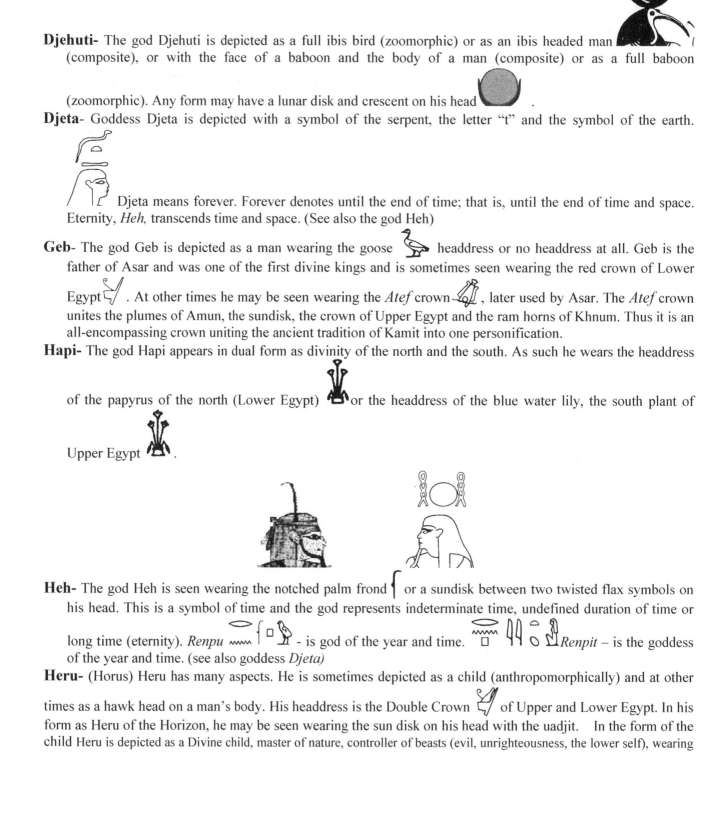

Djehuti- The god Djehuti is depicted as a full ibis bird (zoomorphic) or as an ibis headed man (composite), or with the face of a baboon and the body of a man (composite) or as a full baboon (zoomorphic). Any form may have a lunar disk and crescent on his head   .

Djeta- Goddess Djeta is depicted with a symbol of the serpent, the letter "t" and the symbol of the earth.

Djeta means forever. Forever denotes until the end of time; that is, until the end of time and space. Eternity, *Heh,* transcends time and space. (See also the god Heh)

Geb- The god Geb is depicted as a man wearing the goose   headdress or no headdress at all. Geb is the father of Asar and was one of the first divine kings and is sometimes seen wearing the red crown of Lower Egypt   . At other times he may be seen wearing the *Atef* crown   , later used by Asar. The *Atef* crown unites the plumes of Amun, the sundisk, the crown of Upper Egypt and the ram horns of Khnum. Thus it is an all-encompassing crown uniting the ancient tradition of Kamit into one personification.

Hapi- The god Hapi appears in dual form as divinity of the north and the south. As such he wears the headdress of the papyrus of the north (Lower Egypt)   or the headdress of the blue water lily, the south plant of

Upper Egypt   .

Heh- The god Heh is seen wearing the notched palm frond   or a sundisk between two twisted flax symbols on his head. This is a symbol of time and the god represents indeterminate time, undefined duration of time or long time (eternity). *Renpu*   - is god of the year and time.   *Renpit* – is the goddess of the year and time. (see also goddess *Djeta)*

Heru- (Horus) Heru has many aspects. He is sometimes depicted as a child (anthropomorphically) and at other times as a hawk head on a man's body. His headdress is the Double Crown   of Upper and Lower Egypt. In his form as Heru of the Horizon, he may be seen wearing the sun disk on his head with the uadjit.   In the form of the child Heru is depicted as a Divine child, master of nature, controller of beasts (evil, unrighteousness, the lower self), wearing

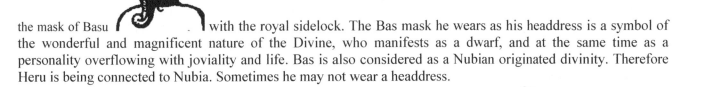

the mask of Basu with the royal sidelock. The Bas mask he wears as his headdress is a symbol of the wonderful and magnificent nature of the Divine, who manifests as a dwarf, and at the same time as a personality overflowing with joviality and life. Bas is also considered as a Nubian originated divinity. Therefore Heru is being connected to Nubia. Sometimes he may not wear a headdress.

Hetheru- The goddess Hetheru is often depicted as a woman (anthropomorphic) with horns of a cow and/or with plumes or/and the vulture (see Mut), and sometimes as a woman with the head of a cow and with horns of a cow that has the sun between them, or also often as a cow wearing the sun disk between her horns. The horns symbolize duality and the sun symbolizes oneness (nonduality) and together they are the trinity. Also, the sun symbolizes the right eye of Ra, which is another aspect of the goddess herself.

Khepri -(Khepera). The God Khepri is most important because he is the Creator who gave rise to Creation and living beings including human beings and the gods and goddesses. He is presented as a man with a scarab for a head of as a frog headed man with a scarab on its head. Khepri is an aspect of the Trinity Khepri-Ra-Atum.

Khonsu –The god Khonsu is usually depicted as a young man or a hawk headed man wearing a crescent and lunar disk on his head. The God Djehuti and Yah, both moon-related deities, also wear the lunar headdress. Khonsu also wears a sidelock. The sidelock is a symbol of youth but also of royalty. It is a symbol of a prince.

Maat- The goddess Maat is shown as a woman wearing an ostrich feather held by a headband - the feather of Maat symbolizes truth, balance, non-violence, order, justice, peace and freedom.

Min- The god Min or Amsu-Min is depicted as a man wearing a crown with twin plumes like those of Amun and Hetheru. Sometimes he is depicted also with a long ribbon that trails down to his feet.

Mut -The goddess Mut is often depicted wearing the vulture  headdress of the New Kingdom queens or the double crown of Egypt. She wore the vulture crown because it symbolizes the power of the vulture to turn carrion into life essence and there is a link between the name for mother in Egyptian and her name. The two words are both *mwt*. In Southern Africa, the name for an Egyptian vulture is synonymous with the term applied to lovers, for vultures like pigeons are always seen in pairs.[129] Thus mother and child remain closely bonded together. The wide wingspan of a vulture may be seen as all encompassing and providing a protective cover to its infants. The vulture when carrying out its role as a mother and giving protection to its infants may exhibit a forceful nature whilst defending her young. All these qualities inspired the imagination of the Ancient Egyptians.

Nefertum- The God Nefertum was depicted as a attractive and captivating young man wearing the lotus flower *(Seshen - the Blue Water Lily)* on his head. The lotus flower is the floral symbol of Upper Egypt. It is related to the sun, and to healing, sensuality and the power of creation as well as perfume and vitality.

Nat- (Net Anet, Anat (Neith to the Greeks)) the goddess Nat may wear the hawk, the crown of Lower Egypt or the weaving spool. Also she may wear the shield that has two crossed arrows, or the red crown of Lower Egypt. Sometimes she is seen wearing a skullcap similar to that of Ptah. The shield represents protection from injury and crossed arrows, neutralization of duality.

Nebethet – The goddess wears the headdress composed of the glyph for "mistress" and "house" i.e. 'Mistress of the House': so she is the controller of the abode. As she represents the opposite of goddess Aset, the higher wisdom, Nebethet represents the "Lower Wisdom," the knowledge of the world, the time and space reality, mortality and that which is finite.

Nut –The goddess Nut is sometimes portrayed as a woman wearing sign for container. She contains the heavens, the outer space, the higher ether.

Ptah – The god Ptah is depicted as a mummified man with a false beard, who wears a close fitting skullcap which exposes only his ears and face. A golden statue of Ptah was discovered in the tomb of Tutankhamen and it has a blue faience cap on its head. The mummification symbolism ties Ptah with Asar in death and resurrection. The blue skullcap represents priesthood and also transcendental consciousness, which ties Ptah to Amun who is depicted with a blue-black body.

Ra, Ra-Herakhti- Ra is one of the most important Kamitan divinities. As the father of the gods and goddesses of Anunian Theology he is the source of the divinities and people. His main headdress symbol if the sundisk encircled by the Serpent. The sundisk is his eye of power, the right eye through which the life force comes in to time and space to sustain life. The serpent goddess Hetheru encircles the sundisk and is also

---

[129] *Ma-Wetu, The Kiswahili-Bantu Research Unit for the Advancement of the Ancient Egyptian Language.*

known as (*Maa-Heru* - Fiery flash from eye of Heru) spits out sunrays like venom, which can nourish life or destroy demons. The serpent also symbolizes immortality, as it makes a full circuit around the sundisk and also it sheds its skin, it symbolizes rebirth and immortality. Ra is an aspect of the Trinity Khepri-Ra-Atum.

Sati or Satit is often depicted wearing long antelope horns and the crown of the south - Upper Egypt . The crown also has a vulture's head and tail coming out from it, uniting her to the mother goddesses (Nut, Mut, Aset, Hetheru, etc) of Egypt.

Serqet is often depicted as a woman with a scorpion as her headdress. She was also shown wearing the headdress of Hetheru, cow horns with solar disk. Actually, the scorpion symbol is a "water-scorpion," an insect that resembles the land-based scorpion. The water-scorpion is a predatory insect that grabs its victims and sucks out their bodily fluids. People should handle it carefully as its bite is painful. A water scorpion can hang upside down perfectly still for hours just waiting. It has a snorkel used for breathing so it can breathe and hunt at the same time.

Sesheta or Seshat is depicted as a woman with a headdress that is also the hieroglyph of her name, which is a stylized seven (or nine) pointed flower on a standard that is held by a headband, all of which is beneath a set of horns that are down-turned. As her name is phonetically related to Sushen, "lotus," she is the scribe of the spirit.

Shesmu, is a God or a Demon-depending on his particular function. He is closely associated with the God Asar as his servant. As a God he presides over the Wine Press, Oils and as a Demon he carries out the function of Slaughterer of the Damned. Shesmu is shown as a man on a boat holding an uas scepter with a uraeus on top of his head.

Shu was usually shown as a man wearing an ostrich feather as his headdress. Sometimes he wore the sun disk on his head. The feather is the same feather of **Maat**, the ostrich feather. His name is derived from the word *shu,* dryness, which is also the root of the words 'parched', 'dry', 'withered', 'empty' and 'sunlight'. His name also has the meaning *'He who Rises Up'.*

Uadjit- The goddess Uadjit is shown as a woman who wears the crown of Lower Egypt or with a cobra on her head. As one of the pharaoh's - *nebty* ('Two Ladies')- she is the goddess of Lower Egypt. Later in history the crown of Lower Egypt was combined with the vulture.

Waset- The goddess Waset or Uaset wears the *uas (was)* symbol. She is the symbol of the west and the personification of the flow of life force energy as well as the power over the abode of blessedness, the western district where the sun sets in heaven, the goal of all aspirants.

THE SCEPTERS OF THE GODS AND GODDESSES

also holds the crook and the flail. (7) The god Bennu holds the uas scepter. (8) The goddess Uachet (Uadjit) holds the papyrus scepters intertwined by the serpent. She has the power of vegetation and the serpent. (9) The god Khonsu holds the palm frond as does goddess Sesheta. Other divinities who are presented with the same scepters control the same powers along with the specific aspects denoted by their particular iconography and energetic personification.

The Neteru use a variety of scepters. The scepters are related to the qualities of the divinity and the potential energies implicit in their powers. The scepters are also artifacts used as conduits to control and project the powers controlled by the divinity. (1) Goddess Sekhmit holds two serpents as her scepters. These relate to the serpent power, which is one of the goddesses primary principles. (2) Goddess Sesheta holds a palm frond on which she records the events of time and space. (3) Goddess Nekhebet holds a lotus scepter intertwined by the serpent. This implies the power of Upper Egypt and the mystic qualities of the lotus and the serpent. (4) Goddess Meskhent holds a papyrus scepter. This relates to the qualities of vegetation, nourishment and greenery. (5) The god Khonsu holds a composite scepter (crook, flail, djed, ankh and uas). This relates to his control over the powers of royalty, resurrection and the source of life force. (6) The god Asar

MAIN WEAPONS OF THE NETERU

Interesting and important aspects of the regalia of the Neteru are certain objects that some of them carry. These objects are ordinarily considered as weapons. However, from a mystical standpoint they have a very atypical function. In Kamitan myth it is related that the god Asar traveled the world to establish order, the worship of the Divine, agriculture and peace. However, there is one part of the saga that relates how he was confronted with evil and the following excerpt from Diodorus provides a description of those events.

Osiris (Asar) was not warlike, nor did he have to organize pitched battles or engagements, since every people received him as a god because of his benefactions...

In Thrace he slew Lycurgus, the king of the barbarians.

Lycurgus was an evil, demoniac personality who used to, when he met wandering wayfarers, have them bound and dragged to his house, and then sacrificed to *Ares* (Greek god of war); they were cut to pieces, and he took their extremities to decorate his gates. Clearly there is a legitimate purpose for weapons. They are to be used to protect what is right and true. Not for imposing one's will on others but to protect life and establish order or to protect order from chaos. In this manner a soldier should protect his/her country but not impose his/her country's will on others. Police and law enforcement should use weapons to protect truth and life and not to act as enforcers of state sponsored terrorism, capitalist economic subjugation or any other form of injustice.

The gods and goddesses use their weapons to vanquish demons and all forms of unrighteousness. The nature of the weapon denotes its function and the type of demon it is used against. Therefore, the weapons of the Neteru are the instruments that they use to oppose the forces of iniquity. Therefore, when a divinity is propitiated and invoked it is this power and weaponry that is brought to bear in the war against the evil forces that prevent an aspirant from attaining enlightenment and even may be trying to hurt or destroy an aspirant. The force of the gods and goddesses is always more powerful because it is based on truth. Falsehood can only stand when there is ignorance. That is why it is said:

"GOD KNOWETH they who acknowledge Him, GOD rewardeth them who serve Him and protects them who follow Him; they who <u>SET Him in their HEART</u>"

"Truth protects from fear."

-Ancient Egyptian Proverbs

Above: the arrows and shield of Goddess Net

The goddess Net uses a bow and arrow as her weapon of choice. The bow and arrow is a subtle instrument of war. Consider what this implies. The practice of archery requires steadiness, control of breath and accurate vision. It also requires the highly evolved ability to gauge distance to the target, and complex mental physics to calculate the elevation and speed of travel necessary for an arrow to hit a mark. Also, it requires compensating for a host of other variables such as wind that can affect the trajectory of an arrow in flight. Then through one pointed concentration the breath is held in order to release the arrow without undue vibration. Certain demoniac qualities in the human psyche must be dealt with this way. The wind that can disturb the trajectory of the arrow is the thought process that can be disturbing the mind. This is caused by passion and desire. So there must be sturdiness and establishment in the Higher Self. Subtle egoism is so elusive, so camouflaged and intertwined with the personality that it is often hard to pinpoint. Through the worship of goddess Net and the practice of her disciplines, meditation on the target, control of breath, one pointed attention on the mark, etc., the demoniac quality cannot escape the gaze of such an aspirant and is destroyed thereby.

Bows and arrows were present in Egyptian culture since the predynastic origins. The arrow is a symbol of divine power, and is personified by goddess Net, who is also the goddess of war. Two crossed arrows symbolize her spiritual tradition. Arrows symbolize the sun's rays. The god Atum is the divine archer who fires sunbeams as though they were arrows. At the time for the Ascension of the king, he symbolically fires an arrow in each of the four cardinal directions which symbolizes his dominion over the *Four Corners* of the world. Arrows are also thoughts. A thought can have a piercing and exacting quality when the mind is razor sharp in its lucid quality. When the mind is clear of egoism and passion it can direct itself one-pointedly to a goal and hit exactly on the mark. Also, it can pinpoint the source of a problem and go directly to its solution without diffidence and it can direct thoughts to counteract negative thoughts with exacting accuracy. The quiver symbolizes a mind that is purified. When the mind is clear and enlightenment is dawning there is an endless source of arrows to fight off the demoniac influences and egoistic notions and then the victory against the inimical forces of the mind is assured and the victory in the battle of life is achieved.

Anat

Goddess Anat is a form of the Ancient Egyptian Goddess Nat that was revered in Kamit as well as in Asia Minor. She displays the axe, spear and shield in her iconography. The shield represents dispassion. Dispassion protects one from the dangers of the world, those weapons that cause pain and suffering. So desire is a weakness and detachment and dispassion shield the personality from the weapons of the demoniac personalities and objects of the world that threaten a person's inner peace and god consciousness. Dispassion is attained by following the path of *Shems*, following the teachings and practicing the disciplines enjoined in the teachings.

The mace is a gross weapon that is wielded with one or both hands. It is used as a club. The movement of the arm and the pivot at the wrist generate immense

force to smash an object into pieces. This has the effect of shattering the object and also a crushing effect. Consider the image above. The king, in the form of Heru, is charged with destroying the enemies of Maat who would bring chaos and confusion to the country. By smashing them he breaks up their ranks, scattering them and rendering their threat neutralized, their order that was used for unrighteousness is broken. So too an aspirant should use the force of Maatian laws, the precepts to smash gross impurities of the personality in the form of unrighteous thoughts and behaviors. When negative thoughts arise in the mind they should be hit with the mace of righteousness and truth and in so doing rendering their threat void so that the personality may maintain peace and balance to practice the teaching and experience higher consciousness.

Similar to the mace, the axe is also a wielded instrument. However, is not as blunt as the mace. It is used when a cutting effect is needed but when more force is needed than what is possible with an ordinary sword or knife. Consider the image above. The king, in the form of Heru, charged with destroying the enemies of Maat, holds the soldiers of the enemy army who are begging for mercy as he raises the axe to them. This instrument is used when a swift stroke is to be used to finish off the enemy. Certain impurities of the heart require swiftness and deliberate movement to be dealt with. An example is the desire to smoke.

This is a most gross impurity that cannot be allowed to exist in any shape or form. An aspirant should not take time pounding at it with the mace, trying to quit over and over again to beat it into submission. This needs to be cut off but with great force and so the axe is used. An aspirant should use the axe with the perspective of Heru, of self-worth, valor, heroism and regalness and not from the perspective of weakness. This requires righteous spiritual aspiration and Shemsu-Heru following the path of Heru, virtue, listening to the enlightening teaching of Aset and living life with the ideal of avenging the murder of his father, Asar, the soul within that has been killed by the same inimical forces that are trying to destroy the aspirant now.

The sword is a wielded instrument for cutting and striking an enemy. It can also be manipulated to thrust at an enemy from a distance. The Nubian Queen above in the form of Heru, holds the enemies of the state as she raises a sword to them. A sword is useful to one who can handle it. Otherwise the handler may hurt him/her self. If not handled properly it can become dull or even break. In this case it will be less useful in a battle and the user will be open to attack. The idea is to engage in slashing motions, keeping the opponent at bay until an opportunity opens to engage a decisive cutting blow or thrust. In the same way, in battling the demons of life an aspirant should use the sword of intellect which cuts away at illusions and unrighteousness and ignorance in order to establish understanding and truth. However, remember that the sword has two edges. So it cuts both ways. A true practitioner of the mysteries cannot cut away at some ignorance and then leave others untouched. Sometimes aspirants want to deal with things that they are comfortable with but not deal with those things that are more difficult. Wisdom cuts both ways and this also means that if an aspirant is ready to slash away at the external world of illusion he/she should prepare also to slice away the internal illusions, closely held beliefs and ignorant notions. Spirituality is a battle that is internal but which reflects externally as well. There is a deeper aspect to this teaching that is beyond the

scope of this present volume but what has been given here give sufficient indication.[130]

sheathed daggers with inlaid handles

Above from left to right: 1- the god Amun holds a sickle shaped knife-sword with which he assists the King, again in the form of the god Heru, to slay the enemies of the state. 2- the god Bes holds two knives. 3- the god Amun as a four-headed ram-man also holds two knives. 4- the god Anpu holds two knives as he battles Apep, the evil serpent. Knives are very useful tools which can be used for many tasks such as preparing foods, cutting materials of construction etc.

---

[130] See also the lecture series *Travels of Asar and His Spiritual Message: Class 4: Mysteries of War and violence.*

When used for warfare knives are fearsome instruments that are used for close-in fighting, stealthiness and swift attack. They are regarded as weapons for battles on to death. The gods and goddesses use these to cut off the heads of evil serpents, the demons which are slithery and slippery, stealthy and smooth. In like manner the ego is slithery, and stealthy. It hides in the shadows of the unconscious mind until ready to strike and when it does the personality is filled with the poison of desire. The knives cut off the head, which delivers that venom and with it the desire that leads to worldly entanglements and delusions. The god Bes is especially venerated for his protective qualities, goodwill, joviality, mirth, music and purity of feeling. So too aspirants should develop these qualities so as to hold in the hands the knives of good intellect, agreeable nature and right discernment, which cut away at the errors that lead to strife and unrest in life.

Above left: Ankhwahibre controlling a snake on top of spine with his staff. Above center: The initiate controls Apep who is in the form of a serpent. Below: the god Heru controls Apep, who appears as a man (anthropomorphic) underwater.

The staff is a blunt instrument that can be used for striking an opponent or tripping them up, that is, to disrupt their footing. Also it can be used to control dangerous animals, such as snakes, that need to be kept at a distance for one's own safety. In the picture above the initiate tries to control Apep so as to not allow him to gain control over the spine, that is the higher spheres of psycho-spiritual consciousness. In the image at right above Heru uses a spear to deal crippling blows to Apep. Unlike the staff, the spear has the capacity to pierce the flesh of the opponent. This signifies that self-effort as a spiritual aspirant goes far to control the lower nature (Apep) but it is Heru, the higher aspiration in an aspirant that defeats Apep completely. This is the difference between effort or battle and freedom and victory. Both are necessary on the Neterian spiritual path.

Chapter 6: The Nubian Gods and Goddesses in the Kamitan Company of Gods and Goddesses

In modern times, the land which was once known as Nubia ("Land of Gold"), is currently known as the Sudan, and the land even further south and east towards the coast of east Africa is referred to as Ethiopia (see map above). The land that is today referred to as Sudan was in ancient times referred to as "Ethiopia" by the Greeks. While the divinity Amun was popular in Nubia, this popularity was exemplified in the later periods of Nubian history which began with the New Kingdom Period in Kamit. The Nubian preference was the ram-headed man while the preference in Kamit was either the ram in a completely zoomorphic (animal) form or the divinity as a man with the body and head of a man (anthropomorphic).

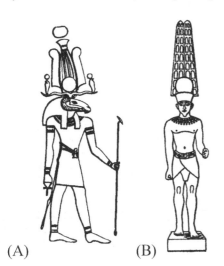 

(A)　　　　　(B)　　　　(C)

Above (A): The God Amun in the form of the Ram headed man. Above (B), the God Amun-Ra from Ancient Egypt as a man. Above (C)- the god Amun-Ra from Ancient Egypt as a full ram.

If we look further back however, we will discover that the mythic association between the Kamitans and the Nubians in Pre-Dynastic times is supported by the earliest writings of Ancient Egypt. Firstly, the god Bas (Basu, Bes), who is usually referred to as a Nubian originated god, is also equated by the Ancient Egyptian scripture and iconography with the divinity Heru. The following panel shows this link most succinctly.

Far left -Heru as a Divine child, master of nature, controller of beasts (evil, unrighteousness, the lower self), wearing mask of Basu.

Right– Basu as the dwarf with the characteristic Nubian plumes as headdress.

In anthropology, pigmies are known as members of any of various peoples, especially of equatorial Africa and parts of southeast Asia, having an average height less than 5 feet (127 centimeters).[131] In the ancient period, the pigmies of Nubia were renowned for knowing "the dance of the God" and for being jovial but forthright people. In this vein they were renowned musicians and lovers of play and festivity, but also leaders in wars of righteousness and protectors of children. These are all attributes of Basu. Basu also appears in the Pyramid Texts along with the other gods and goddesses of Kamit. The Pyramid Texts are the earliest known extensive writings about the myth and philosophy of Kamit (Ancient Egypt). Therefore, any divinity which is mentioned in those texts, emerges with at least the same importance of the other Kamitan gods and goddesses depending on the interrelationships provided in the text itself.

we see the Vulture. These are all traditional and archetypal symbols that reached their height in Kamit.

The god Bes or Bas and a host of other Nubian divinities can be seen as the legendary divinities which appear in the early Kamitan texts, but later take on new Kamitan forms, under which their worship continues. Bas, for example, continues to be worshipped as Heru. Bas also figures prominently as a part of the Kamitan concept of the transcendental divinity, Neberdjer. The iconography of Bas in the form of Neberdjer (below) closely follows that of the representation of Heru as the Divine Child (above) in the following respects. Both are regarded as the all-encompassing Divinity, masters of the animal forces. In the picture of Heru above, this is symbolized by Heru holding and standing on the animals; his nudity is a symbol of transcendentalism (unconditioned consciousness).

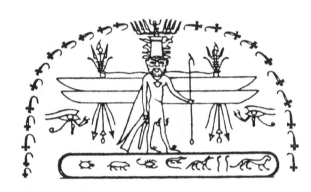

Above: The Kamitan/Nubian god Bas in the form of the all-encompassing divinity, Neberdjer.

The Bas mask he wears as his headdress is a symbol of the wonderful and magnificent nature of the Divine, who manifests as a dwarf, and at the same time as a personality overflowing with joviality and life.

The Nubian iconography above demonstrates that the Nubian people followed the same religion as those of Kamit. Notice the typical headdress composed of the serpents at the forehead. Also, the image of foreign soldiers under control, Heru is seated upon the Queens head. At her feet we find the Lion and above

---

[131] American Heritage Dictionary

Above left: Kamitan depictions of the Kamitan/Nubian God Bas as the Harpist. Above right: Another image of the Kamitan/Nubian god Bas in the form of the all-encompassing divinity, Neberdjer.

Neberdjer represents all of the forces of the other divinities including Ra, Amun and Heru thus representing (see picture above) non-duality and Supreme Divinity. This being is in control of the seven eternal animal forces (seven animals encircled by the serpent with its tail in its mouth-symbolizing eternity).

Other Nubian divinities which were mentioned in the Ancient Egyptian Pyramid Texts include:

𓆄𓅱𓊹𓂻𓅱 *Aahs*

The Nubian divinity Aahs is referred to as the "Regent of the land of the south."

𓆄𓍯𓈖𓆓𓀭 *Ari Hems Nefer*

The Nubian divinity Ari Hems Nefer is referred to as the "beautiful womb." *Ari Hems Nefer* was a divinity of the area 15 miles south of the modern Egyptian city of Aswan, where the temple of Aset is located. In ancient times it was known as Pilak or the limit or southern border of Egypt. Today it is called Pilak (Philae).

𓅃𓈖𓏭𓃭 or 𓈖𓅃𓂋𓃭 *Meril*

The Nubian divinity Meril is referred to as the "beloved lion" divinity of the city of Kalabshah (city located 35 miles south of the modern Egyptian city Aswan), where the temple of Khnum is located. In ancient times it was known as Abu (Greek

Elephantine) by the Greeks or the first cataract of Egypt. Today it is called Aswan. Meril, a Ram-headed divinity like the Heru aspect Hery-shaf (Heryshaf), was recognized as a manifestation of Heru and Ra. He is regarded as the sun-god of northern Nubia. The Greeks identified him with Apollo and Heracles.

Symbol A 𓇳,   Symbol B 𓂋𓈖𓅭𓅃,
Symbol C 𓂋𓈖𓅱𓏏𓏏

The symbols above for the Nubian divinity *Dudun* show the association with one of the oldest most worshipped and most powerful divinities of Kamit, Heru, whose symbol is the falcon (hawk). Symbol *A* shows the characteristic Heruian icon, the hawk, perched on the divine solar boat. Symbol *B* shows one of the full spellings of the name including the phonetic signs and again, including the hawk, this time perched on the standard, meaning *Dudun Sa Heru:* "Dudun the son of Heru." Symbol *C* shows one of the full spellings of the name including the phonetic signs and this time showing the symbol of the two lands, meaning *Dudun Sa Tawi* "Dudun the son of the two lands (i.e. Nubia and Egypt)." The divinity Dudun was important in Kamitan spirituality even into the late period. The evidence of this can be found in the fact that it was Dudun who symbolically burnt the special Nubian incense through which the royalty of Kamit was to be purified for induction to the high offices, including the throne of rulership. Pharaoh Djehutimes III built temples to Dudun in Nubia at *el-Lessya* and *Uronarti.* Below we see the symbols of Heru used in

Kamit. Notice the correlation to the symbols of Dudun.

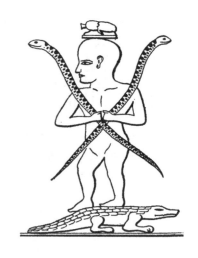

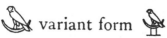 variant form

The symbols of Heru and those of Dudun are a perfect match. Therefore, Dudun was the Nubian name for the same divinity which was called Heru in Kamitan religion. Another strong correlation between Nubian and Kamitan religion is the dwarf figure. We have already been introduced to Basu. This quality of stature and Nubian features is also present in the figure of Asar in his aspect of Ptah-Sokar-Asar. Ptah is sometimes depicted as a Pigmy lord Creator (Khepri) of the primeval matter with two serpents, standing on a crocodile, as Heru.

Ptah-Sokar-Asar (as Pigmy)

Above far-left The god Asar. Middle- is Ptah-Sokar-Asar as an average sized man. Far right- The god Ptah of Memphis.

Ptah-Sokar-Asar unites the three main spiritual traditions of the early Dynastic Period in ancient Kamit, that of Ra, Asar, and Ptah. Asar is part of Anunian theology, which is centered on the divinity Ra, and Ra is associated with the even earlier Heru as the all-encompassing Divinity. Also, Asar is associated with the divinity Heru, as Heru is Asar's son in the Asarian mystical tradition. Ptah is the

central divinity in the theology of the Ancient Egyptian city of *Men-nefer* (also Het-Ka-Ptah), known as Memphis. He is associated, in his work of Creation, with the Divinity Tem, who is a form of Ra. Therefore, the dwarf figure of Ptah-Sokar-Asar united the culture of Nubia with that of Kamit Also the religious iconography of Basu as the dwarf and the characteristic Nubian plumed headdress comes into the later Dynastic Period. Therefore, the impact of Nubian spirituality was felt all the way from the commencement of Kamitan religion through the late period. The figure at above depicts another conceptualization of the Netherworld, which is at the same time the body of Nut in a forward bend posture.

The god Geb is on the ground practicing the Plough Yoga exercise posture. The goddess in the center symbolizes the lower heaven in which the moon traverses, the astral realm. The outermost goddess symbolizes the course of the sun in its astral journey and the causal plane.

Notice the characteristic Nubian headdress of Nut, which is also visible in the iconography of the god Bas and the goddess Anqit. This iconography links the Kamitan religion with that of the Pre-Dynastic era, and with the Nubian origins of Kamitan culture. Geb, who is in the plough sema-yoga posture, symbolizes the physical plane and all solid matter, while the goddesses represent the subtler levels of existence.

Below: Goddess Nut, the Mother of Asar and Aset and Blackness as a Metaphor of Consciousness and as a Description of the gods and goddesses

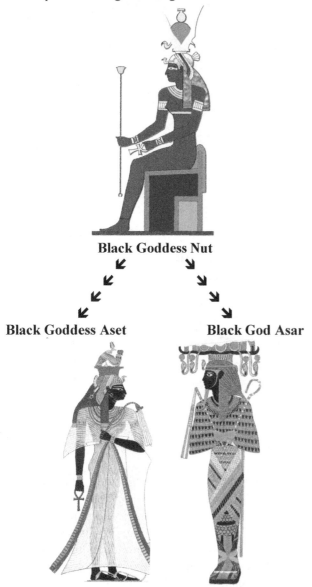

Black Goddess Nut

Black Goddess Aset　　　**Black God Asar**

In Kamitan philosophy, blackness is used as a descriptive nomenclature of the people, certain of the gods and goddesses as well as the concept of the transcendental.

In the Temple of Iunet (Denderah) in Kamit, it is inscribed that the goddess Nut gave birth to the goddess Aset there, and that upon her birth, Nut exclaimed: "As" (behold), I have become thy mother." This was the origin of the name "Ast," later known as Isis to the Greeks and others. It further states that "she was a dark-skinned child and was called Khnemet-ankhet" or "the living lady of love". Thus, Aset also symbolizes the "blackness" of the vast un-manifest regions of existence. In this capacity she is also the ultimate expression of the African ideal prototype of

the Christian Madonna, especially in statues where she is depicted holding the baby Heru in the same manner Mother Mary is portrayed holding baby Jesus. Her identification is also symbolized in her aspect as Amentet, the Duat, itself.

Ament means "hidden." It is a specific reference to the female form of the astral plane or Netherworld known as Amenta (Amentet, Amentat) or the Duat. Like her husband Asar, who was known as the "Lord of the Perfect Black," Aset was the Mistress of the Netherworld (Amentet, Amentat). Thus, Aset also symbolizes the "blackness" of the vast unmanifest regions of existence (the unmanifest). Upon further reflection into the mythology it becomes obvious that since Asar is the Duat, and since the goddess Amentet is also Amentat or the realm of Asar, they are in reality one and the same (both the realms and the deities). So Aset and Asar together form the hidden recesses of Creation. In essence they are the source of Creation, and are therefore both simultaneously considered to be the source of the Life Force which courses through Creation.

The Ethiopian divinity Apedemak, (below center) displays the same leonine trinity concept and the multi-armed motif.

The trinity symbolically relates the nature of the Divine, who is the source and sustenance of the three worlds (physical, astral and causal), the three states of consciousness (conscious, subconscious and unconscious), the three modes of nature (dull, agitated and lucid), the three aspects of human experience (seer, seen and sight), as well as the three stages of initiation (ignorance, aspiration and enlightenment). This triad idea is common to Neterianism, Hinduism and Christianity.

The idea of the multi-armed divinity is common in Indian Iconography. However, the depiction above from Ethiopian-Egyptian spiritual iconography shows that it was present in Africa as well.

Other Nubian Divinities:

Shesmetet- A leonine goddess, similar to Kamitan Sekhmit. In the Pyramid Texts it says that Shesmetet gives birth to the king and she is the mother of the deceased in funerary papyri. Shesmetet is pray to as a force against demons of the slaughter. One of her epithets is 'Lady of Punt.' Punt is the region on the horn of Africa from where Ancient Kamitans obtained incense.

Sebiumeker - Anthropomorphic god of pro-creation in the Meroitic pantheon with worship center at the desert east of the sixth cataract of the Nile.

The Terms "Ethiopia," "Nubia," "Kush" and "Sudan"

The term "Ethiopian," "Nubian," and "Kushite" all relate to the same peoples who lived south of Egypt. Recent research has shown that the modern Nubian word *kiji* means "fertile land, dark gray mud, silt, or black land." Since the sound of this word is close to the Ancient Egyptian name 𓀀𓆓 Kash- (Kush- from the tomb of *Amen-m-Hat* at Beni Hasan 12 dyn) Kish or Kush, referring to the land south of Egypt, it is believed that the name Kush also meant "the land of dark silt" or "the black land." Sudan is an Arabic translation of *sûd* which is the plural form of *aswad*, which means "black," and *ân* which means "of the." So, Sudan means "of the blacks." In the modern Nubian language, *nugud* means "black." Also, *nuger*, *nugur*, and *nubi* mean "black" as well. All of this indicates that the words Kush, Nubia, and Sudan all mean the same thing — the "black land" and/or the "land of the blacks."[132]

Summary

Thus, it is clear that the Ancient Egyptians, while recognizing the geographical differences (Egypt is in the north and Kush is in the south) between their land and the land of the Nubians (Kush), also recognized the similitude of the lands. In effect the name of lands of Egypt and Nubia actually mean the same thing "black land" or "land of the blacks." The different words used to identify the two cultures (Kush and Kamit) simply denote the relative geographical locations and the ethnic (tribal) differentiation of inhabitants. The ethnic differences here do not relate to race or religion as these have been shown to be the same, but of customs and traditions that developed independently due to differences in distance from each other. This is done for the purpose of showing an underlying unity while at the same time denoting the practical differences of the two lands. This of course points to the underlying ethnic homogeneity between the two peoples, and at the same time acknowledges the cultural differences which developed due to the language changes and the accelerated development of the Ancient Egyptians.

Another force, which spurred the Ancient Egyptians to develop at a faster pace, was the interaction they had with the Asiatic peoples. Since the Ancient Egyptians were geographically located closer to Asia Minor, they encountered more Asiatics and Europeans than the Ethiopians, who were in an area that afforded them a relative form of seclusion. Some of the interactions were peaceful while others were hostile and this prompted (stimulated) the Ancient Egyptians to mature and advance in the areas of building technology, farming, warfare and social as well as spiritual philosophy.

Recent archaeological finds have revealed that the region's people were producing sophisticated ceramics by 8000 B.C.E. Indeed, it seems evident that Nubia contributed as much to Ancient Egypt's development as Egypt did to Nubia's.[133] Nubian-Egyptian pottery from the Pre-Dynastic Period is important evidence that demonstrates the link between the Ancient Nubian (Ethiopians), the Ancient Egyptians and the Ancient Indus Valley culture.

---

[132]"Nubia," *Microsoft® Encarta® Africana.* © 1999 Microsoft Corporation. All rights reserved.

[133] "Kush, Early Kingdom of," *Microsoft® Encarta® Africana.* ©&(p) 1999 Microsoft Corporation. All rights reserved.

Epílog

Men and Women as Gods and Goddesses

"The purpose of all human life is to achieve a state of consciousness apart from bodily concerns."

-Ancient Neterian Proverb

Right: Queen Nefertari as initiate Asar

The hieroglyphic inscription reads *"Asar Nefertari, the great queen, beloved of goddess Mut and Maakheru (spiritually victorious) is in the presence of Asar, the Great God"*

In Ancient Egyptian Asarian mysticism, all initiates were given the spiritual name *"Asar"* regardless of if they were male or female. Thus, in the Papyrus of Ani, Ani, who was a man, was renamed Asar Ani. Likewise, Nefertari, who was a woman, also received the name Asar Nefertari. Thus, in the same manner, other papyruses of the *Prt m Hru* prepared for other initiates, were not prepared for the man or woman, but for the spiritual aspirant. While Asar is usually seen as a male divinity his higher attributes include those which relate him as an androgynous, transcendental Spirit. The term "ren" relating to the aspect of the personality of a human being therefore refers to the ego and not to the Higher Self. So every human being has a Divine Name and an ego name.

What is the deeper implication of this? This is a very important mystical teaching relating that the deeper Self within Ani is Asar, the Divine Self. That is, his true identity is not the birth name, but the Divinity which transcends mortal existence. In modern times, John would be Asar John, Cynthia would be Asar Cynthia, etc. It is an affirmation and acceptance of one's Divine true essential nature not only as an expression of God, but as God in fact. Thus the entire journey of self-discovery revolves around your discovering that the deeper reality within you is God. This does not contradict other religions. In Buddhism, the deeper reality a Buddhist is looking for is Buddha Consciousness. Thus, in Ancient Egyptian terms as related in the *Book of Coming Forth By Day,* the deeper reality to be sought is Asar. So as you live your life, see your existence as a journey of discovery.

The even deeper implication of the Divine Name of every human being is that it relates the essential and true nature of every man and woman. This means that in reality every man and every woman is a god or goddess. There is a special Neterian saying that provides insight into this great teaching: *men and women are mortal gods and goddesses and the gods and goddesses are immortal men and women.* Therefore, there are *billions* of gods and goddesses on earth or at least potential gods and goddesses. A human being becomes a god or goddess when they attain the realization of their higher nature. So when a human being attains that level of consciousness they are regarded as Asar, one with the Divine Self and also one of the Company of Gods and Goddesses. This is the true teaching behind referring to the initiate as Asar, for all humanity. It is also reflected in the teaching of placing the initiate, the king or queen in the Boat of Ra. Becoming Asar or joining with the Company of Gods and Goddesses, as one of them is the highest attainment of life. That is what it means to accomplish the goal exhorted by the teachings:

"Men and women are to become God-like through a life of virtue and the cultivation of the spirit through scientific knowledge, practice and bodily discipline."

ASAR MEETS ASAR[134]

The momentous meeting of the initiate with the Divine is the central issue of the Pert m Hru (Book of the Dead) teaching. When a human being realizes that their true name is The Divine and not the individual given name. This means that there has been a realization of the identity with the Divine, a communion, i.e. a Smai or yoga. This is the goal of all efforts and it is the purpose of all disciplines and spiritual practices.

Following the judgment, Asar Ani is taken by the androgynous Heru (note the female-left breast) and introduced to a mummified Asar who holds the *Flail, Crook* and *Was* staffs and is enthroned in a shrine surmounted by a Hawk - Heru. Asar wears a crown symbolic of Upper and Lower Egypt and is assisted by Nebthet and Aset. When Ani reaches the shrine, he is justified and glorified as symbolized by the anointment *"grease cone"* on his head (the Anointed One), and kneels with upraised right arm, holding a Sekhem staff in the left. In front of him there is a table of offerings including flowers, fruit and a **khepesh** or "foreleg of ox". Above him there are vessels of wine, beer and oils, and at the topmost compartment of the register, there is another offering table with bread, cakes, a wreath and a *"set"* or duck.

Above: Asar Ani meets Asar (The Supreme Being)

After being judged and having been found to be worthy (pure of heart), Ani is led by Heru, the Lord of Heaven and Earth (Upper and Lower Egypt), who is Ani's own androgynous soul, to Asar who is Ani's higher self. Ani has acquired the spiritual strength (Sekhem) to become one with Asar and thus will join Asar in Amenta. Ani's offering of the **"khepesh and set"** (symbols of male and female principles) represents Ani's relinquishment of his earthly - dualistic consciousness. Thus Ani is offering his ego-consciousness so that he may realize his non-dualistic - all-encompassing cosmic higher self in Asar. Therefore, this is the culmination of all Neterian endeavors, when a human being realizes his/her true essence as a god/dess. In that realization there is a remembrance, a meeting of a person with their true self. Thus it is God meeting God, the most glorious and most sublime experience of life. This is Nehast, the great spiritual awakening, the Akh or spiritual enlightenment, that is so much spoken of in the teachings, the ultimate *destiny* for all who tread the path of Neterianism.

HTP

Sebai Maa (Dr. Muata Ashby)

---

[134] For more on the Book of the dead see *The Book of the Dead* by Seba Muata Ashby

Index

Other Books by Muata Ashby

P.O.Box 570459
Miami, Florida, 33257
(305) 378-6253 Fax: (305) 378-6253

This book is part of a series on the study and practice of Ancient Egyptian Yoga and Mystical Spirituality based on the writings of Dr. Muata Abhaya Ashby. They are also part of the Egyptian Yoga Course provided by the Sema Institute of Yoga. Below you will find a listing of the other books in this series. For more information send for the Egyptian Yoga Book-Audio-Video Catalog or the Egyptian Yoga Course Catalog.

Now you can study the teachings of Egyptian and Indian Yoga wisdom and Spirituality with the Egyptian Yoga Mystical Spirituality Series. The Egyptian Yoga Series takes you through the Initiation process and lead you to understand the mysteries of the soul and the Divine and to attain the highest goal of life: ENLIGHTENMENT. The *Egyptian Yoga Series*, takes you on an in depth study of Ancient Egyptian mythology and their inner mystical meaning. Each Book is prepared for the serious student of the mystical sciences and provides a study of the teachings along with exercises, assignments and projects to make the teachings understood and effective in real life. The Series is part of the Egyptian Yoga course but may be purchased even if you are not taking the course. The series is ideal for study groups.

THE EGYPTIAN MYSTIERIES BOOK SERIES

Coming Soon

EGYPTIAN MYSTERIES VOLUME 2: Shetaut Neteru- The Mysteries of the Gods and Goddesses

EGYPTIAN MYSTERIES VOLUME 3: Shetaut Hemu Neter- The Secret Science of the Ancient Egyptian Priests and Priestesses

EGYPTIAN MYSTERIES VOLUME 4: Shetaut Medu Neter- The Philosophy of Egyptian Grammar

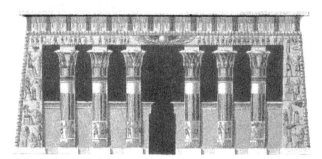

1. EGYPTIAN YOGA: THE PHILOSOPHY OF ENLIGHTENMENT An original, fully illustrated work, including hieroglyphs, detailing the meaning of the Egyptian mysteries, tantric yoga, psycho-spiritual and physical exercises. Egyptian Yoga is a guide to the practice of the highest spiritual philosophy which leads to absolute freedom from human misery and to immortality. It is well known by scholars that Egyptian philosophy is the basis of Western and Middle Eastern religious philosophies such as *Christianity, Islam, Judaism,* the *Kabala*, and Greek philosophy, but what about Indian philosophy, Yoga and Taoism? What were the original teachings? How can they be practiced today? What is the source of pain and suffering in the world and what is the solution? Discover the deepest mysteries of the mind and universe within and outside of your self. 8.5" X 11" ISBN: 1-884564-01-1 Soft $19.95

2. EGYPTIAN YOGA II: The Supreme Wisdom of Enlightenment by Dr. Muata Ashby ISBN 1-884564-39-9 $22.95 U.S. In this long awaited sequel to *Egyptian Yoga: The Philosophy of Enlightenment* you will take a fascinating and enlightening journey back in time and discover the teachings which constituted the epitome of Ancient Egyptian spiritual wisdom. What are the disciplines which lead to the fulfillment of all desires? Delve into the three states of consciousness (waking, dream and deep sleep) and the fourth state which transcends them all, Neberdjer, "The Absolute." These teachings of the city of Waset (Thebes) were the crowning achievement of the Sages of Ancient Egypt. They establish the standard mystical keys for understanding the profound mystical symbolism of the Triad of human consciousness.

3. THE KAMITAN DIET GUIDE TO HEALTH, DIET AND FASTING Health issues have always been important to human beings since the beginning of time. The earliest records of history show that the art of healing was held in high esteem since the time of Ancient Egypt. In the early 20th century, medical doctors had almost attained the status of sainthood by the promotion of the idea that they alone were "scientists" while other healing modalities and traditional healers who did not follow the "scientific method' were nothing but superstitious, ignorant charlatans who at best would take the money of their clients and at worst kill them with the unscientific "snake oils" and "irrational theories". In the late 20th century, the failure of the modern medical establishment's ability to lead the general public to good health, promoted the move by many in society towards "alternative medicine". Alternative medicine disciplines are those healing modalities which do not adhere to the philosophy of allopathic medicine. Allopathic medicine is what medical doctors practice by an large. It is the theory that disease is caused by agencies outside the body such as bacteria, viruses or physical means which affect the body. These can therefore be treated by medicines and therapies The natural healing method began in the absence of extensive technologies with the idea that all the answers for health may be found in nature or rather, the deviation from nature. Therefore, the health of the body can be restored by correcting the aberration and thereby restoring balance. This is the area that will be covered in this volume. Allopathic techniques have their place in the art of healing. However, we should not forget that the body is a grand achievement of the spirit and built into it is the capacity to maintain itself and heal itself. Ashby, Muata ISBN: 1-884564-49-6 $24.95

4. INITIATION INTO EGYPTIAN YOGA Shedy: Spiritual discipline or program, to go deeply into the mysteries, to study the mystery teachings and literature profoundly, to penetrate the mysteries. You will learn about the mysteries of initiation into the teachings and practice of Yoga and how to become an Initiate of the mystical sciences. This insightful manual is the first in a series which introduces you to the goals of daily spiritual and yoga practices: Meditation, Diet, Words of Power and the ancient wisdom teachings. 8.5" X 11" ISBN 1-884564-02-X Soft Cover $24.95 U.S.

5. *THE AFRICAN ORIGINS OF CIVILIZATION, MYSTICAL RELIGION AND YOGA PHILOSOPHY* HARD COVER EDITION ISBN: 1-884564-50-X $80.00 U.S.   81/2" X 11"   Part 1, Part 2, Part 3 in one volume 683 Pages Hard Cover First Edition Three volumes in one. Over the past several years I have been asked to put together in one volume the most important evidences showing the correlations and common teachings between Kamitan (Ancient Egyptian) culture and religion and that of India. The questions of the history of Ancient Egypt, and the latest archeological evidences showing civilization and culture in Ancient Egypt and its spread to other countries, has intrigued many scholars as well as mystics over the years. Also, the possibility that Ancient Egyptian Priests and Priestesses migrated to Greece, India and other countries to carry on the traditions of the Ancient Egyptian Mysteries, has been speculated over the years as well. In chapter 1 of the book *Egyptian Yoga The Philosophy of Enlightenment,* 1995, I first introduced the deepest comparison between Ancient Egypt and India that had been brought forth up to that time. Now, in the year

2001 this new book, *THE AFRICAN ORIGINS OF CIVILIZATION, MYSTICAL RELIGION AND YOGA PHILOSOPHY,* more fully explores the motifs, symbols and philosophical correlations between Ancient Egyptian and Indian mysticism and clearly shows not only that Ancient Egypt and India were connected culturally but also spiritually. How does this knowledge help the spiritual aspirant? This discovery has great importance for the Yogis and mystics who follow the philosophy of Ancient Egypt and the mysticism of India. It means that India has a longer history and heritage than was previously understood. It shows that the mysteries of Ancient Egypt were essentially a yoga tradition which did not die but rather developed into the modern day systems of Yoga technology of India. It further shows that African culture developed Yoga Mysticism earlier than any other civilization in history. All of this expands our understanding of the unity of culture and the deep legacy of Yoga, which stretches into the distant past, beyond the Indus Valley civilization, the earliest known high culture in India as well as the Vedic tradition of Aryan culture. Therefore, Yoga culture and mysticism is the oldest known tradition of spiritual development and Indian mysticism is an extension of the Ancient Egyptian mysticism. By understanding the legacy which Ancient Egypt gave to India the mysticism of India is better understood and by comprehending the heritage of Indian Yoga, which is rooted in Ancient Egypt the Mysticism of Ancient Egypt is also better understood. This expanded understanding allows us to prove the underlying kinship of humanity, through the common symbols, motifs and philosophies which are not disparate and confusing teachings but in reality expressions of the same study of truth through metaphysics and mystical realization of Self. (HARD COVER)

6. AFRICAN ORIGINS BOOK 1 PART 1 African Origins of African Civilization, Religion, Yoga Mysticism and Ethics Philosophy-<u>Soft Cover</u> $24.95 ISBN: 1-884564-55-0

7. AFRICAN ORIGINS BOOK 2 PART 2 African Origins of Western Civilization, Religion and Philosophy(Soft) -<u>Soft Cover</u> $24.95 ISBN: 1-884564-56-9

8. EGYPT AND INDIA (AFRICAN ORIGINS BOOK 3 PART 3) African Origins of Eastern Civilization, Religion, Yoga Mysticism and Philosophy-<u>Soft Cover</u> $29.95 (Soft) ISBN: 1-884564-57-7

9. THE MYSTERIES OF ISIS: The Path of Wisdom, Immortality and Enlightenment   Through the study of ancient myth and the illumination of initiatic understanding the idea of God is expanded from the mythological comprehension to the metaphysical. Then this metaphysical understanding is related to you, the student, so as to begin understanding your true divine nature. ISBN 1-884564-24-0 $24.99

10. EGYPTIAN PROVERBS: TEMT TCHAAS *Temt Tchaas* means: collection of ——Ancient Egyptian Proverbs How to live according to MAAT Philosophy. Beginning Meditation. All proverbs are indexed for easy searches. For the first time in one volume, ——Ancient Egyptian Proverbs, wisdom teachings and meditations, fully illustrated with hieroglyphic text and symbols. EGYPTIAN PROVERBS is a unique collection of knowledge and wisdom which you can put into practice today and transform your life. 5.5"x 8.5" $14.95 U.S   ISBN: 1-884564-00-3

11. THE PATH OF DIVINE LOVE The Process of Mystical Transformation and The Path of Divine Love This Volume will focus on the ancient wisdom teachings and how to use them in a scientific process for self-transformation. Also, this volume will detail the process of transformation from ordinary consciousness to cosmic consciousness through the integrated practice of the teachings and the path of Devotional Love toward the Divine. 5.5"x 8.5" ISBN 1-884564-11-9 $22.99

12. INTRODUCTION TO MAAT PHILOSOPHY: Spiritual Enlightenment Through the Path of Virtue Known as Karma Yoga in India, the teachings of MAAT for living virtuously and with orderly wisdom are explained and the student is to begin practicing the precepts of Maat in daily life so as to promote the process of purification of the heart in preparation for the judgment of the soul. This judgment will be understood not as an event that will occur at the time of death but as an event that occurs continuously, at every moment in the life of the individual. The student will learn how to become allied with the forces of the Higher Self and to thereby begin cleansing the mind (heart) of impurities so as to attain a higher vision of reality. ISBN 1-884564-20-8 $22.99

13. MEDITATION The Ancient Egyptian Path to Enlightenment   Many people do not know about the rich

history of meditation practice in Ancient Egypt. This volume outlines the theory of meditation and presents the Ancient Egyptian Hieroglyphic text which give instruction as to the nature of the mind and its three modes of expression. It also presents the texts which give instruction on the practice of meditation for spiritual Enlightenment and unity with the Divine. This volume allows the reader to begin practicing meditation by explaining, in easy to understand terms, the simplest form of meditation and working up to the most advanced form which was practiced in ancient times and which is still practiced by yogis around the world in modern times. ISBN 1-884564-27-7 $24.99

14. THE GLORIOUS LIGHT MEDITATION TECHNIQUE OF ANCIENT EGYPT ISBN: 1-884564-15-1 $14.95 (PB) New for the year 2000. This volume is based on the earliest known instruction in history given for the practice of formal meditation. Discovered by Dr. Muata Ashby, it is inscribed on the walls of the Tomb of Seti I in Thebes Egypt. This volume details the philosophy and practice of this unique system of meditation originated in Ancient Egypt and the earliest practice of meditation known in the world which occurred in the most advanced African Culture.

15. THE SERPENT POWER: The Ancient Egyptian Mystical Wisdom of the Inner Life Force.   This Volume specifically deals with the latent life Force energy of the universe and in the human body, its control and sublimation. How to develop the Life Force energy of the subtle body. This Volume will introduce the esoteric wisdom of the science of how virtuous living acts in a subtle and mysterious way to cleanse the latent psychic energy conduits and vortices of the spiritual body. ISBN 1-884564-19-4 $22.95

16. EGYPTIAN YOGA MEDITATION IN MOTION Thef Neteru: *The Movement of The Gods and Goddesses* Discover the physical postures and exercises practiced thousands of years ago in Ancient Egypt which are today known as Yoga exercises. This work is based on the pictures and teachings from the Creation story of Ra, The Asarian Resurrection Myth and the carvings and reliefs from various Temples in Ancient Egypt 8.5" X 11" ISBN 1-884564-10-0 Soft Cover $18.99   Exercise video $21.99

17. EGYPTIAN TANTRA YOGA: The Art of Sex Sublimation and Universal Consciousness This Volume will expand on the male and female principles within the human body and in the universe and further detail the sublimation of sexual energy into spiritual energy. The student will study the deities Min and Hathor, Asar and Aset, Geb and Nut and discover the mystical implications for a practical spiritual discipline. This Volume will also focus on the Tantric aspects of Ancient Egyptian and Indian mysticism, the purpose of sex and the mystical teachings of sexual sublimation which lead to self-knowledge and Enlightenment. 5.5"x 8.5" ISBN 1-884564-03-8 $24.95

18. ASARIAN RELIGION: RESURRECTING OSIRIS The path of Mystical Awakening and the Keys to Immortality NEW REVISED AND EXPANDED EDITION!   The Ancient Sages created stories based on human and superhuman beings whose struggles, aspirations, needs and desires ultimately lead them to discover their true Self. The myth of Aset, Asar and Heru is no exception in this area. While there is no one source where the entire story may be found, pieces of it are inscribed in various ancient Temples walls, tombs, steles and papyri. For the first time available, the complete myth of Asar, Aset and Heru has been compiled from original Ancient Egyptian, Greek and Coptic Texts. This epic myth has been richly illustrated with reliefs from the Temple of Heru at Edfu, the Temple of Aset at Philae, the Temple of Asar at Abydos, the Temple of Hathor at Denderah and various papyri, inscriptions and reliefs. Discover the myth which inspired the teachings of the *Shetaut Neter* (Egyptian Mystery System - Egyptian Yoga) and the Egyptian Book of Coming Forth By Day. Also, discover the three levels of Ancient Egyptian Religion, how to understand the mysteries of the Duat or Astral World and how to discover the abode of the Supreme in the Amenta, *The Other World*   The ancient religion of Asar, Aset and Heru, if properly understood, contains all of the elements necessary to lead the sincere aspirant to attain immortality through inner self-discovery. This volume presents the entire myth and explores the main mystical themes and rituals associated with the myth for understating human existence, creation and the way to achieve spiritual emancipation - *Resurrection.* The Asarian myth is so powerful that it influenced and is still having an effect on the major world religions. Discover the origins and mystical meaning of the Christian Trinity, the Eucharist ritual and the ancient origin of the birthday of Jesus Christ. Soft Cover ISBN: 1-884564-27-5 $24.95

19.   THE EGYPTIAN BOOK OF THE DEAD MYSTICISM OF THE PERT EM HERU $26.95   ISBN# 1-884564-28-3 Size: 8½" X 11" I Know myself, I know myself, I am One With God!–From the Pert Em Heru "The Ru Pert em Heru" or "Ancient Egyptian Book of The Dead," or "Book of Coming Forth By Day" as it is more popularly known, has fascinated the world since the successful translation of Ancient Egyptian hieroglyphic scripture over 150 years ago. The astonishing writings in it reveal that the Ancient Egyptians believed in life after death and in an ultimate destiny to discover the Divine. The elegance and aesthetic beauty of the hieroglyphic text itself has inspired many see it as an art form in and of itself. But is there more to it than that? Did the Ancient Egyptian wisdom contain more than just aphorisms and hopes of eternal life beyond death? In this volume Dr. Muata Ashby, the author of over 25 books on Ancient Egyptian Yoga Philosophy has produced a new translation of the original texts which uncovers a mystical teaching underlying the sayings and rituals instituted by the Ancient Egyptian Sages and Saints. "Once the philosophy of Ancient Egypt is understood as a mystical tradition instead of as a religion or primitive mythology, it reveals its secrets which if practiced today will lead anyone to discover the glory of spiritual self-discovery. The Pert em Heru is in every way comparable to the Indian Upanishads or the Tibetan Book of the Dead." Muata Abhaya Ashby

20.   ANUNIAN THEOLOGY THE MYSTERIES OF RA The Philosophy of Anu and The Mystical Teachings of The Ancient Egyptian Creation Myth Discover the mystical teachings contained in the Creation Myth and the gods and goddesses who brought creation and human beings into existence. The Creation Myth holds the key to understanding the universe and for attaining spiritual Enlightenment. ISBN: 1-884564-38-0 40 pages $14.95

21.   MYSTERIES OF MIND AND MEMPHITE THEOLOGY Mysticism of Ptah, Egyptian Physics and Yoga Metaphysics and the Hidden properties of Matter   This Volume will go deeper into the philosophy of God as creation and will explore the concepts of modern science and how they correlate with ancient teachings. This Volume will lay the ground work for the understanding of the philosophy of universal consciousness and the initiatic/yogic insight into who or what is God? ISBN 1-884564-07-0 $21.95

22.   THE GODDESS AND THE EGYPTIAN MYSTERIESTHE PATH OF THE GODDESS THE GODDESS PATH The Secret Forms of the Goddess and the Rituals of Resurrection The Supreme Being may be worshipped as father or as mother. *Ushet Rekhat* or *Mother Worship*, is the spiritual process of worshipping the Divine in the form of the Divine Goddess. It celebrates the most important forms of the Goddess including *Nathor, Maat, Aset, Arat, Amentet and Hathor* and explores their mystical meaning as well as the rising of *Sirius,* the star of Aset (Aset) and the new birth of Hor (Heru). The end of the year is a time of reckoning, reflection and engendering a new or renewed positive movement toward attaining spiritual Enlightenment. The Mother Worship devotional meditation ritual, performed on five days during the month of December and on New Year's Eve, is based on the Ushet Rekhit. During the ceremony, the cosmic forces, symbolized by Sirius - and the constellation of Orion ---, are harnessed through the understanding and devotional attitude of the participant. This propitiation draws the light of wisdom and health to all those who share in the ritual, leading to prosperity and wisdom. $14.95 ISBN 1-884564-18-6

23.   *THE MYSTICAL JOURNEY FROM JESUS TO CHRIST* $24.95   ISBN# 1-884564-05-4 size: 8½" X 11" Discover the ancient Egyptian origins of Christianity before the Catholic Church and learn the mystical teachings given by Jesus to assist all humanity in becoming Christlike. Discover the secret meaning of the Gospels that were discovered in Egypt. Also discover how and why so many Christian churches came into being. Discover that the Bible still holds the keys to mystical realization even though its original writings were changed by the church. Discover how to practice the original teachings of Christianity which leads to the Kingdom of Heaven.

24.   THE STORY OF ASAR, ASET AND HERU: An Ancient Egyptian Legend (For Children)   Now for the first time, the most ancient myth of Ancient Egypt comes alive for children. Inspired by the books *The Asarian Resurrection: The Ancient Egyptian Bible* and *The Mystical Teachings of The Asarian Resurrection, The Story of Asar, Aset and Heru* is an easy to understand and thrilling tale which inspired the children of Ancient Egypt to aspire to greatness and righteousness. If you and your child have enjoyed stories like *The Lion King* and *Star Wars you will love The Story of Asar, Aset and Heru.* Also, if you know

the story of Jesus and Krishna you will discover than Ancient Egypt had a similar myth and that this myth carries important spiritual teachings for living a fruitful and fulfilling life. This book may be used along with *The Parents Guide To The Asarian Resurrection Myth: How to Teach Yourself and Your Child the Principles of Universal Mystical Religion.* The guide provides some background to the Asarian Resurrection myth and it also gives insight into the mystical teachings contained in it which you may introduce to your child. It is designed for parents who wish to grow spiritually with their children and it serves as an introduction for those who would like to study the Asarian Resurrection Myth in depth and to practice its teachings. 41 pages 8.5" X 11"   ISBN: 1-884564-31-3 $12.95

25. THE PARENTS GUIDE TO THE AUSARIAN RESURRECTION MYTH: How to Teach Yourself and Your Child the Principles of Universal Mystical Religion.   This insightful manual brings for the timeless wisdom of the ancient through the Ancient Egyptian myth of Asar, Aset and Heru and the mystical teachings contained in it for parents who want to guide their children to understand and practice the teachings of mystical spirituality. This manual may be used with the children's storybook *The Story of Asar, Aset and Heru* by Dr. Muata Abhaya Ashby. 5.5"x 8.5"   ISBN: 1-884564-30-5 $14.95

26. HEALING THE CRIMINAL HEART BOOK 1 Introduction to Maat Philosophy, Yoga and Spiritual Redemption Through the Path of Virtue   Who is a criminal? Is there such a thing as a criminal heart? What is the source of evil and sinfulness and is there any way to rise above it? Is there redemption for those who have committed sins, even the worst crimes?   Ancient Egyptian mystical psychology holds important answers to these questions. Over ten thousand years ago mystical psychologists, the Sages of Ancient Egypt, studied and charted the human mind and spirit and laid out a path which will lead to spiritual redemption, prosperity and Enlightenment.   This introductory volume brings forth the teachings of the Asarian Resurrection, the most important myth of Ancient Egypt, with relation to the faults of human existence: anger, hatred, greed, lust, animosity, discontent, ignorance, egoism jealousy, bitterness, and a myriad of psycho-spiritual ailments which keep a human being in a state of negativity and adversity. 5.5"x 8.5"   ISBN: 1-884564-17-8 $15.95

27. THEATER & DRAMA OF THE ANCIENT EGYPTIAN MYSTERIES: Featuring the Ancient Egyptian stage play-"The Enlightenment of Hathor' Based on an Ancient Egyptian Drama, The original Theater - Mysticism of the Temple of Hetheru $14.95 By Dr. Muata Ashby

28. GUIDE TO PRINT ON DEMAND: SELF-PUBLISH FOR PROFIT, SPIRITUAL FULFILLMENT AND SERVICE TO HUMANITY Everyone asks us how we produced so many books in such a short time. Here are the secrets to writing and producing books that uplift humanity and how to get them printed for a fraction of the regular cost. Anyone can become an author even if they have limited funds. All that is necessary is the willingness to learn how the printing and book business work and the desire to follow the special instructions given here for preparing your manuscript format. Then you take your work directly to the non-traditional companies who can produce your books for less than the traditional book printer can. ISBN: 1-884564-40-2 $16.95 U. S.

29. Egyptian Mysteries: Vol. 1, Shetaut Neter ISBN: 1-884564-41-0 $19.99 What are the Mysteries? For thousands of years the spiritual tradition of Ancient Egypt, S*hetaut Neter,* "The Egyptian Mysteries," "The Secret Teachings," have fascinated, tantalized and amazed the world. At one time exalted and recognized as the highest culture of the world, by Africans, Europeans, Asiatics, Hindus, Buddhists and other cultures of the ancient world, in time it was shunned by the emerging orthodox world religions. Its temples desecrated, its philosophy maligned, its tradition spurned, its philosophy dormant in the mystical *Medu Neter*, the mysterious hieroglyphic texts which hold the secret symbolic meaning that has scarcely been discerned up to now. What are the secrets of *Nehast* {spiritual awakening and emancipation, resurrection}. More than just a literal translation, this volume is for awakening to the secret code *Shetitu* of the teaching which was not deciphered by Egyptologists, nor could be understood by ordinary spiritualists. This book is a reinstatement of the original science made available for our times, to the reincarnated followers of Ancient Egyptian culture and the prospect of spiritual freedom to break the bonds of *Khemn,* "ignorance," and slavery to evil forces: *Sâaa* .

30.   EGYPTIAN MYSTERIES VOL 2: Dictionary of Gods and Goddesses ISBN: 1-884564-23-2 $19.99
This book is about the mystery of neteru, the gods and goddesses of Ancient Egypt (Kamit, Kemet). Neteru
means "Gods and Goddesses." But the Neterian teaching of Neteru represents more than the usual limited
modern day concept of "divinities" or "spirits." The Neteru of Kamit are also metaphors, cosmic principles
and vehicles for the enlightening teachings of Shetaut Neter (Ancient Egyptian-African Religion). Actually
they are the elements for one of the most advanced systems of spirituality ever conceived in human history.
Understanding the concept of neteru provides a firm basis for spiritual evolution and the pathway for viable
culture, peace on earth and a healthy human society.   Why is it important to have gods and goddesses in
our lives? In order for spiritual evolution to be possible, once a human being has accepted that there is
existence after death and there is a transcendental being who exists beyond time and space knowledge,
human beings need a connection to that which transcends the ordinary experience of human life in time and
space and a means to understand the transcendental reality beyond the mundane reality.

31.   EGYPTIAN MYSTERIES VOL. 3 The Priests and Priestesses of Ancient Egypt ISBN: 1-884564-53-4
$22.95 This volume details the path of Neterian priesthood, the joys, challenges and rewards of advanced
Neterian life, the teachings that allowed the priests and priestesses to manage the most long lived
civilization in human history and how that path can be adopted today; for those who want to tread the path
of the Clergy of Shetaut Neter.

32.   THE KING OF EGYPT: The Struggle of Good and Evil for Control of the World and The Human Soul
ISBN 1-8840564-44-5 $18.95   Have you seen movies like The Lion King, Hamlet, The Odyssey, or The
Little Buddha? These have been some of the most popular movies in modern times. The Sema Institute of
Yoga is dedicated to researching and presenting the wisdom and culture of ancient Africa. The Script is
designed to be produced as a motion picture but may be addapted for the theater as well. 160 pages bound
or unbound (specify with your order) $19.95   copyright 1998 By Dr. Muata Ashby

33.   FROM EGYPT TO GREECE: The Kamitan Origins of Greek Culture and Religion ISBN: 1-884564-47-X
$22.95 U.S. FROM EGYPT TO GREECE   This insightful manual is a quick reference to Ancient Egyptian
mythology and philosophy and its correlation to what later became known as Greek and Rome mythology
and philosophy. It outlines the basic tenets of the mythologies and shoes the ancient origins of Greek
culture in Ancient Egypt. This volume also acts as a resource for Colleges students who would like to set
up fraternities and sororities based on the original Ancient Egyptian principles of Sheti and Maat
philosophy. ISBN: 1-884564-47-X $22.95 U.S.

34.   THE FORTY TWO PRECEPTS OF MAAT, THE PHILOSOPHY OF RIGHTEOUS ACTION AND THE
ANCIENT EGYPTIAN WISDOM TEXTS ADVANCED STUDIES This manual is designed for use with
the 1998 Maat Philosophy Class conducted by Dr. Muata Ashby. This is a detailed study of Maat
Philosophy. It contains a compilation of the 42 laws or precepts of Maat and the corresponding principles
which they represent along with the teachings of the ancient Egyptian Sages relating to each. Maat
philosophy was the basis of Ancient Egyptian society and government as well as the heart of Ancient
Egyptian myth and spirituality. Maat is at once a goddess, a cosmic force and a living social doctrine,
which promotes social harmony and thereby paves the way for spiritual evolution in all levels of society.
ISBN: 1-884564-48-8 $16.95 U.S.

Music Based on the Prt M Hru and other Kemetic Texts

Available on Compact Disc $14.99 and Audio Cassette $9.99

Adorations to the Goddess

Music for Worship of the Goddess

**NEW Egyptian Yoga Music CD
by Sehu Maa
Ancient Egyptian Music CD**
Instrumental Music played on reproductions of Ancient Egyptian Instruments– Ideal for <u>meditation</u> and
reflection on the Divine and for the practice of spiritual programs and <u>Yoga exercise sessions.</u>

©1999 By Muata Ashby
CD $14.99 –

MERIT'S INSPIRATION
**NEW Egyptian Yoga Music CD
by Sehu Maa
Ancient Egyptian Music CD**
Instrumental Music played on

reproductions of Ancient Egyptian Instruments– Ideal for <u>meditation</u> and reflection on the Divine and for the practice of spiritual programs and <u>Yoga exercise sessions.</u>
©1999 By
Muata Ashby
CD $14.99 –
UPC# 761527100429

ANORATIONS TO RA AND HETHERU
**NEW Egyptian Yoga Music CD
By Sehu Maa (Muata Ashby)
Based on the Words of Power of Ra and HetHeru**
played on reproductions of Ancient Egyptian Instruments **Ancient Egyptian Instruments used: Voice, Clapping, Nefer Lute, Tar Drum, Sistrums, Cymbals** – The Chants, Devotions, Rhythms and Festive Songs Of the Neteru – Ideal for meditation, and devotional singing and dancing.
©1999 By Muata Ashby
CD $14.99 –
UPC# 761527100221

SONGS TO ASAR ASET AND HERU
NEW
Egyptian Yoga Music CD
By Sehu Maa
played on reproductions of Ancient Egyptian Instruments– The Chants, Devotions, Rhythms and
Festive Songs Of the Neteru - Ideal for meditation, and devotional singing and dancing.
Based on the Words of Power of Asar (Asar), Aset (Aset) and Heru (Heru) Om Asar Aset Heru is the third in a series of musical explorations of the Kemetic (Ancient Egyptian) tradition of music. Its ideas are based on the Ancient Egyptian Religion of Asar, Aset and Heru and it is designed for listening, meditation and worship. ©1999 By Muata Ashby
CD $14.99 –
UPC# 761527100122

HAARI OM: ANCIENT EGYPT MEETS INDIA IN MUSIC
NEW Music CD
By Sehu Maa

The Chants, Devotions, Rhythms and Festive Songs Of the Ancient Egypt and India, harmonized and played on reproductions of ancient instruments along with modern instruments and beats. Ideal for meditation, and devotional singing and dancing.

Haari Om is the fourth in a series of musical explorations of the Kemetic (Ancient Egyptian) and Indian traditions of music, chanting and devotional spiritual practice. Its ideas are based on the Ancient Egyptian Yoga spirituality and Indian Yoga spirituality.
©1999 By Muata Ashby
CD $14.99 –
UPC# 761527100528

RA AKHU: THE GLORIOUS LIGHT
NEW
Egyptian Yoga Music CD
By Sehu Maa
The fifth collection of original music compositions based on the Teachings and Words of The Trinity, the God Asar and the Goddess Nebethet, the Divinity Aten, the God Heru, and the Special Meditation Hekau or Words of Power of Ra from the Ancient Egyptian Tomb of Seti I and more... played on reproductions of Ancient Egyptian Instruments and modern instruments - **Ancient Egyptian Instruments used: Voice, Clapping, Nefer Lute, Tar Drum, Sistrums, Cymbals**
— The Chants, Devotions, Rhythms and Festive Songs Of the Neteru – Ideal for meditation, and devotional singing and dancing.
©1999 By Muata Ashby
CD $14.99 –
UPC# 761527100825

GLORIES OF THE DIVINE MOTHER
Based on the hieroglyphic text of the
worship of Goddess Net.
The Glories of The Great Mother
©2000 Muata Ashby
CD $14.99 UPC# 761527101129`

Order Form

Telephone orders: Call Toll Free: 1(305) 378-6253. Have your AMEX, Optima, Visa or MasterCard ready.

    Fax orders: 1-(305) 378-6253   E-MAIL ADDRESS: Semayoga@aol.com

Postal Orders: Sema Institute of Yoga, P.O. Box 570459, Miami, Fl. 33257. USA.

Please send the following books and / or tapes.

ITEM

_____Cost $_____

_____Cost $_____

_____Cost $_____

_____Cost $_____

_____Cost $_____

Total $_____

Name:_____

Physical Address:_____

City:_____ State:_____ Zip:_____

Sales tax: Please add 6.5% for books shipped to Florida addresses

_____Shipping: $6.50 for first book and .50¢ for each additional

_____Shipping: Outside US $5.00 for first book and $3.00 for each additional

_____Payment:_____

_____Check -Include Driver License #:

    _____

_____Credit card: _____ Visa, _____ MasterCard, _____ Optima, _____ AMEX.

Card number:_____

Name on card:_____ Exp. date:_____/_____

Copyright 1995-2005 Dr. R. Muata Abhaya Ashby

Sema Institute of Yoga

P.O.Box 570459, Miami, Florida, 33257

(305) 378-6253 Fax: (305) 378-6253